Investment Appraisal
and related decisions

A. B. ROBERTSON

Investment Appraisal

and related decisions

Stephen Lumby

London School of Economics
and Political Science

Nelson

To my Mother and Father

Thomas Nelson and Sons Ltd
Nelson House   Mayfield Road
Walton-on-Thames   Surrey KT12 5PL

P.O. Box 18123   Nairobi   Kenya

116-D JTC Factory Building
Lorong 3   Geylang Square   Singapore 1438

Thomas Nelson Australia Pty Ltd
19–39 Jeffcott Street   West Melbourne   Victoria 3003

Nelson Canada Ltd
81 Curlew Drive   Don Mills   Ontario M3A 2R1

Thomas Nelson (Hong Kong) Ltd
Watson Estate   Block A   13 Floor
Watson Road   Causeway Bay   Hong Kong

Thomas Nelson (Nigeria) Limited
8 Ilupeju Bypass   PMB 21303   Ikeja   Lagos

Typeset by Santype International Ltd, Salisbury, Wilts
Printed and bound in Hong Kong

British Library Cataloguing in Publication Data

Lumby, Stephen
   Investment appraisal and related decisions.
   —(Nelson series in accounting and finance).
   1. Capital investments—Decision making
   I. Title
   658.1′527   HG4028.C4

   ISBN 0-17-761055-7
   ISBN 0-17-771060-8 Pbk

Publishers' Note
Model answers to the Selected Questions on pp. 220–39 of this volume
are available to lecturers and instructors free of charge on application
to the Publishers.

Contents

BR PEII DEC '82

v

Preface

There is a popular feeling that 'theory' is opposed to 'practice' and the merits lie with 'practice'. This is a false conclusion, based on a false supposition. If practice has long been successful and does not conform to theory, the theory is bad and in need of revision ... The distinction should not be between theory and practice; it should be between good theory and bad theory, between good practice and bad practice ... Practice is brick; theory is mortar. Both are essential and both must be good if we are to erect a worthy structure.

D. Paarlberg, *Great Myths of Economics*

This book takes the above quotation as its starting point. It has been mainly based on my undergraduate lectures on financial decision theory, given at the London School of Economics over the past few years. These have been supplemented with additional material from a number of sources, including lecture notes and class problems used in the teaching of Financial Management to professional accounting students both of the Institute of Chartered Accountants in England and Wales and the Association of Certified Accountants. In all these lectures, it has been my intention to present a thorough and rigorous grounding in the concepts and principles of long-term financial decision making, whilst leaving the more institutional and descriptive aspects to be developed by readings from one of the many competent textbooks available.

In writing this book I have continued to follow this philosophy by keeping institutional material to an absolute minimum, so as to make the essential theoretical framework stand out sharply and also to keep the text to a manageable length. To this end also, it has been necessary to omit any review or discussion of the empirical testing of the theoretical arguments, a task which would really require a book to itself if it were to be well done and of real value to the reader. At the outset, I have tried to make it clear that this is not a cook-book of capital investment decision making, but is an attempt at a fairly detailed exposition of a normative theory of financial decision making. Therefore, examples that have used real-world data are there for the purposes of exposition, rather than to encourage the unthinking application of the theory to practical decision making. The aim is not to put forward theoretical solutions to practical problems, but to promote more thought and reflection on how decisions are actually made and, maybe, how they can be improved.

As far as possible, the presentation has been argued in descriptive and graphical terms, rather than using a strict mathematical analysis. The reasons for this are two-fold. First a mathematical treatment often excludes a great many potential enquirers and reduces the subject matter to a degree of terseness that makes unrealistic demands upon the concentration of readers. Second, a mathematical treatment, although often elegant, can sometimes fail to make clear the full significance of important conclusions. However, it has been impossible to exclude mathematics completely – indeed it would have been counterproductive to do so in certain areas – but its complexity has been kept to an absolute minimum.

At the end of the book there is a small collection of exercises, designed to assist the student to grasp some of the points made and to promote further thought. In addition, at the end of each chapter there is a limited bibliography which should be used by the reader to help rediscover many of the origins of this book's subject-matter, to fill out the institutional detail and to provide an introduction to some of the empirical evidence.

Throughout my time at the LSE, from 1972 when I first arrived as a graduate student, many people have extended a beneficial influence over my thoughts and ideas, which have now manifested themselves in this book. In particular I would like to thank all my colleagues and teachers at the LSE, both past and present, and especially Professors Bryan Carsberg, Harold Edey and Peter Watson. But despite this glittering array of talent, I have unfortunately not taken all their advice and so must accept responsibility for the errors that remain. Thanks are also due to Professors John Grinyer and John Perrin for specific criticism and advice (again, not all heeded!) and also to Dominic Recaldin of Thomas Nelson and Sons for his gentle, but necessarily persistent, prodding. Their collective help has been invaluable. My thanks also to Vicky Scriven, Lyn Holtham and Jane Savage, who between them have converted my unreadable scrawl into perfect typescript.

Finally, my thanks must go to Vanessa, whom I met when I first started this book and whom I married when I had finished it. For her patience and understanding of the trials and tribulations of writing, go my heart-felt thanks.

S.P.L.

1 Introduction

1.1 An overview

This book covers an area of managerial economics which is relatively new in terms of university and professional examination courses: the theory of business financial decisions. It is concerned with how management within companies[1] *should* make[2] financial decisions,[3] and so it can be called a normative theory because it sets out to establish a standard or norm. But such a theory cannot hope to succeed in its task if it is developed in isolation from what actually does happen in practice, and so we shall also examine how financial decisions *are* made, in order to guide the development of the normative theory.

The value base However, it is important to realize that financial decisions are no different in their fundamental aspects from other decisions of a non-financial nature, be they in industry or commerce or elsewhere, such as marketing decisions, international diplomacy decisions or even marriage decisions. In essence, *all* decisions are based on the concept of the comparison of alternatives, and it is in this sense that the theory of financial decisions really has its roots in valuation theory, because all the alternatives in any decision-making situation have to be valued in order to be compared. Therefore, although we can say that all types of decisions involve the same fundamental process, each is given its own unique characteristics by the valuation basis which it employs.

The financial decision theory developed in this book is founded on the valuation basis of capitalism[4] and the idea of the free market economy. It is important that this is specified from the outset, as a different valuation basis is likely to produce a different overall theory of financial decisions. However, many parts of our financial theory will be applicable to other types of economic organization, and the reader may wish to occasionally consider and reflect upon the implications of our theory for more socialistic value bases, such as those which might be appropriate to the UK nationalized industries.

The 'model' approach The theory will be developed by examining the three major areas of financial decisions: the investment, financing and dividend decisions. In the course of this development a considerable number of abstractions from and simplications of the 'real world' will be made, in order to distil the difficulties and focus attention on areas of major importance. Thus we are going to take a 'modelling' approach, but we must be careful not to fall into the trap of oversimplifying the real world and, in so doing, leaving out important and relevant factors which should properly be included. This is particularly important because we are developing a normative theory and are therefore attempting to give advice on how financial decisions should be taken. If we work with oversimplified models and the theory is followed in practice, the quality of financial decisions made in business may deteriorate rather than improve. Thus the difficulties caused by taxation, inflation and capital scarcity will all be taken into account, as will the concept of risk and the fact that the future is uncertain.[5] All these real world realities will be added layer by layer, and so we shall begin with a model which, although a poor reflection of the real world, provides a logically sound framework upon which to build.

A warning As a final point, the reader should be constantly aware that the theory of financial decisions which is presented here is neither in a state of general detailed agreement, nor does it yet provide complete solutions to many of the important problems of financial decision making. In order to reflect this state of affairs, we shall examine the causes and evidence of these controversies and point out the irrationalities, ambiguities and inconsistencies that necessarily accompany the development of any theory that aspires to real world application.

1.2 The decision process

In order to examine the decision process and to answer the question: 'How do we make a decision?', we have first to discuss the circumstances in which a decision needs to be made. We can specify two necessary conditions for a decision situation: the existence of alternatives and the existence of an objective or goal.

The first necessary condition The existence of alternatives is necessary for, if there are no alternatives amongst which to choose, then there is no need for a decision. This condition can be specified further in that not only must alternatives exist, but they must be seen to exist by the potential decision maker. There are two points of interest here. First, notice that we talk of a decision *situation* and of a *potential* decision maker. This is because the mere existence of perceived alternatives does not necessarily mean that a decision will be made. For instance, the potential decision maker may well procrastinate, and therefore the passage of time takes him (or her) out of a decision situation into a situation where there is only one possible course of action and no alternatives are available. (Death is the ultimate example of the passage of time removing a decision situation from an individual.) The second point of interest is that we are *not* specifying that all possible alternatives are perceived (if they were we could call this an optimal decision situation), because we are examining how decisions are made, given a decision situation exists; whether the decision is optimal or non-optimal is of no concern at present.

The second necessary condition The second necessary condition for a decision situation arises from the fact that the actual process of 'making a decision' is liable to cause the decision maker to expend both time and effort. Rationally he will be unwilling to do so unless he expects that some of the perceived alternatives will be preferred to others in relation to attaining the desired objective. This is the second necessary condition. If it does not exist, there will be no purpose in making a decision.[6]

Valuation of alternatives Together, these two necessary conditions give the rationale for making decisions: if the decision maker does not perceive alternatives or sees no reason to choose between the alternatives if they are perceived, then no decision will be made (except one of a totally arbitrary kind, as in note 6). But once these conditions do exist, a decision cannot actually be made until values are placed upon the alternatives. In fact, we can assert that the *only* reason why any alternative course of action is ever evaluated is in order to make a decision about it; therefore, the valuation method used must be related to the objective involved in making the decision and the way in which that objective is expressed. For example, if our objective were to drive from A to B in the shortest possible time, then we should value the alternative routes from A to B by a common value criterion which was related to our objective of time, and choose whichever route took the shortest time. Suppose there were three alternative routes and one we valued by time, one by distance and one by scenic beauty. We obviously could not make a decision because the alternatives have different measures or yardsticks of value and so cannot be compared. Alternatively, if all three routes were measured in terms of scenic beauty, we should again be unable to make a decision even though we could compare the routes – because the basis of the comparison is not the one which gives the rationale for the decision: the value base of the objective, which in this example is 'time'.[7]

Therefore, any decision making process consists of these three components: a series of perceived alternatives, an expectation that these alternatives are not all equally desirable in terms of attaining an objective held by the decision maker, and a common value base related to the decision objective. So it is with all financial decisions made in business.

1.3 Financial decision making

This book focuses attention on only two of the three components that we have identified in the decision process and examines how they relate to the making of financial decisions: the expectation that the perceived alternatives are not all equally desirable in terms of attaining a specific objective, and the common value base that is related to this objective and is used to compare the alternatives.

The remaining component of the decision process is the series of perceived alternatives. We shall not be examining it in the main body of the text as it is primarily a necessary condition for the decision situation, and we are concentrating on the actual decision making, assuming that the decision situation already exists. However, this omission does not mean that the 'search process' (as it is called) for alternatives is unimportant. It is in fact extremely important. If this search process is not efficient in seeking out alternatives, then there is a grave danger that the decision itself will not be optimal because the 'most preferred' alternative may go unperceived.

The decision objective Turning to the two decision process components that we shall examine in detail, we immediately become involved in value judgements, because the objective we use for financial decision making, and the consequent value base, will completely determine the decision reached on which alternative is selected. Therefore, what objective are we going to use and what valuation base are we going to set up for our theory of financial decisions?

We stated earlier that the fundamental value judgement upon which this theory is based is capitalism. So it is a theory that is essentially (but by no means exclusively) applicable to companies operating in largely unregulated, competitive economies. In such economies, companies exist for one overriding purpose: in order to benefit their owners.[8] Certainly it may be said that companies provide a source of employment for local populations, that they supply the needs of a particular market or even that they are the vanguard in technological advance, but the fact still remains that the fundamental rationale for their existence must be to bring benefit to their owners. Once a company ceases to perform this function, whatever else it might be doing, it is likely to come to an end very rapidly; certainly it will cease to exist in its present form, because at least its directors and top management will be replaced.

This rationale for existence undoubtedly holds true for the great majority of privately owned[9] companies (and also, to some extent, for the nationalized industries although their rationale for existence can be more complex[10]). Therefore, management's objective in making financial decisions should be to further the very reason for the company's existence, of benefiting the owners, i.e., the shareholders. If that is to be their decision objective, what is the value base to be used for the comparison of alternatives? To answer this question, we have to examine the decision objective more closely. It is obvious from what we have already said that not only should company managements make financial decisions so as to benefit the shareholders but they should also strive to maximize the benefit, otherwise shareholders will be interested in replacing them with a set of decision makers who will do this. Therefore, what is meant by the term 'maximizing owners' or shareholders' benefit'?

Maximizing shareholder wealth We are going to assume that maximizing benefit means maximizing wealth, and although there is nothing surprising about this, we have to be careful here because we are going to assume that maximizing the increase in the owners' wealth is the *only* way in which management decisions can benefit owners. This is a slight simplification of the real world because it is quite possible for shareholders to gain benefit from a company other than by increases in wealth. For example, many owners of the original Rolls Royce company (before it went bankrupt and was rescued by the Government) gained benefit from ownership in terms of pride in owning part of Britain's 'Industrial Heritage'. However, this a comparatively minor simplification, and we shall proceed on the relatively sound assumption that increase in wealth is the sole source of benefit from company ownership.

What about firms selling military arms to countries with repugnant policies, or firms causing pollution to land, air or water resources? Do these types of activity enter into our decision objective? On the basis of our underlying assumption about the nature of the economy, our answer must be that they should not, because if these activities were thought to be truly undesirable, governments would legislate to constrain companies' decision–choice alternatives so as to exclude them (as in many cases they do). Company decision makers should only need to perceive and analyse the decision alternatives in terms of maximizing the owners' wealth. Under the market economies of western countries, we develop a theory of financial decisions for privately owned firms in this way because of the workings of the market system for company capital. Ordinary share capital, the substance of ownership, is normally provided through supply and demand markets (i.e., stock exchanges), which means that potential shareholders will wish to own companies that are expected to provide them with the greatest possible increase in wealth (i.e., shareholders have to make financial decisions in much the same way as management, choosing between alternative ownership opportunities), and existing shareholders will change their ownership allegiances if they see other companies providing greater increases to their owners' wealth than they are receiving. (An important concept here, and one we have yet to deal with, is that the future is uncertain and so any decision amongst alternatives usually has a risk attached to it: the risk that the alternative chosen may not turn out as expected. Some alternatives are riskier than others and so shareholders will really want to own companies that give them the greatest possible increase in wealth, *for a given level of risk.* This concept we shall consider much more fully later.) Therefore, if a company in its financial decision process starts consistently to take into account factors other than that of maximizing shareholder wealth, the whole rationale for the company's existence – so far as shareholders are concerned – is cast into doubt and they are likely to take their investment funds elsewhere. In the extreme case, company law provides the opportunity for shareholders to replace a company's decision makers if enough of them believe that decisions are not being taken in their best interests.

Defining wealth However, we still cannot determine the value base for financial decision making until we have defined 'wealth', because the purpose of the value base is to act as a common denominator with which to make the alternative courses of action directly comparable and to see which one leads furthest towards the decision objective. As the objective of financial decisions is assumed to be to 'maximize the increase in owners' wealth', let us define 'wealth' and so determine the value base.

Wealth can be defined as purchasing power or, to put it in more straightforward terms, money or cash.[11] Thus company management's objective becomes the maximization of shareholders' purchasing power, which can be achieved by maximizing the amount of cash paid out to shareholders in the form of dividends. But which dividend should a company's management try to maximize, this year's, next year's or what? The point here is that it would be a relatively easy task for a company to maximize a single year's dividend, simply by selling up all the assets and paying a final liquidation dividend! (We are ignoring the niceties of company law here, but the point still remains.) Obviously this is not what is meant by our decision objective of maximizing dividends, and the trouble arises through the omission of the time dimension. When fully defined, including the time dimension, the objective of a company's financial decision makers becomes the maximization of the *flow* of dividends to shareholders *over or through time.*

The role of accounting profit Now there are two points of fundamental importance that arise from the development of this decision objective. Firstly, the word 'profit' has not been mentioned and the emphasis has been laid on wealth defined as cash. Secondly, the introduction of time means that decisions must be analysed not only in terms of immediate cash gains and losses, but also in terms of *future* gains and losses.

The two points are interlinked. The absence of the word 'profit' can be explained by the introduction of the time dimension. Profit, when used in a business sense, is purely an accounting concept introduced by accountants in order to perform their stewardship function as auditors for the owners of companies. In very general terms, profit represents the increased wealth of a company that has been achieved by management within the confines of an arbitrary period of time: the accounting year. But profit is only a very, very rough approximation of increased wealth as we have defined it in our decision objective, as it is based on a whole range of arbitrary and somewhat inconsistent accounting conventions that have been made necessary in order to split what is a continuous flow (i.e., changes in wealth) into artificial time periods. A company does not increase its wealth in discrete twelve-month steps, but in a continuous (although not necessarily constant) flow through time. In making financial decisions, it is increases in this flow that we wish to maximize, and hence accounting profit is a concept both ill-defined and ill-suited for this purpose.

However, we cannot discard the accounting profit concept completely. To do so would be rather like a sports team whose policy is that they do not mind whether they win or lose, so long as in playing they give maximum entertainment to their supporters. This is fine, and it is probably the correct attitude; but often it is on winning and losing that the success of the team is ultimately judged and therefore that part of the game cannot be ignored. So it is with accounting profit. The company's financial decision makers should have as their major concern the maximization of the flow of cash through time to the shareholders, but they should always do so with an eye to reported profit. Profitability, as expressed in annual published accounts, forms a major criterion by which shareholders and prospective shareholders judge a company's success and, as we shall see later, it is important that people do form correct judgements about a company's performance.

A further reason why the effects of financial decisions on reported profits cannot be completely ignored is provided by the fact that the level of retained profits in company law can form a very substantial maximum barrier to an annual dividend payment. Thus a company that wishes to maximize its dividend flow must ensure that its dividend payout intentions are legally within the confines of company law.

Therefore, with the exception of these two provisos, we can say that the financial decision theory developed here is built on an analytical framework that is largely devoid of the accounting profit concept, although it would be correct to assume that, in the longer run, good company cash flows will result in good reported profits.

The time dimension Turning to the second point of importance in our decision objective, the introduction of the time dimension, we have already noted that the arbitrary time segmentation of a continuous flow process has been the cause of major problems for the accounting profit concept, but to see the true significance of the introduction of this factor we have to return to our discussion on value. An asset (in its widest sense) is given a value on the basis of the gains and losses that an individual receives as a result of ownership, and these gains and losses do not refer to just one period of time but to the whole period of time for which the asset exists.

Let us consider an asset of company ownership: an ordinary share. Ordinary shares are traded (i.e., bought and sold) in supply and demand markets and so its market valuation represents an equilibrium value, a value at which demand for the share by people who wish to buy it equates with the supply of the share by people who wish to sell it. But what process actually gives a share its equilibrium price, what makes prospective purchasers wish to buy it at that price and what makes prospective sellers wish to sell it at that price? Let us examine the prospective purchaser's reasons. Suppose an ordinary share of XYZ Ltd has a stock market value of £1.[12] A prospective owner will be willing to buy that share for £1 only if he believes that the gain received as a result of ownership will have a value of at least £1. These gains of ownership consist of two elements: the flow of dividends through time for as long as he owns the share, and the selling price received when ownership is finally relinquished. But this future selling price of the XYZ share is based on the value the succeeding owner puts on the benefits that he in turn expects to receive from ownership, which again consists of the dividend flow and the selling price that he will receive upon selling the share at some future time, and so on. Thus we can see that although a potential owner sees two types of benefit arising from share ownership, the dividend stream and the future selling price, both types of benefit are derived from a single source: the future dividend stream that the share will produce over its life-span. As a result, our theory will assume that shares derive their (equilibrium) stock market price on the basis of the dividend flow that they will produce through time. (As the future is uncertain it is more correct to talk of valuation based on the *expected* dividend flow, but we shall return to this later.) Thus the greater the future dividend flow, the more highly are the shares valued. Therefore if our financial decision makers are taking decisions so as to maximize dividend flow through time, then via the direct link between dividend flow and a share's market price, this action will result in the maximization of the market value of the company's shares.

The objective hierarchy So let us summarize our assumed hierarchy of decision objectives:

1 Decisions are taken by companies so as to maximize owners' wealth.
2 Owners' wealth can be maximized through maximizing owners' purchasing power.
3 Purchasing power can be maximized through maximizing the amount of cash the company pays out to shareholders in the form of dividends.
4 With the introduction of the time dimension the objective becomes the maximizing of the value of the dividend flow through time to the shareholders.
5 The maximization of the value of the dividend flow through time maximizes the stock market's valuation of the company's ordinary share capital.

It is this final restatement of the objective function that we shall use in developing our theory, but it is important to realize that it is really only a surrogate objective for maximizing shareholder wealth.

A fundamental assumption As a final point in this introduction to financial decision making let us state the assumptions about the shareholder which have been implied in the analysis. It was earlier argued that the maximization of shareholders' wealth had to be the fundamental decision objective because of the nature of the capital markets. However, the validity of this assertion depends entirely upon the assumptions that shareholders perceive wealth in the way we have postulated and that in this perception they are rational. In essence this means that we have assumed that shareholders see wealth as the receipt of cash flows (dividends) through time and that they will always prefer a greater to a lesser cash flow. These appear reasonably safe assumptions, but we shall consider situations where they may not hold when we look later at dividend policies.

The next stage Having discussed in general terms the problem of choice in relation to financial decisions, we are now ready to examine closely the investment decision which is the most fundamental of all the three decision areas covered by this book. But before doing so, it is perhaps prudent to emphasize at this point that although our analysis will appear to separate out the three decision areas – investment, financing and dividend – in practice they are inexorably interlinked. For example, the investment and dividend decision may well be competing for the same cash resources within the company, the financing decision may be closely bound to what investment decision is made and vice versa, and the dividend decision is likely to have a direct bearing on the financing decision. It is only for the sake of clarity of exposition that these three decisions have been artificially segregated, and each should really be seen as just another complex layer of the whole financial decision 'cake'; but, to continue the metaphor, it is the investment decision that forms the foundation layer.

Selected references

R. Bird, 'A Reappraisal of the Share Price Maximation Criterion', *Accounting and Business Research*, Spring 1974.

G. Donaldson, 'Financial Goals: Management vs. Stockholder', *Harvard Business Review*, May–June 1963.

W. W. Haynes and M. B. Solomon, 'A Misplaced Emphasis in Capital Budgeting', *Quarterly Review of Economics and Business*, February 1962.

J. Y. Kamin and J. Ronen, 'The Effects of Corporate Control on Apparent Profit Performance', *Southern Economic Journal*, July 1978.

R. J. Larner, *Management Control and the Large Corporation*, New Jersey, Dunellan Publishing Co., 1970.

E. M. Lerner and W. T. Carleton, 'The Integration of Capital Budgeting and Stock Validation', *American Economic Review*, September 1964.

H. A. Simon, 'Theories of Decision Making in Economics and Behavioural Science', *American Economic Review*, June 1959.

2 Traditional Methods of Investment Appraisal

2.1 Introduction

In its simplest form, an investment decision can be defined as one which involves the firm in a cash outlay with the aim of receiving, in return, future cash inflows. Numerous variations on this definition are possible, such as a cash outlay with the aim of reducing or saving further cash outlays, but these can all generally adapt to the initial definition with little trouble.[1] Therefore decisions about buying a new machine, building a factory, extending a warehouse, improving a delivery service, instituting a staff training scheme or launching a new product line are all examples of the investment decisions that may be made by industry. In order to help in making such decisions, and to ensure that they are consistent with each other, a common method of appraisal is required which can be applied equally to the whole spectrum of investment decisions and which should, in terms of the decision structure so far outlined, help to decide whether any particular investment will assist the company in maximizing shareholder wealth (via dividend or share price maximization).

A warning In looking for such an investment appraisal method we shall begin by examining the two most widely used[2.] methods, Payback and Return on Capital Employed, to see how well they fit in with our financial decision objective and value base. However, before doing so we should be clear that neither of these two methods nor any other method of investment appraisal can give a *definitive* decision. They cannot tell a company's financial decision maker to 'invest' or 'not invest', but can only act as a decision *guide*. This extremely important point will become obvious as we develop our theory, but it is all too easy to slip back into the erroneous (and sometimes comforting) belief that the techniques that we shall develop here will make decisions for us. They will not do this. All they will do is help to communicate information to the decision maker; but when the actual decision is finally made, it is based on a whole range of very diverse considerations which are beyond our present capabilities to encompass in 'overall' decision making formulae.[3]

There has always been a considerable amount of resistance and resentment by financial management to the introduction of any new investment appraisal technique, based partially on the belief that with such methods their decision making function would be replaced by a formula, 'handle-turning' function. Such a belief is ill-founded, not only for the reason already given, but also because any investment appraisal will always consist of making forecasts/estimates/guesses about the investment's future performance, and it is upon these forecasts that the appraisal techniques are applied. However the future, almost without exception, is uncertain and so any investment technique can give only investment *advice* on these forecasts and not a definitive decision. Such techniques can never replace managerial judgement, but they can help to make that judgement more sound.

2.2 The Payback method

Let us start by looking at the first of these two traditional methods of investment appraisal: the Payback method.[4] This is one of the most tried and trusted of all methods and its name neatly describes its operation, referring to how quickly the incremental benefits that accrue to a company from an investment project 'pay back' the initial capital invested – the benefits being normally defined in terms of after-tax cash flows.

The payback method can be used as a guide to investment decision making in two ways. When faced with a straight accept-or-reject decision it can provide a rule where projects are only accepted if they pay back the initial investment outlay within a certain predetermined time. In addition, the payback method can provide a rule when a comparison is required of the relative desirability of a number of mutually exclusive investments.[5] In such cases projects can be ranked in terms of 'speed of payback', with the fastest paying-back project being the most favoured and the slowest paying-back project the least favoured. Thus the project which paid back quickest would be chosen for investment.

Given below are examples of the payback method operating in both decision making situations. With Project A1, assuming that the criterion for project acceptance is a four-year (maximum) payback, then we can see that it should be accepted because it pays back the initial outlay of £4000 within this time period:

Project A1

Year[6]	Cash flow	
0	−£4,000	
1	+£1,000	
2	+£1,000	
3	+£2,000	Payback period
4	+£3,000	
5	+£1,000	

If projects A2 and A3 are mutually exclusive, Project A3 has the faster 'speed of payback' and so is the preferred investment. A2 pays back within three years (i.e., $2\frac{3}{5}$ years: years 1 and 2 profit plus three fifths of year 3 profit) whilst A3 pays back in two years exactly:

Project A2		*Project A3*	
Year	Cash flow	Year	Cash flow
0	−£10,000	0	−£112,500
1	+£ 3,000	1	+£ 5,000
2	+£ 4,000	2	+£ 7,500
3	+£ 5,000	3	+£ 1,000
4	+£ 6,000	4	+£ 1,000
		5	+£ 1,000

As can be seen from these two examples, the payback period is quick and simple to calculate (once the project's cash forecasts have been made) and is likely to be readily understood by management. In fact the rationale for decision advice conveyed by the method is almost intuitive, concentrating as it does on the *speed* of return. Such a factor can become a dominant short-run consideration for companies with tight liquidity. Additionally, concentration on speed of return is often viewed as being in accord with management's wish to avoid or minimize risk. This is on the basis that, given that the investment decision is made on estimates of future cash flows and that the further ahead in time to which those estimates refer the less reliable they become, then selecting the fastest ones repaying projects automatically means selecting the least risky ones. This is a complex point that we shall return to later when looking at risk and uncertainty. In theoretical terms this claimed advantage of the payback method is not fully justified, but the point may well be more valid in practical terms.

Disadvantages of payback Having looked at the advantages – true or otherwise – claimed for the method, let us now turn to the disadvantages. The first is the problem of what is meant by 'initial investment outlay' and how the start of the payback period is defined. Looking at the example of Project A4 (overleaf), given a three-year payback criterion, the project should be accepted if the payback starts from the end of the last capital outflow (year 1) because it pays back in 3 years, but if the payback period is defined as starting from the time of the initial outlay (year 0), then the project should be rejected because it does not pay back within the three year criterion.

Project A4

Year	Cash flow
0	−£10,000
1	−£ 5,000
2	+£ 4,000
3	+£ 5,000
4	+£ 6,000

Just how is the initial investment outlay to be defined in this example: £10,000 or £15,000, given that both the £10,000 and the £5,000 are capital expense? Or more problematical still, how should it be defined in Project A5?

Project A5

Year	Cash flow
0	−£5,000
1	+£1,000
2	−£5,000
3	+£3,000
4	+£3,000
5	+£4,000

The point is that in each case we *can* come to a decision, say to accept Project A4 and reject A5, but the decision rule as it stands is too ambiguous in its definition of terminology to give a definitive ruling. (It should be mentioned that when a technique, designed to be a decision making aid, is open to ambiguity in interpretation, then it is likely to be manipulated in order to lend backing for a desired decision. Any decision rule open to such misuse is dangerous).

A second problem with the method is found in the setting of the maximum payback period criterion. In the examples so far, we have assumed either a three- or a four-year payback rule but have said nothing about how these particular periods were formulated. This is because there are no specific guidelines on how the maximum payback period should be determined, save advice such as, 'This size of firm usually has a five-year payback rule'; but the setting of the maximum payback period is fundamental to the decision advice the method gives.

Another problem arises from the fact that the decision is concentrated purely on the cash flows that arise within the payback period, and flows that arise outside this period are ignored. Projects A6 and A7 illustrate the problem that this can cause:

Project A6				Project A7			
Year	Cash flow			Year	Cash flow		
0	−£100,000			0	−£100,000		
1	+£ 10,000			1	+£ 50,000		
2	+£ 20,000			2	+£ 50,000		
3	+£ 40,000			3	+£ 10,000		
4	+£ 80,000						
5	+£160,000						
6	+£320,000						

According to the payback rule, if the two projects are mutually exclusive, project A7 is preferred because it pays back the more quickly. If the two projects are independent[7] (i.e., either one or both could be accepted or rejected) and the company had a three-year payback period criterion, again project A7 would be accepted and A6 rejected. In both situations, looking at the cash flows over the whole life of the projects, we can see that the wisdom of the decision advice given by the payback method is open to some doubt.

The time value of money Finally there is a further serious problem with the payback method. It is that the payback method (in its original form) suffers from the fundamental drawback that it fails to allow for the 'time value' of money. Although this is a fundamental drawback of the payback method in its original form this problem, like the previous one, can be easily overcome in practice by using the method in terms of net present values – the so-called 'discounted payback' method. (See the next chapter for a full discussion on the meaning of net present values).[8] This is a very important concept as far as financial decision theory is concerned, and we shall develop it formally in the next chapter; but essentially what is meant by the time value of money is that a given sum of money has a different value depending upon when it occurs in time. The idea is not directly concerned with inflation or deflation (let us assume that neither exist, so that price levels are stable through time) but really concerns the fact that money can be invested so as to earn *interest*. Suppose you were owed £100 and were given the choice of having your £100 returned to you either now or in one year's time (assume that if you choose £100 in a year's time the event is 'certain' – i.e., you are certain to be alive then and you are certain to be paid the money). Most people would instinctively take the £100 now – even if they did not need the money – and this would be the correct decision in terms of the time value of money. £100 in a year's time has a smaller value than £100 now, because if you took the £100 now the money could be placed on deposit at (say) a 6% interest rate and so turn into £106 in one year's time. Therefore if the person who was in debt to you offered the choice of £100 now or £106 in one year's time (again both events are certain to occur), you would have no preference for either alternative. Thus we could say that the *present value* of £106 received in a year's time is £100 or that the *future value* of £100 now is £106 in a year's time, assuming a 6% interest rate.

This concept of the time value of money will be much more fully discussed when we talk about the cash flow methods of investment appraisal, but the point to be made here is that the payback method does not make any allowance for the time value of money, its emphasis on the speed of return being purely a consideration of risk and uncertainty. For example, the payback method would be indifferent between Projects A8 and A9 whereas, as the reader may well discern, if allowance is made for the time value of money, Project A9 is preferable to Project A8.

Project A8		Project A9	
Year	Cash flow	Year	Cash flow
0	−£4,000	0	−£4,000
1	+£ 100	1	+£3,900
2	+£3,900	2	+£ 100

In conclusion Despite these criticisms it is still possible to say that, to some extent, payback has been unfairly maligned in the literature on financial decisions. However it obviously has a robust ability to survive, because it remains one of the most popular of appraisal methods. This popularity stems mainly from the two reasons that we have already given, that of ease of computation and ease of comprehension, and indeed it can be strongly argued that the payback method does provide a very useful 'rule of thumb' check mechanism for the very many minor investment decisions that companies have to make, which are financially too small (either in relative or absolute terms) to justify the time and expense that would necessarily be incurred in using a more theoretically correct appraisal method.[9]

The real problem does not stem from the payback concept itself, but more from the way the method is *used* in the decision making process. Except in the case of very minor investment decisions, it should not really be used to give decision *advice* at all, but only to give *information* on the speed of return of the initial outlay, which may, or may not, be of relevance (depending upon the firm's liquidity) in the decision process. It cannot really be considered as an investment appraisal technique because of its major defect: its inability to report the expected return over the whole life of an investment, through its disregard of the investment's post-payback period flows. Using the payback method to choose between alternative investments or to set a minimum criterion for investment acceptance is really applying it to a task which is well beyond its ability to handle. At best, for large investments, it can act successfully only as an initial screening device before more powerful methods of appraisal are applied.[10]

2.3 Return on Capital Employed

The second traditional approach of investment appraisal is the Return on Capital Employed (ROCE) which, like payback, has many different names (perhaps the most common is the Accounting Rate of Return) and a wide variety of different methods of computation. In its basic form, it is calculated as the ratio of the accounting profit generated by an investment project to the required capital outlay, expressed as a percentage. There are many variations in the way these two figures are actually calculated, but normal practice in its use for investment appraisal is to calculate profit after depreciation but before any allowance for taxation, and to include in capital employed any increases in working capital that would be required if the project were accepted.

The measure is normally (but by no means exclusively) expressed as the ratio of the annual average profit generated over the life of the investment to the average annual capital value, and stated as a percentage. For example, Project B1 requires an initial capital outlay of £10,000 and has a life of 5 years, at the end of which it can be sold as scrap for £1,500. The expected annual profits over the project's life are given below, together with the calculation of the return on capital employed.

Project B1

Year	Capital flow	Profit flow
0	−£10,000	
1	—	+£1,000
2	—	+£1,500
3	—	+£2,500
4	—	+£3,000
5	+£ 1,500	+£3,000

Average Capital Employed:
$$\frac{£10,000 + £1,500}{2} = £5,750^{[11]}$$

Average Annual Profit:
$$\frac{£(1,000 + 1,500 + 2,500 + 3,000 + 3,000)}{5} = £2,200$$

Return on Capital Employed:
$$\frac{2,200}{5,750} \times 100 = 38.26\%$$

The return on capital employed calculation can act as an investment decision guide in two ways. First, it can help in a straightforward 'accept or reject' decision by providing a rule that projects may only be accepted if their ROCE exceeds some minimum or 'target' rate of return. Second, in a decision situation where projects have to be placed in an order of investment preference (e.g., when several investment alternatives are mutually exclusive), the higher a project's ROCE, the more it is preferred.

The method owes much of its popularity as an investment appraisal technique to its superiority over payback, having the advantage of not only being relatively quick and easy to calculate (once the initial profit forecasts have been made), but also producing a percentage rate of return – a concept with which financial management is very familiar. In addition, it overcomes the greatest criticism of the payback method, by considering the profit flows over the *whole* of a project's life. Thus, in the comparison of projects A6 and A7 the ROCE method, unlike payback, would prefer A6 to A7.

Disadvantages of return on capital employed Nevertheless, to set against these advantages, there are a number of disadvantages. The first of which is the ambiguous nature of the ROCE concept. There are so many variants that no general agreement exists on how capital employed should be calculated, on whether initial or average capital employed should be used, or on how profit should be defined. As a result, the method lays itself open to abuse as a technique of investment appraisal by allowing the decision maker to select a definition of ROCE which best suits his prejudgement of a project's desirability. Second, because the method measures a potential investment's worth in percentage terms (i.e., it uses an absolute rather than relative measure), it is unable – in an unadjusted form – to take into account the financial size of a project when alternatives are compared. A third problem is that although the method does take into account the profit flows over the whole of a project's life, it ignores the possibility of differing lengths of lives. When comparing alternative projects, a difference in length of life may be of crucial importance for a number of reasons, e.g., uncertainty, liquidity, technological change. Finally, like payback, ROCE suffers from the disability of ignoring the time value of money and concentrating on a project's accounting-defined financial flows rather than cash flows.

However, despite these criticisms, the method is still widely applied to investment decisions in industry and it may be fair to say that, like payback, although there are many problems associated with its application, it may give acceptable decision advice when applied to relatively minor, short-run investment projects.

In conclusion Comparing these two 'traditional' investment appraisal techniques, each has its own advantages and disadvantages and it is not clear whether either is superior. Each has its own group of advocates and it is common to find both used in conjunction so as to produce a 'two-tier' decision rule, e.g., projects may be accepted only if (say) they payback within five years *and* have a minimum ROCE of 12%.

In the final analysis, our conclusion must be that, apart from the possible exception of the analysis of relatively small, short-lived investments, neither method has sufficient advantages to offset its disadvantages, particularly the failure of both to allow for the time value of money.[12] In the next chapter we shall start to examine investment appraisal methods that do attempt to make such an allowance.

Selected references

J. Dean, 'Measuring the Productivity of Capital', *Harvard Business Review*, January–February 1954.

M. J. Gordon, 'The Payoff Period and the Rate of Profit', *Journal of Business*, October 1955.

H. Levy, 'A Note on the Payback Method', *Journal of Financial and Quantitative Analysis*, December 1968.

M. J. Mepham, 'A Reinstatement of the Accounting Rate of Return', *Accounting and Business Research*, Summer 1978.

A. Rappaport, 'The Discounted Payback Period', *Management Sciences*, July–August 1965.

E. A. Ravenscroft, 'Return on Investment: Fit the Method to your Need', *Harvard Business Review*, March–April 1960.

M. Sarnat and H. Levy, 'The Relationship of Rules of Thumb: Restatement and Generalization', *Journal of Finance*, June 1969.

M. H. Weingartner, 'Some New Views on the Payback Period and Capital Budgeting Decisions', *Management Science*, August 1969.

3 The Two Period Investment–Consumption Decision Model

3.1 Introduction to the model

There are two main approaches to the investment decision using discounted cash flow methods: the Net Present Value method (NPV) and the Internal Rate of Return (IRR) or Yield method. Unlike the two investment appraisal methods we have examined so far, both NPV and IRR focus on cash flows rather than on accounting profit flows as the major decision variable (we have already dealt with the economic logic behind this), and both explicitly allow for the time value of money through a process of discounting the cash flows. (The simple mathematics of compounding and discounting are dealt with in a separate appendix and the reader is advised to become familiar with its contents.)

Before we examine these two discounted cash flow methods of investment appraisal in detail, we first have to expand our initial discussion on the time value of money so as to be able to place both appraisal methods in their correct decision making context. In order to do so, we are going to develop a simple graphical analysis of the underpinning framework of investment decisions.[1]

The basic assumptions So as to simplify the analysis and to lay bare the problem of investment decision making we shall specify six assumptions about the real world environment within which investment decisions are made:

Assumption 1 There are only two periods of time facing the decision maker – 'now' (i.e., t_0 or period 0) and 'next year' (i.e., t_1 or period 1). Thus all the available investment opportunities possess the general characteristics of requiring a cash outlay 'now' in return for a cash inflow 'next year'. No investment cash flows extend beyond period 1.[2]

Assumption 2 The size and timing of any investment's cash outflow and subsequent cash inflow is known with certainty by the decision maker and so no risk is involved in the investment decision.[3]

Assumption 3 Only 'physical' investment opportunities are available, i.e., investments involving the use of factors of production (land, labour and machinery) to produce a future return. This means that there is no 'capital market' where money can be lent or borrowed at a rate of interest.[4]

Assumption 4 All investment projects are infinitely divisible, so that fractions of projects may be undertaken, and exhibit decreasing returns to scale.

Assumption 5 All investment project cash flows are entirely independent of each other. Therefore the return produced 'next year' from any investment 'now' is fixed and known for certain and is unaffected by any other investment decision.

Assumption 6 The person in receipt of the benefits from investment decisions is rational in that 'more cash' is always preferred to 'less cash' in any period.

These are the six major assumptions that we are going to make initially (although there are several other assumptions which we shall specify later as we develop the analysis), and obviously most of them are very unrealistic and in no way reflect the real world: investors are almost invariably faced with making decisions of which the effects stretch over many periods; the future is largely unknown and so future cash flows cannot be certain; non-physical investments, such as placing money on deposit at a bank, are usually available to investors; investment projects are often indivisible and so must either be undertaken completely or not at all; many investment project cash flows depend upon what other investment decisions have or have not been made. However, such simplifying assumptions do provide a starting point for our analysis; we shall examine later the effect of replacing them with more realistic descriptions of the real world, but for the moment let us accept them.

The marginal rate of time preference We have already defined an investment decision by a company as one which involves the company in a cash outlay (now) with the aim of receiving a (future) cash inflow in return. If we also make the simplistic but basically correct assumption that a company can do either of two things with any 'spare' cash[5] it has – pay it out to shareholders as a dividend[6] or retain it within the company and invest it – then if a company makes a decision to invest, it is in fact deciding not to pay that cash to shareholders now but instead to put it into a project with the aim of obtaining an increased amount of cash in the future, which can then be paid out as a dividend. Therefore, a decision to invest by a company means that shareholders forego the opportunity of consumption *now* (i.e., a dividend now) with the aim of increasing *future* consumption (i.e., an enlarged dividend later). This is what investment decisions are all about: the delaying of current consumption in order to increase future consumption. (Or in non-economic terms, not spending money on consuming goods and services now, but investing the money instead so as to produce *more* money later which can then be spent on an increased quantity of goods and services.)

To look more closely at the investment decision, let us first consider the case of the owner-firm (i.e., one in which the company has only one shareholder, who owns all the shares), in which the owner is also the decision maker. In deciding to invest, the owner is forgoing some present consumption in order to increase future consumption and, in taking such action, he must also have decided that the future consumption so gained is somehow of greater value than the present consumption sacrificed in making the investment. To make such investment decisions in a consistent manner,[7] the owner requires a specific criterion that will enable him to judge whether or not any particular investment opportunity will produce sufficient compensation, in terms of increased future consumption, for having to reduce current consumption in order to make the investment. For example, dealing with the simple two-period situation of 'now' and 'next year', if the owner requires a minimum £1·20 next year in order to persuade him to forgo £1 of consumption now (i.e., he requires an *extra* 20p) then his 'exchange rate' between the two periods is given by $120/100 - 1 = 0.20$ or, in percentage terms, 20%. So the company will invest in a project only if the owner receives at least a 20% return; he is not willing to forgo current consumption to invest in a project which produces less than a 20% return. This 'exchange rate' between periods is called the Marginal Rate of Time Preference (MRTP)[8] and it is important to realize that it is unlikely to remain a constant but will probably increase as more and more present consumption is sacrificed for investment so as to produce a greater amount of future consumption. That is to say, with each successive reduction in current consumption the owner is likely to demand a higher and higher minimum future return in order to persuade him to invest, because each additional £1 of current consumption forgone is likely to be of increasing value (in terms of the benefits received from consumption), and each additional £1 of future consumption gained is likely to be of decreasing value. This is an example of the economic concept of diminishing marginal utility.

3.2 The basic graphical analysis

The owner-firm case The two-period graphical analysis, made under our six assumptions, is shown in Figure 3.1. The curve AB is called the 'physical investment line'[9] (PIL) and represents the complete range of maximum consumption combinations that the owner can obtain between the two periods[10] by applying varying amounts of the company's existing resources to physical investment opportunities.

Therefore as the owner gives up increasing amounts of current consumption in order to make physical investments, the company locates further and further up and around the physical investment line. (For instance if it locates at point A, no investment is undertaken and if it locates at point B, all possible physical investments are undertaken.) The physical investment line is composed of all the physical investment opportunities available to the company at period O, arranged in order of decreasing return.[11] (Thus the most 'profitable' investment – in terms of greatest return – would be undertaken first.)

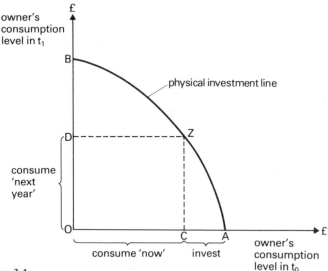

Figure 3.1

Using Figure 3.1, OA represents the owner's total wealth now (i.e., at t_0) and can be regarded as the (unforced) liquidation value of the company. If all this wealth is consumed now and none is invested, then there will be zero wealth available for consumption next year (i.e., t_1). If only part of this year's wealth is consumed, say OC, and the rest, CA, invested, then the company locates itself at point Z on the physical investment line and this level of investment will produce OD available for consumption next year. The return received by the company from the last (i.e., marginal) £1 of investment made in time period O – the final piece of investment that brings the company to locate at point Z – can be found from the slope of the physical investment line at that point.[12] But besides being the return on the marginal investment, this slope also represents something else. The company has located at point Z because the owner must feel that *further* investment is not worth while (i.e., the gain in next year's consumption generated by a marginal increase in investment does not provide sufficient compensation for the further reduction in present consumption that would be necessary to finance the increased investment), therefore the marginal return on investment being obtained at Z must be equal to the owner's marginal rate of time preference (MRTP). If the marginal return at Z was greater than his MRTP the company would continue to invest, and if it was less than his MRTP the company would have stopped investing *before* reaching point Z (because the return gained from a move along the PIL from below Z to point Z would have been insufficient compensation for the present consumption that would have to be forgone to make the investment).

We can derive this result better by asking the question: Given that the physical investment line represents a whole series of infinitely divisible and independent opportunities for investment projects, arranged in decreasing order of rate of return, so that the investment with the greatest return is ranked (and undertaken) first and the one with the smallest return last, how does the company know when to stop investing? In order to answer this fully, we have to use another economic concept: the Utility Curve. (It is assumed that the reader is familiar with the derivation and meaning of this term – it is explained in most basic economic textbooks. In rough terms, utility curves are curves of constant utility or welfare, and when mapped on to our graph of consumption 'now' and consumption 'next year', an individual utility curve indicates all possible combinations of consumption in the two periods which give the same level of utility. The curves are convex to the origin, indicating that there is diminishing marginal utility attached to any one period's consumption, and each utility curve, moving from left to right, gives the individual a higher overall level of utility.) Their place here concerns the fact that the set of utility curves belonging to the company's owner can be mapped on to the Figure 3.1 graph, as shown in Figure 3.2, and can be used to indicate at what point the company should stop investing; it is that point on the physical investment line which enables him to achieve his highest utility curve. This is found (on the basis of the assumption that utility curves are smooth and convex to the origin) at the point of tangency between a utility curve and the physical investment line. In terms of Figure 3.2, the company invests CA 'now' because the two-period pattern of consumption that results for the owner – OC 'now' and OD 'next year' – places him on his highest possible utility curve and so maximizes his welfare. The point of tangency between the two curves represents a point where the slopes of each equate. As the slope of the utility curve reflects an individual's rate of time preference and the slope of the physical investment line represents the rate of return on the marginal project, then the point where the slopes of these two curves equate must be the point at which the owner's marginal rate of time preference equals the return on the marginal investment made by the company. Thus the company continues to make physical investments until the return from the marginal investment (i.e., the last one made) equals the owner's rate of time preference. Any further investment will not produce the necessary return required and so will have the effect, in terms of our utility curve analysis, of placing the owner on a lower utility curve.[13]

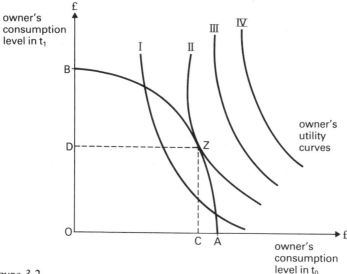

Figure 3.2

3.3 Introduction of capital markets

From this simple analysis, under a series of restrictive assumptions about the real world, we have seen how investment decisions would be made and why money is said to possess a 'time value' because individuals have rates of time preference. If we now make our analysis slightly more realistic by relaxing our third assumption so as to make available to the owner-firm the opportunity of being able to lend and borrow money on a 'capital market' at a rate of interest, we can then develop a second reason for money having a time value.

With the introduction of capital markets, the owner-firm is faced with three available courses of action at period O: consumption, physical investment, capital market investment. Assuming that there is a 'perfect' capital market[14] and therefore only one market rate of interest[15] (which is both the borrowing and lending rate), we can use the two-period graphical analysis to illustrate how the company makes investment decisions so as to allow the owner to distribute his consumption between the two periods in such a way that he maximizes his welfare.

The financial market line In terms of Figure 3.3, suppose an owner-firm has amount OG available for consumption in time period O and OH available in period 1. The capital market can be represented by a straight line, AE, which passes through point F, the co-ordinate of the existing consumption distribution. The slope of this line is given by $1 + r$, where r is the perfect capital market rate of interest, and the line is termed the Financial Market Line (FML). This line shows the range of capital market transactions available to the owner-firm, given the existing distribution of cash resources of OG now (i.e., t_0) and OH next year (i.e., t_1). A move *down* the financial investment line to (say) point L means that the owner-firm borrows GM on the capital market now – so increasing consumption from OG to OM – and repays (capital plus interest) HN next year – so reducing consumption from OH to ON. Notice that the maximum that can be borrowed now is amount GA; if the owner-firm attempts to borrow more than this, there will not be sufficient resources available next year to repay the capital and accrued interest. A move *up* the finan-

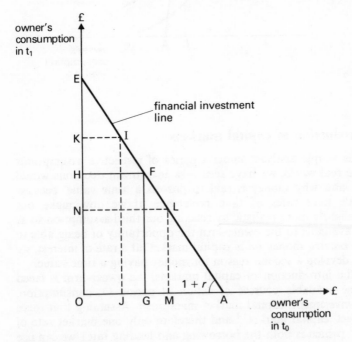

Figure 3.3

cial market line to (say) point I means that the owner-firm is lending on the capital market so as to reduce consumption now (to OJ) and to increase consumption next year (to OK). Again notice that a maximum of OG can be lent now – reducing current consumption to zero – and this results in having OE available for consumption next year.

The separation theorem Having seen how the financial investment line works, we can now combine the physical and financial investment lines so as to examine how both physical investment decisions *and* capital market borrowing or lending decisions are made in conjunction with each other, in order to allow the owner to achieve his highest possible utility curve and so optimize his consumption spread between the two periods. However, up to this point we have taken as our decision making entity the owner-firm, where the investment decision maker and the owner were one and the same person. Introducing the possibility of using the capital market allows us to analyse the investment decision process not only in the owner-firm case, but also in the much more important situation where there are *many* owners (i.e., shareholders) and they are separate from the investment decision makers (i.e., management). This is the Separation Theorem which gives the following investment decision rules: the company (i.e., managers) make physical investments until the return from the marginal physical investment equates with the perfect capital market interest rate/rate of return. This level of physical investment results in some two-period dividend flow to the shareholders. The shareholders then make financial investment decisions (by either borrowing or lending on the capital market) until their marginal rate of time preference equals the capital market rate of interest. Such action will result in their achieving their highest possible utility curve by producing a distribution of consumption between the two periods, which maximizes their individual welfare.

Graphical derivation of the decision rules We can see how these Separation Theorem decision rules are derived and why they help to maximize the shareholder's welfare by examining Figure 3.4. Here the financial investment line is superimposed on the Figure 3.1 situation. Let us assume for the moment that although ownership is separate from management, the company has only one shareholder.

The current liquidation value is OA. In the absence of a capital market we know that the company management will make physical investments up to point Z on the physical investment line. At this point the return from the marginal investment (derived from the slope of the physical investment line) equates with the shareholder's marginal rate of time preference (given by the slope of the utility curve tangential to point Z). Thus, in our two-period world, the shareholder would receive a 'dividend' of OC now and OD next year.

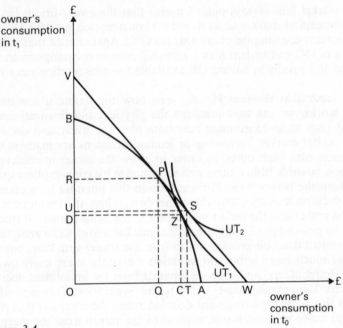

Figure 3.4

This distribution of consumption between the two periods places him on his highest attainable utility curve: UT_1, and so maximizes his welfare.

With the introduction of a capital market, the company's management now undertake physical investments up to the point where the return on the marginal physical investment equates with the capital market interest rate/rate of return (derived from the slope of the financial investment line). This occurs at point P where the financial investment line is tangent to the physical investment line. Thus the shareholder receives a different dividend distribution: OQ now and OR next year. The company has undertaken physical investments up to point P because this has the effect of placing the shareholder on the highest possible financial investment line.

Unlike the situation where capital market opportunities did not exist, the shareholder does *not* have to accept the two-period dividend distribution given by the company for consumption. Instead, he can borrow or lend on the capital market (i.e., move down or up VW from point P) so as to adjust his received dividend flow to suit whatever consumption pattern is preferred. This preferred pattern is given by the point on the financial investment line which is tangent to one of his utility curves, because this utility curve will be the highest attainable. Thus the shareholder either lends or borrows on the capital market until his marginal rate of time preference (derived from the slope of the utility curve) equates with the perfect capital market rate of interest. In Figure 3.4 the shareholder achieves this point, S, by moving down the financial investment line and borrowing an amount QT to make a total of OT available for consumption 'now' and OU available for consumption 'next year'. (A dividend of OR is received from the company next year, but part of this, RU, is used to repay the borrowed capital and accrued interest.) Whether the shareholder lends or borrows or even omits to use the capital market at all depends solely upon the location of the point of tangency between the financial investment line and the shareholder's utility curve, as Figure 3.5 shows. What Figure 3.4 illustrates is how, by taking advantage of both physical *and* financial investment opportunities, the shareholder can attain a higher utility curve, UT_2 (and so increase his welfare), than would have been possible from making physical investments alone. In fact this can unambiguously be seen occurring in Figure 3.4, because the shareholder has managed to increase his consumption in *both* periods through using the capital market: by amount CT 'now' and UD 'next year'.[16]

The multi-owner firm The development of this Separation Theorem is extremely important. It results in a company's management making only *physical* investment decisions and leaving individual shareholders to adjust their received dividend pattern to fit their particular requirements by using the capital market. In the owner-firm and in the situation where ownership and management are separate but there is only *one* owner, it makes no difference to the analysis whether the individual owner/shareholder uses the capital markets or the company uses the capital markets on the owner's/shareholder's behalf (as long as, in the case where owner and management are separate, the managers are aware of the owner's marginal rate of time preference). However, the crucial importance of the Separation Theorem comes when ownership is separated from management and there is more than one owner. Quite simply, different individuals have different rates of time preference, and so a company would be able to undertake the physical investment decisions but *not* the financial investment decisions, because there would be more than one marginal rate of time preference.[17] The use of the Separation Theorem avoids this problem by leaving the financial investment decisions to the individual shareholders. Figure 3.6 shows a situation where a company is owned by two shareholders: one with 75% of the equity (Shareholder 1) and the other, 25% of the equity (Shareholder 2). The firm continues to make physical investments until the marginal return on investment equates with the market rate of investment, and then pays out the resulting dividend in each period to each shareholder in

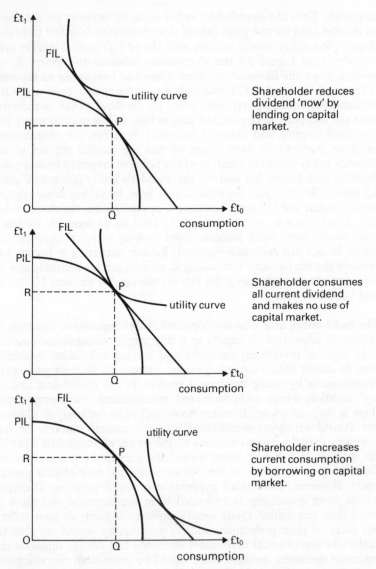

Figure 3.5

proportion to his equity holding. In so doing, the company would be still ensuring that each individual shareholder is placed on the highest possible financial investment line. It is then up to the individual shareholder to make whatever decision is best, in the knowledge of his own set of utility curves and marginal rate of time preference, with

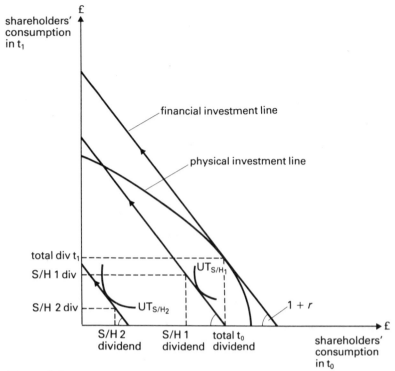

Figure 3.6

regard to using the capital market in order to adjust his received dividend flow. In the example shown in Figure 3.6, Shareholder 1 (75% holding) uses the capital market to borrow and so increases consumption 'now' at the expense of a reduced future consumption level. Shareholder 2 uses the capital market to lend, thereby reducing consumption 'now' but, in return, having an increased level of consumption 'next year'.

The conclusions of the basic model This development of the two period investment–consumption model, as it is called, is important not only for illustrating how and why money has a time value, but also as acting as an introduction to financial decision making in general. In this respect, we stated that management's objective must be to try to maximize shareholder's wealth and this would be achieved through the maximization of the dividend flow through time. The Separation Theorem placed this latter statement in a clearer light. Management must make investment decisions so as to maximize the dividend flow to shareholders, but this is only the first stage of a two-stage process, because the individual shareholder then uses the capital market to adjust the timing of this dividend flow so that it accords with his desired patterns of consumption.

These conclusions of our two-period investment–consumption model *and the assumptions upon which it is based* are important and wide-ranging (as we shall see later). The model implies that we require a technique of investment appraisal which will ensure that companies undertake physical investment until the return from the marginal investment equates with the perfect capital market rate of return. In other words, companies should undertake investment in projects as long as the return generated (from each one) is *not less* than the market rate of interest.

Clearly, the Payback method does not meet this requirement (even if it can be adapted to allow for the time value of money) because it uses 'time' rather than 'rate of return' as its criterion of project desirability. Equally unsuitable is the Return on Capital Employed because, although it is a rate-of-return concept, it ignores the time value of money.[18, 19] In the next chapter we shall turn to the discounted cash flow methods of investment appraisal and examine the extent to which they meet the requirements of our model.[20]

Selected references

I. Fisher, *The Theory of Interest*, New York, Augustus M. Kelley, 1965.

J. R. Hicks, *Value and Capital*, 2nd ed., Oxford, Clarendon Press, 1946.

J. Hirshleifer, 'On the Theory of Optimal Investment Decisions', *Journal of Political Economy*, August 1958.

J. Hirshleifer, *Investment, Interest and Capital*, Englewood Cliffs, N.J., Prentice-Hall, 1970.

4 The Discounted Cash Flow Approach

4.1 Net Present Value

Introduction There are basically two discounted cash flow (DCF) methods of investment appraisal, the net present value (NPV) and the internal rate of return (IRR) methods. We shall start by first examining the net present value method.

The NPV investment appraisal method works on the simple but fundamental principle that an investment is worth undertaking only if the money got out of the investment is at least equal to, if not greater than, the money put in. (Indeed, we could almost define 'investment' in this way.) On this commonsense principle, Project B2 is worth investing in, because for an outlay of £500 it produces £600 in return; but Project B3 is not worth while, because an outlay of £1,000 returns only £850. With Project B2 we can say this net value is +£100, whilst the net value of Project B3 is −£150:

Project B2			*Project B3*		
Year	Cash flow		Year	Cash flow	
0	−£500		0	−£400	
1	+£200		1	−£600	
2	+£200		2	+£400	
3	+£200		3	+£250	
			4	+£200	
Net value	+£100		Net value	−£150	

We can easily see that with such a straightforward approach, the decision criterion would be: accept all investments with a zero or a positive net value (as they produce a return equal to or greater than their cost) and reject all those with a negative net value. This is the decision rule that the NPV method uses but with just one difference, which is that the time value of money is taken into account in assessing whether an investment has a positive or negative net value.

The discounting process Allowance for the time value of money is achieved through 'discounting' the cash flow. These discounting techniques, including the effects of different discount rates and a discussion on the basic mathematics of the present and terminal values of annuities and their variants are developed in an appendix and the reader is advised to become familiar with its contents. However, it will help us to explain the NPV method if the basic discounting approach is also developed here.

We have already seen from our initial discussion on the time value of money that, given the choice between £100 now or £100 in twelve months' time, most people would 'intuitively' take the £100 now (even if both alternatives were certain) because the money could be put on deposit at the Bank to earn (say) 6% interest and so turn the £100 into £106 in twelve months' time. In such a case, if offered the choice between £100 now or £106 in twelve months' time, we should have no preference, because each alternative would be equally attractive. We can say that £100 is the '*present* value' of £106 to be received in twelve months' time.

The mathematics of this process works through the compound interest formula:

$$A \cdot (1 + r)^N$$

where A is the initial amount invested or deposited, r is the (annual) rate of interest and N is the number of years for which A is left deposited. In the example used above, these three letters (or 'unknowns') have the respective values of: £100, 0·06 and 1. So, £100 left on deposit for twelve months is turned into:

$$£100 \cdot (1 + 0·06)^1 = £100 + £6 = £106$$

Using this compound interest formula, but switching it around, we can also calculate that to receive £106 in twelve months' time, the amount to be invested now is:

$$£106 \cdot \frac{1}{(1 + 0·06)} = \frac{£106}{(1 + 0·06)} = £100$$

We can term £100 the 'present value' of £106 received in twelve months' time, and £106 the 'terminal value' of £100 deposited twelve months' previously, assuming a 6% interest rate in each case.

Similarly, £100 invested for two years at a 6% compound interest rate would turn into:

$$£100 \cdot (1 + 0·06) \cdot (1 + 0·06) = £100(1 + 0·06)^2 = £112·36$$

and £112·36 received in two years' time is equal to:

$$£112·36 \cdot \frac{1}{(1 + 0·06)(1 + 0·06)} = \frac{£112·36}{(1 + 0·06)^2} = £100 \text{ now}$$

Thus the terminal value in two years' time of £100 invested now is £112·36, whilst the present value of £112·36 received in two years' time is £100. In each case we are assuming an annual compound interest rate of 6%.

In general terms: $A(1 + r)^N$ is the terminal value in N years time of an amount A which is invested now at an annual compound interest rate of r. Similarly: $A \cdot [1/(1 + r)^N]$ is the present value of an amount A received in N years' time, where r is the annual compound interest rate (or the *discount* rate as it is called in calculations of present value). The NPV method makes use of the idea of present values, although it could be quite easily expressed in terms of net *terminal* value rather than net *present* value. To see how the NPV method works, let us return to Project B2, but this time, instead of just netting out the cash inflows and outflows to produce a net value of $+£100$, we first of all convert (or 'discount') the cash flows to *present value* cash flows in order to allow for the time value of money and then net out the inflows and outflows. Thus with a discount rate of (say) 8%, the net present value of Project B2 is $+£15 \cdot 40$.

Project B2

Year	Cash flow	×	Present value factor			Present value cash
0	$-£500$		$1/(1 + 0 \cdot 08)^0$	$= -£500 \cdot 1$		$= -£500 \cdot 00$
1	$+£200$		$1/(1 + 0 \cdot 08)^1$	$= +£200 \cdot 0 \cdot 9259$		$= +£185 \cdot 18$
2	$+£200$		$1/(1 + 0 \cdot 08)^2$	$= +£200 \cdot 0 \cdot 8573$		$= +£171 \cdot 46$
3	$+£200$		$1/(1 + 0 \cdot 08)^3$	$= +£200 \cdot 0 \cdot 7938$		$= +£158 \cdot 76$
Net value	$+£100$				Net present value	$+£ \ 15 \cdot 40$

From this analysis we can see that Project B2 is worth undertaking because the cash outflows associated with it are exceeded by the cash inflows produced by it. The time value of money has been taken into account by the fact that all the cash flows of the project, for the purposes of comparison, are converted to values at one point in time: the present. To emphasize this important point further, it is vital to understand that once the fact is accepted that money has a time value, then it follows that money at different points in time is not directly comparable: £1 now cannot be directly compared with £1 next year, and so the cash flows of a project that arise at different points through time all have to be converted to a value at one particular point in time. By convention, and because it has many practical advantages, the point in time normally chosen is the present. Thus our original netting procedure with Project B2 which produced a net value of $+£100$ was nonsensical, because we were not comparing like with like but were trying to compare directly the net money flows arising at different points in time without first converting them to a common point in time. Our NPV approach tells us that in terms of present values (i.e., converting all the cash flows to money values *now*) Project B2 produces a return which is £15·40 in excess of the investment outlay (i.e., in present value terms the cash outflow is £500 and the total cash inflow is £515·40) and is therefore a worthwhile investment.

Evaluating Project B4 without taking into account the time value of money, the cash inflows exceed the cash outflows by £50 and so the project appears to be a worthwhile investment. However if we do take into account the time value of money by discounting the cash flows into present values at an 8% discount rate, then we can see that Project B4 is *not* a worthwhile investment because the cash outflow required exceeds the cash inflows produced, resulting in a negative net present value:

Project B4

Year	Cash flow	×	Present value factor	=	Present value cash flow
0	−£1,000		$1/(1 + 0·08)^0$		−£1,000·00
1	+£ 100		$1/(1 + 0·08)^1$		+£ 92·59
2	+£ 200		$1/(1 + 0·08)^2$		+£ 171·46
3	+£ 200		$1/(1 + 0·08)^3$		+£ 158·76
4	+£ 550		$1/(1 + 0·08)^4$		+£ 404·25
Net value +£ 50			Net present value −£ 172·94		

The NPV model In general terms, we can express the net present value of an investment project as the sum of its discounted future cash flows:

$$\sum_{t=0}^{N} \frac{A_t}{(1 + r)^t}$$

where A_t is the project's cash flow (either positive or negative) in period t (t takes on values from period 0 to period N) and r is the annual rate of discount (which is here assumed to remain a constant over the life of the project). If the expression has a zero or positive value, the company should invest in the project; if it has a negative value, it should not invest.[1,2] (This general mathematical expression for the net present value of an investment project is more fully explained in the appendix on compounding and discounting.)

Let us take a closer look at Project B4 to see why the NPV method tells us not to invest. Project B4 requires an outlay of £1,000 and would produce cash inflows for the four following years. However, if we did not invest £1,000 in B4 we could presumably put the money on deposit (i.e., lend the money on the capital market) at the going rate of interest of 8%. At the end of four years this would produce £1,000 . $(1 + 0·08)^4 = £1,360·49$.

Suppose we *did* invest in Project B4 and as they arose we placed on deposit (at 8% compound interest) the cash inflows that the project produced. What value would this accumulate to by the end of four years (i.e., by the time the life of the project was completed)? This is shown in the table below, where the £100 Project B4 produces can be invested for three years, the £200 it produces in twenty-four months' time can be invested for two years, and so on:

Year	Project's cash × inflow	Compound interest factor	Terminal value (end of year 4)
1	+£100	$(1 + 0.08)^3$	= +£ 125.97
2	+£200	$(1 + 0.08)^2$	= +£ 233.28
3	+£200	$(1 + 0.08)^1$	= +£ 216.00
4	+£550	$(1 + 0.08)^0$	= +£ 550.00
		Total terminal value =	+£1,125.25

So putting the £1,000 on deposit for four years produces £1,360.49, whilst if we invest our £1,000 in Project B4 and place on deposit any cash flows that arise, at the end of four years this will produce £1,125.25. Therefore, looking at the two alternatives, the project is not the most desirable investment: we should be better off placing the £1,000 on deposit in the capital market. This is the basis of the advice given by the NPV appraisal method.

Also notice that the present value of £1,360.49 received in four year's time with an 8% discount rate is:

$$£1,360.49 \cdot \frac{1}{(1 + 0.08)^4} = £1,000$$

whilst the present value of £1,125.25 received in four years' time with an 8% discount rate is:

$$£1,125.25 \cdot \frac{1}{(1 + 0.08)^4} = £827.06$$

The difference between these two sums (£1,000 − £827.06) is £172.94, which is the amount of Project B4's negative net present value.

So we can see that the net present value method of investment appraisal evaluates projects by looking at the *alternative* to investment in that project, that is, lending the money out on the capital market at the market rate of interest. It automatically carries out this comparison of alternatives through the decision rule: only invest in projects which produce zero or positive NPVs. As we have seen, the value of a project's NPV represents the increase or decrease (depending upon whether the NPV is positive or negative) in return that would arise from investing in the project rather than lending the money on the capital market at the market rate of interest, and it is this rate that is used as the discount rate.

NPV method and the investment–consumption model When looking
at our two-period investment–consumption model, we saw that in
order best to further the interests of its owners, a company should
move along the physical investment line until the return from the
marginal investment becomes equal to the return given by the capital
market (i.e., the market rate of interest). How does the NPV method
of investment appraisal help us achieve this point? Returning to
Project B2, we saw that, using an 8% discount rate, the project had
an NPV of +£15.40 whilst Project B4 had an NPV of −£172.94.
Collaterally to what we already understand about the net present
value, we can also say – using the two examples above – that as
Project B2 has a positive NPV when discounted at 8%, it must be
producing a rate of return greater than 8%, and similarly as Project
B4 has a negative NPV when discounted at 8%, then it must produce
a rate of return of less than 8%. Just what the exact rate of return is
in each case we shall consider later, but looking at Project B5, since it
gives a zero NPV when discounted at 8% we can conclude that it has
a rate of return *exactly* equal to 8%.

Project B5

Year	Cash flow	$\times$ 8% Present value factor	= Present value cash flow
0	-400	$1/(1 + 0.08)^0$	$-£400.00$
1	$+200$	$1/(1 + 0.08)^1$	$+£185.18$
2	$+100$	$1/(1 + 0.08)^2$	$+£\ 85.73$
3	$+163$	$1/(1 + 0.08)^3$	$+£129.09$
		Net present value	$£\ \ 0$

Therefore, if a company follows the NPV rule and invests in all
physical investment opportunities that possess either zero or positive
net present values, using the market rate of interest as the discount
rate, it will automatically move along the physical investment line
until a point of tangency is reached with the financial investment line.
If a company makes physical investments beyond this optimal point,
these projects will have a rate of return which is less than the market
rate of interest and therefore negative net present values. As long as
investment decision makers within companies follow the NPV decision rule and *only* invest in projects with zero or positive NPVs, then
the company is ensured of optimally locating on the physical investment line. However, it is important to remember that this analysis of
the discounted cash flow appraisal methods (both NPV and IRR) is
being carried out (for the time being) under the six assumptions
which were made at the outset of the discussion on the two-period
investment–consumption model.

In Figure 4.1, if management assess the company's total resources (i.e., the full, liquidated value of the company at time t_0) as OA and they have sought out all possible investment alternatives available, expressed by the physical investment line AB, then using the NPV method of investment appraisal, they will invest in all projects with positive or zero NPVs when discounted at the market rate of interest.

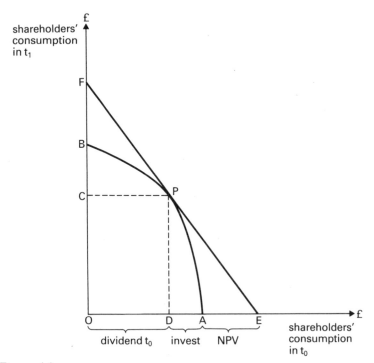

Figure 4.1

This simple decision rule will lead to DA of the company's resources being put into productive investments and the remainder, OD, being paid out to shareholders as dividends. Shareholders can then adjust their individual dividends to fit their desired consumption pattern by lending or borrowing on the capital market. This two-stage process, with the company first making physical investment decisions and then the individual shareholder making financial investment decisions, will ensure that the individual shareholder will achieve his highest possible utility curve and hence maximize his level of welfare.

We should also note that if the company does invest up to the optimal point P in Figure 4.1 (i.e., the point of tangency between the physical and financial investment lines), then the present value of the cash *inflows* generated by all the company's investment project undertakings is given by DE, the cash expenditure made on these investments is given by DA and so, by difference, AE represents the total *net* present value of the investment projects undertaken by the firm. (Alternatively, OE represents the present value of the sum of dividend OD at t_0 and dividend OC at t_1.)

In general, the two-period investment–consumption diagram can measure the NPV of a company's total physical investments as the distance between the point at which the physical investment line cuts the horizontal axis and where the financial investment line, passing through the point at which the firm has located on the physical investment line, also cuts the horizontal axis.[3] As can be seen from Figure 4.2, if a company either underinvests and locates at point X, or overinvests and locates at point Y, or optimally invests and locates at point Z on the physical investment line, in each case the total NPV

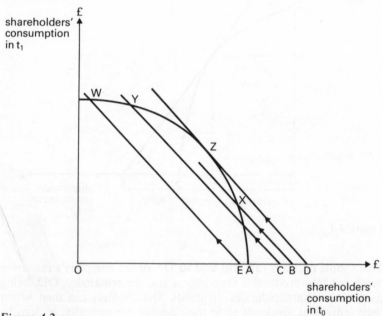

Figure 4.2

earned by the company's investment decision is given by the distance on the horizontal axis between the physical investment line and the financial investment line passing through the location point: respectively AB, AC and AD.[4] Locating at the optimal point on the physical investment line (at the point of tangency with the market line), also maximizes NPV and so here is yet another surrogate for the financial decision making objective of maximizing shareholder wealth, that of maximizing total net present value.

One final point of interest from this graphical analysis is to use it to look at the effect of a change in the market rate of interest. A fall in the market rate of interest will cause the financial investment line to pivot anticlockwise and become flatter. This would then have the effect of moving the point of tangency (and hence the optimal physical investment point) higher up the physical investment line, thus increasing the amount of investment that a company must undertake to reach its point of optimality. This is just as we would expect, as is with the case where the market rate of interest rises and the reverse effect is observed.

4.2 Internal rate of return

Before looking more carefully at this analysis and specifically at the implicit and explicit assumptions that lie behind the NPV method, let us turn to the second major discounted cash flow investment appraisal technique, the Internal Rate of Return (IRR) or Yield.[5] As we shall see later on in the discussion, the IRR has some very great theoretical and practical difficulties as a method of investment appraisal, and indeed it may be questioned whether it is truly a method of appraisal at all or just an arithmetical result.

The IRR model To discover what the IRR is, let us return briefly to our discussion of NPV, where we stated that if a project had a positive NPV at a certain discount rate (say) 10%, this meant, amongst other things, that the project's return was actually greater than 10%, whilst if the project had a negative NPV then its return was less than the discount rate, and if it had a zero NPV, then its return was equal to the discount rate. The internal rate of return of a project is the rate of discount that, when applied to the project's cash flows, produces a zero NPV (hence the method could be seen as just an arithmetical result of the NPV method). In general terms, the IRR is the value for r which satisfies the expression:

$$\sum_{t=0}^{n} \frac{A_t}{(1 + r)^t} = 0$$

For a very simple project such as B6, where cash flows only extend over two periods, the internal rate of return is easy to calculate using simple algebra.

Project B6

Year	Cash flow	
		IRR = r, where:
0	−£200	$-200 + \dfrac{218}{1 + r} = 0$
1	+£218	multiplying both sides by $(1 + r)$:
		$-200(1 + r) + 218 = 0$
		$218 = 200 + 200r$
		$218 - 200 = 200r$
		$18 = 200r$
		$18/200 = r = \underline{0\cdot09} = 9\%$

Thus if Project B6's cash flows were discounted by 9% they would have a zero NPV:

Project B6

Year	Cash flow	9% Present value factor	= Present value factor
0	−£200	$1/(1 + 0\cdot09)^0$	−£200
1	+£218	$1/(1 + 0\cdot09)^1$	+£200
		Net present value	£ 0

And with a slightly more complex project, with cash flows occurring in three periods, 0, 1 and 2, the IRR can still be easily found through the solution to a quadratic equation, as with Project B7:

Project B7

Year	Cash flow	
		IRR = r, where:
0	−£100	$-100 + \dfrac{60}{1 + r} + \dfrac{70}{(1 + r)^2} = 0$
1	+£ 60	
2	+£ 70	multiplying both sides by $(1 + r)^2$, we produce a quadratic equation in $1 + r$ that can be solved via the quadratic formula:
		$-100(1 + r)^2 + 60(1 + r) + 70 = 0$
		$(1 + r) = \dfrac{-60 \pm \sqrt{60^2 - (4. - 100 . 70)}}{(2. - 100)}$
		$1 + r = +1\cdot1888$ or $1 + r = -0\cdot5888$

This second (negative) result can be discarded as meaningless for our purposes, so that $1 + r = 1\cdot1888$ and so $r = 0\cdot1888$ or $18\cdot88\%$. This is the internal rate of return of Project B7, and therefore if the project's cash flows were discounted at this rate they would have a zero NPV.

Calculating the IRR via linear interpolation However, to find the IRR of projects whose cash flows extend over more than three periods, we become involved with finding solutions to complex polynomial equations. There are several computer package programmes that will carry out this task, but a fairly good *approximation* of an investment project's IRR can be found through the mathematical technique called linear interpolation. Returning to Project B7, although we have found its IRR to be 18·88%, let us now calculate it by using the linear interpolation method. The approach is to choose two discount rates to apply to the project, so that one produces a positive NPV and the other a negative NPV. Discounting Project B7 by 18% and 20% produces this required result:

Project B7

Year	Cash flow	18% Present value factor	Present value cash flow
0	−£100	$1/(1 + 0·18)^0$	−£100·00
1	+£ 60	$1/(1 + 0·18)^1$	+£ 50·85
2	+£ 70	$1/(1 + 0·18)^2$	+£ 50·27
		Net present value	−£ +1·12

Year	Cash flow	20% Present value factor	Present value cash flow
0	−£100	$1/(1 + 0·20)^0$	−£100·00
1	+£ 60	$1/(1 + 0·20)^1$	+£ 50·00
2	+£ 70	$1/(1 + 0·20)^2$	+£ 48·61
		Net present value	−£ −1·39

Figure 4.3 shows diagrammatically how Project B7's 'net present value profile' can be constructed by applying a variety of rates of discount to the cash flow. On the basis of the two NPVs calculated above and using the principle of 'similar triangles', we can approximate the IRR of Project B7 as:

$$0·18 + \left[\frac{1·12}{1·12 + 1·39} (0·20 - 0·18) \right] = \underline{\underline{0·1889}}$$

This 'bracketing' of discount rates around the true IRR so as to produce a positive and a negative NPV is not necessary;[6] but it does make the approximation calculations easier, and the narrower the bracketing the closer the approximation and vice versa. For example, in Project B7 using 18% and 20% discount rates we achieved a very good approximation of the IRR: 18·89% as against a 'true' rate of

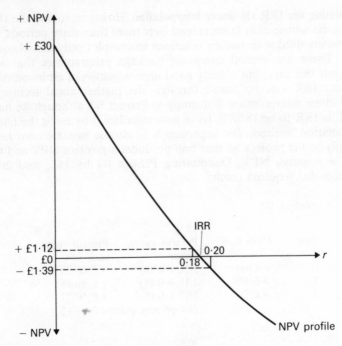

Figure 4.3   NVP profile, Project B7

18·88%; but using 15% and 25% discount rates produces an approximation of the IRR of 19·15%. The reason for this is that in calculating IRR in this way, we are assuming that the project's 'present value profile' is a straight line when in fact it will normally be a curve. Thus, the greater the interval between the two discount rates, the less satisfactory this assumption becomes and the more approximate becomes the calculation of the IRR. Figure 4.4 illustrates this approximation.

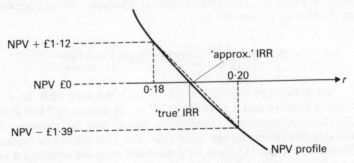

Figure 4.4

IRR and the investment–consumption model Having seen how to calculate a project's internal rate of return, how are we to use it for investment appraisal purposes? The decision rule is that only projects with an IRR greater than or equal to some predetermined 'cut-off' rate should be accepted. This cut-off rate is usually the company's discount rate (i.e., the market rate of interest). All other investment project opportunities should be rejected.

The reasoning behind the IRR decision rule is similar to that behind the NPV rule in so far as the market rate of interest is what the project 'costs'[7] the company in having the capital tied up in the investment; and so the project must earn at least that rate of return in order to be accepted. If a project's IRR is less than the market rate of interest, then the company will not undertake the investment because the project will not earn a sufficient return, and in any case a higher return could be obtained through lending the money on the capital market.

Again, just as the NPV method fitted into our two period investment–consumption model so too does the IRR method. We originally described the physical investment line as representing the whole series of infinitely divisible physical investment projects which were available to the company, arranged in order of decreasing rate of return. This rate of return is the individual project's internal rate of return and can be derived (as we have already seen) from the slope of the physical investment line. In Figure 4.5 therefore, moving progressively along the line from point A to B, the slope gets less and less steep, indicating that the company initially invest in projects with high internal rates of return and then works its way through to projects with much smaller IRRs. Thus from the slope of the physical investment line at point C can be derived the IRR of the marginal physical investment represented by that point. The IRR decision rule tells a company to invest in all projects with IRRs greater than or equal to the market rate of interest. Thus a company will move up and around its physical investment line until it reaches the point of tangency with the financial investment line. Up to this point, all investment projects that the company has undertaken will have IRRs greater than the market rate of interest. At point D on Figure 4.5, the marginal project will have an IRR equal to the market interest rate, and it is at this point that the company will cease further investment, because the remaining investment opportunities will all have IRRs which are less than the market interest rate. Therefore, the internal rate of return investment appraisal rule will, like the NPV rule, ensure that a company locates at the optimal point on its physical investment line.

The assumptions Having seen that both the discounted cash flow methods of investment appraisal allow companies successfully to attain the first stage of the two-stage optimal decision process (i.e., they allow

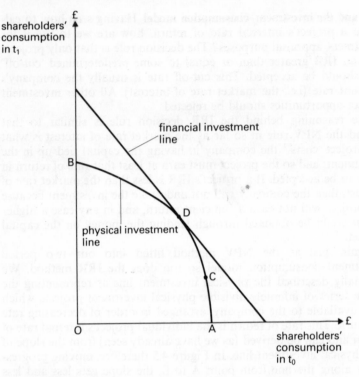

Figure 4.5

management to make 'correct' physical investment decisions), let us now turn to see whether either or both the DCF methods continue to give such seemingly good investment advice in the real world. On the basis of our analysis so far, they only give such good advice under the rather unrealistic assumptions of our two period investment–consumption model. Briefly relisting them, the six assumptions[8] we have adopted are:

1 Two periods.
2 Certainty.
3 All investments are infinitely divisible.
4 All investment cash flows are independent.
5 Shareholders are rational.
6 Perfect capital markets.

At best, all that can be said about these six assumptions is that they give a very doubtful reflection of the real world. In later chapters, we shall examine the 'reality' of each assumption and analyse the effects of relaxing them (or making them more realistic) on the validity of the investment advice given by the NPV and IRR appraisal methods. To this end, we now shall relax assumptions 1 and 4 as we attempt to compare the two appraisal methods.

4.3 Relaxation of the project independence assumption

Mutually exclusive projects Let us now examine what happens to the effectiveness of the two DCF rules of investment appraisal when the assumption of project independence is dropped. There are several types of project interdependence. The first, a very common situation in practice, is where a company is faced with a choice amongst competing alternative investments (in fact, it is probably much more common than a situation concerning a single independent project). In such circumstances the decision is not just simply to accept or reject a particular investment, but is first to choose the 'best' amongst a series of alternative investments and then to decide whether that 'best alternative' is a worthwhile investment to undertake. Thus we are moving away from the simple decision on independent projects to a decision involving choice amongst mutually exclusive projects.[9]

We have already seen from the two-period investment-consumption model that, in terms of net present value (and under the assumptions of the model), the higher the aggregate NPV of a firm's investments, the higher will be the level of wealth achieved by its shareholders. Therefore, as far as deciding between mutually exclusive investment alternatives is concerned, the solution would appear to be quite straightforward in terms of using the NPV rule: accept whichever alternative produces the greatest positive NPV because this will produce the greatest addition to the shareholders' wealth.

An Example Suppose a company has to make an investment decision concerning two mutually exclusive projects, B8 and B9, whose cash flows are set out below:[10]

Project B8

Year	Cash flow	10% Discount rate	= Present value
0	− 1500	1	− 1500
1	+ 500	0·9091	+ 454·55
2	+ 800	0·8264	+ 661·12
3	+ 1000	0·7513	+ 751·30
		Net present value	+ 366·97

Project B9

Year	Cash flow	10% Discount rate	= Present value
0	− 1900	1	− 1900
1	+ 500	0·9091	+ 454·55
2	+ 800	0·8264	+ 661·12
3	+ 1000	0·7513	+ 751·30
4	+ 447	0·6830	+ 305·30
		Net present value	+ 272·27

Assuming the appropriate discount rate is 10%, when the project cash flows are converted to present values, Project B8 is preferred to B9 because it has the larger positive NPV. It is important to realize that the appraisal method in such circumstances is entirely unaffected by the fact that these two projects have differing capital outlays and life-spans. The whole decision is based purely on the absolute size of the positive NPV. A decision can be made in this way, using only a slight (and rather obvious) modification of the basic NPV decision rule, because of the underlying assumption of a perfect capital market. Therefore, the fact that one project requires only £1,500 of capital as against £1,900 for the other project is irrelevant, because investment funds are freely available. The fact that one project has a life of four years and the other a life of three years is also irrelevant. The cash flows are being discounted at the market interest rate and so a full allowance is being made for their different timings.

However, the operation of this modified NPV rule for mutually exclusive projects requires an additional assumption in the face of unequal project lives (but not unequal investment outlays). This is that the mutually exclusive projects are 'isolated' investments in the sense that they do not form part of a replacement chain. In other words, it is assumed that the nature of the mutually exclusive projects is such that, when whichever project is chosen, it will not be replaced when it reaches the end of its life. If this assumption does *not* hold, then we are involved with a different type of project interdependence which requires a more complex decision rule.

The replacement cycle problem In a simple world of unchanging technology, the problem presented by this second type of project interdependence is relatively straightforward. Suppose a company requires a machine to perform an essential job in its factory (and this requirement will not change). Because the job undertaken by the machine is essential, the machine will have to be replaced when it reaches the end of its operational life. The assumption of unchanging technology implies that the replacement machine will be identical with the machine initially chosen for the task.[11] The choice of machine is between two alternatives C1 and C2, which have the following cash flows, lives and net present values when discounted at the market interest rate of 10%:

Project C1

Year	Cash flow	×	10% Discount factor	= Present value
0	− 1500		1	− 1500
1	+ 550		0·9091	+ 500·01
2	+ 1400		0·8264	+ 1156·96
			Net present value +	156·97

Project C2

Year	Cash flow	×	10% Discount factor	= Present value
0	− 1900		1	− 1900
1	+ 400		0·9091	+ 363·64
2	+ 800		0·8264	+ 661·12
3	+ 800		0·7513	+ 601·04
4	+ 700		0·6830	+ 478·10
			Net present value +	203·90

Using the modified NPV rule for mutually exclusive projects, Project C2 would be the preferred alternative because it has the larger positive NPV. However, we cannot consider these machines as two mutually exclusive projects in isolation, because they form an interdependent part of a continuous replacement cycle. Therefore, when projects must be replaced when they come to the end of their operational life, alternative projects *with differing lives* cannot be compared directly, because like is not being compared with like.

One approach to the problem is to take a period which represents the lowest common denominator of the life-spans of the investment alternatives. In this example, where project C1 has a life-span of two years and C2 has a life-span of four years, the period we would take is four years. Over this span of time, if Project C1 were chosen to perform the required task, a replacement would be required at the end of year 2, whilst, if Project C2 were chosen, no replacement would be required over the period. Table 4.1 sets out, for both alternatives, the cash flows that would occur over the four-year period and calculates the resulting NPVs.

Looking at the results of Table 4.1 we can see that, when comparing the alternative projects over a common time-span, Project C1 is preferred to C2, on the basis of having a larger positive NPV. This process of comparing projects over a span of time equal to the lowest common denominator of their individual life spans can be very tedious,[12] and so, as a simpler alternative which produces identical decision advice, annual equivalent factors[13] are usually employed. The results of applying these factors to the two projects in the example used are shown in Table 4.2. The annual equivalent factor for Project C1 indicates that a positive NPV of £156·97 produced over a two-year period is equivalent to an annual net cash inflow of £90·45; whilst the positive NPV of £203·90 produced over a four-year

Table 4.1 4-year replacement cycle

Project C1

Year	Cash flow + M/C 1	Cash flow M/C 2	×	10% Discount factor	= Present value
0	− 1500			1	− 1500
1	+ 550			0·9091	+ 500·01
2	+ 1400	− 1500		0·8264	− 82·64
3		+ 550		0·7513	+ 413·21
4		+ 1400		0·6830	+ 956·20
				Net present value	+ 286·78

Project C2

Year	Cash flow	×	10% Discount value	= Present value
0	− 1900		1	− 1900
1	+ 400		0·9091	+ 363·64
2	+ 800		0·8264	+ 661·12
3	+ 800		0·7513	+ 601·04
4	+ 700		0·6830	+ 478·10
			Net present value	+ 203·90

Table 4.2

Project C1

At a 10% discount rate: NPV = +£156·97
The appropriate annual equivalent factor, at a 10% discount rate, for a project with a two-year life is:

$$A_{2|\cdot10}^{-1} = 0{\cdot}5762$$

Thus Project C1's positive NPV of £156·97, generated over a two year time period, is equivalent to an annual cash flow (over these two years) of:

$$£156{\cdot}97 . 0{\cdot}5762 = £90{\cdot}45$$

Project C2

Similarly, Project C2 yielded: NPV = +£203·90
The appropriate annual equivalent factor, at a 10% discount rate, for a project with a four-year life is:

$$A_{4|·10}^{-1} = 0·3155$$

Therefore, Project C2's positive NPV of £203·90, generated over a four-year period, is equivalent to an annual cash flow (over these four years) of:

$$£203·90 . 0·3155 = \underline{£64·33}$$

period by Project C2 is equivalent to an annual net cash inflow of £64·33. The larger net cash inflow is obviously preferable (on the assumption of rational shareholders) and it is on this basis that the investment choice is made.[14] Therefore, in a situation of mutually exclusive projects which form part of a continuous replacement chain – and so have to be replaced at the end of their operational lives – *and the alternative projects have differing lives*, choice cannot be based on the absolute size of positive NPV, but must be based on the size of the annual net cash flow equivalent of the NPV. The project which produces the largest such annual equivalent is then preferred.

This analysis has been carried out under the important assumption of unchanging technology, so that if Project C1 is chosen, it is assumed that it will be replaced – *ad infinitum* – by a similar Project C1. The presence of, and allowance for, technological change complicates the analysis somewhat because allowance has to be made for the possibility that a shorter-lived alternative may have the additional advantage of allowing a company to take speedier advantage of technological improvements at lower cost. This problem will not be examined here, but will be referred to in Chapter 11, which deals with the problem of risk and uncertainty.

Interlinked projects A third type of project interdependence can arise when a project's cash flows are affected by investment decisions taken elsewhere. It would be highly unlikely to find *any* project which had truly independent cash flows, as almost certainly the magnitude and timing of a project's cash flows will be affected to some extent by other investment decisions. However, this problem really arises out of uncertainty about the future, and will be examined later in that context (see Chapter 11).

The case of interdependence to be examined here is the simpler case in which the cash flows of an investment opportunity are directly affected by the company's decision regarding another investment project. For example, when two *non*-mutually exclusive projects C3 and C4 are appraised it is found that Project C3 has the following cash flows, which are independent of any other investment decisions made by the company:

Project C3

Year	Cash flow	×	10% Present value factor	= Present value
0	− 1000		1	− 1000
1	+ 400		0·9091	+ 363·64
2	+ 500		0·8264	+ 413·20
3	+ 200		0·7513	+ 150·26
			Net present value	− £ 72·90

When discounted by 10% (assumed to be the appropriate rate) it has a negative NPV of £72·90. Viewed in isolation, and following the NPV rule for independent projects, it would be rejected as an unsuitable investment.

Table 4.3

Project C4

Year	Cash flow 1	×	10% Present value factor	= Present value cash flow
0	− 2000		1	− 2000
1	+ 500		0·9091	+ 454·55
2	+ 800		0·8264	+ 661·12
3	+ 1000		0·7513	+ 751·30
4	+ 1000		0·6830	+ 683·00
			Net present value +	549·97

Year	Cash flow 2	×	10% Present value factor	= Present value cash flow
0	− 2000		1	− 2000
1	+ 500		0·9091	+ 454·55
2	+ 800		0·8264	+ 661·12
3	+ 1200		0·7513	+ 901·56
			Net present value +	17·23

However, suppose Project C4, which is also under consideration, has *two* alternative sets of cash flows and NPVs, depending upon whether Project C3 is accepted by the company (cash flow 1) or rejected (cash flow 2). (Table 4.3 provides the details.) The correct way to analyse this situation, within the assumptions made, is to treat the problem as *three* mutually exclusive investments: Project C3, Project C4, and Project C3 + C4. Whichever alternative produces the largest positive NPV should be accepted. In this example:

Project C3 = −£72·90

Project C4 = +£17·23

Project C3 + C4 = −£72·90 + £549·97 = +£477·07

Thus the correct investment decision, in terms of maximizing shareholder wealth, is to accept Projects C3 and C4 jointly, because it is this alternative which produces the largest net present value.[15]

IRR rule and interdependent projects We have seen that in the face of these three types of non-independent cash flow, the NPV investment decision rule can be fairly easily modified so as to produce the correct decision advice. In terms of the two-period investment–consumption model, these modified decision rules would ensure a company's attainment of the optimal point on the physical investment line. But what modifications would have to be made to the IRR decision rule?

In a situation of mutually exclusive investment projects, a modification, apparently similar to that made to the NPV rule, is often advocated: accept whichever project has the greatest IRR, as long as it exceeds the investment cut-off/market interest rate. Such an approach is incorrect, but it has been widely advocated because of a misunderstanding concerning the process involved in using both NPV and IRR as criteria for investment decisions. We have already seen that when an individual project is evaluated by NPV, an 'automatic' comparison is made between the cash flows produced by the project and the cash flows that *would* have been produced (but were forgone, and so represent an opportunity cost under the assumption of a perfect capital market) if the project's outlay had been invested on the capital market for the period of the project's life-span. There the decision whether to accept or reject the project is not an absolute decision, but a *relative* one – relative to what the forgone alternative would yield. Therefore, when faced with mutually exclusive investments, the choice between projects is carried out on the basis of this automatic comparison with the capital market. Whichever project performs best, relative to the capital market, is chosen – given that the chosen alternative out-performs the capital market alternative, i.e., has a positive NPV.

Incremental cash flows We can approach this idea another way. Returning to Projects C1 and C2 when used as an example of the simple mutually exclusive investments problem, we could say that if these projects had *identical* cash flows, in both magnitude and timing, then we should be indifferent as to which one was chosen. However, as

Table 4.4

Year	Project C1 C/F	−	Project C2 C/F	=	Incremental C1 − C2 C/F	×	10% P.V. Factor	=	Present value C/F
0	− 1500		− 1900		+ 400		1		+ 400
1	+ 550		+ 400		+ 150		0·9091		+ 136·36
2	+ 1400		+ 800		+ 600		0·8264		+ 495·84
3			+ 800		− 800		0·7513		− 601·04
4			+ 700		− 700		0·6830		− 478·10
							Net present value		− 46·94

Year	Incremental C2 − C1 C/F	×	10% P.V. Factor	=	Present value C/F
0	− 400		1		− 400
1	− 150		0·9091		− 136·36
2	− 600		0·8264		− 495·84
3	+ 800		0·7513		+ 601·04
4	+ 700		·6830		+ 478·10
			Net present value		+ 46·94

they do not have identical cash flows, let us examine the extra (or incremental) cash flows that would be obtained from investing in Project C1 rather than C2, and vice versa. Table 4.4 lists these incremental cash flows and calculates their NPVs using a 10% discount rate.

In our original analysis of this decision problem, Project C2 was preferred to C1. The incremental analysis of Table 4.4 helps to explain further the reason for the decision: if C2 is chosen in preference to C1, this will produce an NPV which will be £46·94 greater than if C1 was preferred to C2. Therefore, C2 is chosen.

In the case of mutually exclusive investments, use of the IRR decision rule causes problems because, unlike the NPV calculation which automatically compares the project with the alternative capital market investment forgone, the IRR method only makes this comparison on the decision rule: does the project yield a greater or lesser return than the capital market? Using linear interpolation, the IRRs of the two projects, C1 and C2, can be estimated. For C1 the IRR is estimated at 17%, and for C2 at 15%. As C1 has the larger of the two IRRs and this is greater than the cut-off/market interest rate (10%), the IRR decision rule would suggest that Project C1 is accepted and C2 rejected. However, to formulate decision advice on this basis is to forget that the IRR method only compares a project with the capital market alternative in the operation of the accept/reject decision rule. Thus the IRR method can correctly advise in this case that both projects are worth while (their IRRs ≥ cut off rate), but it has *no*

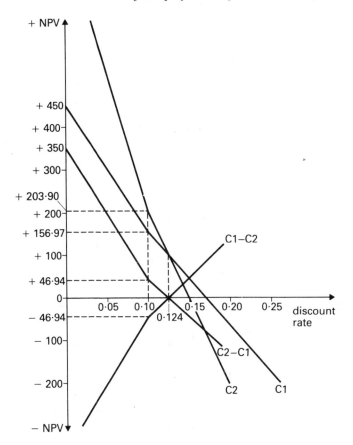

Figure 4.6

basis upon which to advise that C1 is *preferred* to C2. Indeed, we know that this ádvice is incorrect. Selecting C1 instead of C2 will result in a £46·94 reduction in NPV.

IRR and incremental cash flows The correct approach to evaluating mutually exclusive investments using the IRR is to examine the incremental cash flows between the alternatives. In order to clarify the problem and derive the correct IRR decision rule in such circumstances, we shall make use of a device which was used earlier to examine the IRR concept: the net present value profile.

Figure 4.6 graphs the NPV profiles of Projects C1 and C2 and both the differential cash flows (C1 − C2, C2 − C1). It is this figure that demonstrates one of the real problems of using the IRR as a decision criterion when choice amongst alternatives is involved. Project C1 always has a higher IRR than C2, whatever the rate of discount, and therefore, basing the choice between mutually exclusive investments on size of IRR, the decision is independent of the capital market rate of interest. In contrast, when the decision is based on the NPV rule, the choice of project changes as the discount rate/market rate of interest changes. It can be seen from Figure 4.6 that at rates of discount below 12·4%, Project C2 is preferred because it has the higher NPV; but at discount rates above 12·4%, Project C1 is preferred. The intersection point of the two cash flow profiles is at a discount rate of 12·4% and so, at this rate, the decision would be indifferent between the two projects because they both produce the same NPV. Also notice that, as we would expect at that discount rate, the NPV of both differential cash flows is zero: both projects are equally acceptable, and the differential cash flows reflect this indifference.

On the basis of Figure 4.6, a number of firm conclusions can be made about the use of both methods in appraising mutually exclusive projects. The NPV can be used to give the correct decision advice with just a small (and commonsense) modification to the basic rule: accept whichever alternative has the highest positive NPV when discounted at the perfect capital market rate of interest. The use of the IRR involves a more complex decision rule. This complexity arises both from the fact that the IRRs of the differential cash flows have to be computed and (as can be seen from Figure 4.6) from the fact that the IRRs of both incremental cash flows are identical. The decision rule is as follows. Calculate the IRRs of the two projects and the IRR of *either* of the differential cash flows, then:

1 If the differential cash flow IRR is greater than the cut-off rate, and
   (*a*) less than both project IRRs, then accept the project with the *smallest* IRR.
   (*b*) greater than both project IRRs, then accept the project with the *highest* IRR.

2 If the differential cash flow IRR is less than the cut-off rate, and
   (*a*) the IRRs of one or both projects are higher than the cut-off rate, then accept the project with the *highest* IRR.
   (*b*) If neither project's IRR is greater than the cut-off rate, *reject* both.

In the example used therefore, using the NPV decision rule, Project C2 should be accepted because it has the highest positive NPV when discounted at 10% – the perfect capital market interest rate. The IRR decision rule also leads to the acceptance of C2 because the IRR of the differential cash flow (12·4%) is greater than the cut-off rate (10%) and less than the IRR of both projects (15% and 17%). Therefore, the project with the smallest IRR, C2, is chosen.

From this we can see that the IRR decision rule is excessively complex and unwieldly. What is more, the example used only two mutually exclusive projects. If faced with a choice between (say) a dozen alternatives, the NPV rule simply requires the calculation of each project's NPV and the project with the largest positive NPV is selected. With the IRR rule, the IRRs of *pairs* of the projects and their differential cash flow have to be calculated, making a choice between each pair of projects in turn, until an outright 'winner' is found – an extremely tedious operation.

The 'opportunity cost of cash' assumption The fact that, in a decision choice involving mutually exclusive projects, selecting the project with the highest positive NPV will give a correct decision but selecting the project with the highest IRR will only, *by chance*, give the correct decision, has been explained on the basis that the IRR ranks projects in an order of preference which is independent of the capital market interest rate. But we have not really answered the question why, in the example used, does the NPV rule accept Project C2 and reject C1? After all, Project C1 produces a higher return (17%) than C2 (15%). The reason lies in what is (somewhat misleadingly) called the 'reinvestment assumption' of each decision rule. Perhaps a more apt description would be the 'opportunity cost of capital' assumption.

In very simple terms, the basic NPV decision rule can be said to assume that the cash flows produced by an investment have an opportunity cost (or yield an opportunity benefit) equal to the discount rate used. The basic IRR decision rule assumes that the opportunity cost of these cash flows is equal to the IRR of the particular investment which generated them. We have already examined what is *meant* by the NPV of a project. It is – in present value terms – the excess cash that the particular project will produce, in relation to a similar sized investment on the capital market. This difference can be seen in the general forms of the two models. With the NPV model, the discount rate used is the market rate of interest (and hence the 'automatic' comparison between the project and the capital market alternative):

$$\sum_{t=0}^{N} \frac{A_t}{(1 + i)^t} = \text{NPV}$$

where A_t = project cash flow in time period t.
$\quad i$ = market interest/discount rate.
$\quad N$ = number of periods of the project's life.

However, with the IRR model, the discount rate used is the project's own internal rate of return:

$$\sum_{t=0}^{N} \frac{A_t}{(1 + r)^t} = 0 \qquad \text{where } r = \text{project's IRR.}$$

Therefore, the IRR model, in effect, carries out an automatic comparison, not with the capital market investment, but with a hypothetical investment which produces a return equal to the project's own return. Now the important point is that investments yielding such returns may well be available to the company, but these investments will be available independently of whether or not the company accepts the particular project under consideration. The NPV model accepts this reasoning and takes as the opportunity cost of the project cash flows, the market rate of interest. The market rate of interest is viewed as the opportunity cost because, even if a project's cash flow is used by a company to undertake an investment with a very high yield, if that cash flow were *not* available, the high-yielding investment could still be undertaken by using money borrowed from the capital market, *at the market rate of interest*. What the IRR model does is to credit some of the profitability of those other investments to the project being appraised, by assuming that the opportunity cost of the project-generated cash flows is equal to the project's own IRR or yield.

Therefore, we can conclude that, given the presence of a perfect capital market, it is the NPV model and not the IRR model which makes the correct assumption about the opportunity cost of a project's cash flow. In addition to this, there is a logical inconsistency in the IRR's assumption, which can be easily illustrated by means of an example. If two independent projects are appraised and their IRRs are estimated at 20% and 30% respectively, the IRR model is implicitly assuming that, in a particular period, the opportunity cost/benefit of the cash flow generated by one project is 20%, whilst the cash flow generated by the other project is valued at 30%. There is no logical reason why cash flows which arise at the same time from two different sources should be valued differently in terms of opportunity cost.

In conclusion At this point there is perhaps no need to state the obvious that, although we have examined the use of the IRR only in the simple case of mutually exclusive projects, similar problems arise when using it for decision making in the replacement cycle problem and with interdependent project cash flows (which are both special cases of the basic problem). Although these problems can be surmounted by the use of similar adaptations of the IRR decision rule, the process remains complex, tedious and unnecessarily time-consuming.

4.4 Extending the time horizon

Introduction Having relaxed the assumption of independent projects, we shall now reassume it and instead, relax another of the assumptions of the graphical investment–consumption analysis: that of only two periods. Certainly, since starting to examine the DCF methods of investment appraisal, examples have been used of projects which involve cash flows extending over more than two periods. But what we must now ask is whether, given all the other assumptions of the two-period investment–consumption model, the assumption of a two-period time horizon is simply an assumption of convenience which allows the model to be developed graphically. In short, the answer to the question is that it is not. In a two-period world we have seen that both the NPV and IRR decision rules will give the same, correct decision advice (even if some fairly complex adjustments sometimes have to be made to the IRR rule). Both methods should enable a company to locate optimally on its physical investment line. However, problems can occur for the IRR decision rule once this two-dimensional world is left behind.

Average and marginal rates of return As soon as the assumption of only two periods (0 and 1) is explicitly relaxed, we get new support for the rationale of the NPV approach (to the detriment of IRR) and a new perspective from which to view the 'reinvestment' assumption. So far, in all the examples used, we have implicitly assumed that the capital market interest rate remains fixed over time. However, suppose a company is evaluating Project C5, whose cash flows are given below. In this case, the annual market interest/discount rate is expected to be 10% over the coming year and 15% over the following year. The project's NPV and IRR are as follows:

Project C5

Year	Cash flow
0	− 100
1	+ 60
2	+ 60

$$\underline{\text{IRR} \approx 13\%}$$

$$\text{NPV} = -100 + \frac{60}{(1 + 0{\cdot}1)} + \frac{60}{(1 + 0{\cdot}1)(1 + 0{\cdot}15)} = \underline{\underline{£ + 1{\cdot}98}}$$

As far as the NPV decision rule is concerned, known fluctuations in the discount rate (under an assumption of certainty) do not cause any problems. Project C5 has a positive NPV after its cash flows have been discounted by the appropriate market discount rate for each period. But what of the IRR decision rule? Project C5 should be accepted if its IRR is greater than the market interest rate/cut-off rate, but in this example, the IRR of C5 is greater than the market interest rate in one period, and less than the rate in the other period. In such circumstances, a single figure IRR is just not valid for decision making purposes.

This is a very real problem with the IRR decision rule. Unless future market interest rates are assumed to be, at least, approximately constant, the rule breaks down. What we are seeing in this example is that, although both DCF methods recognize that money has a time value and so cash flows that occur at differing points of time cannot be directly compared but first have to be converted to values at just one point of time via a weighting mechanism,[16] the IRR uses the *average* or long-run rate of return for weighting whilst the NPV uses the *marginal* or period-by-period rate of interest.

Multiple IRRs Another problem for the IRR decision rule, which arises out of the mathematics of its computation, comes to light when the investment time horizon is extended. The IRR of a project's cash flow is the root of a polynomial equation, the mathematics of which are explained in a note.[17] The problem is that any particular investment project may have more than one internal rate of return (i.e., there may be more than one rate of discount which will reduce the project's cash flow to a zero NPV), or it may not have any IRR at all. This important (and not uncommon) phenomena can be examined in terms of the NPV profiles of projects on the basis that the IRR is given by the point at which the profile line cuts the graph's horizontal axis (along which the discount rate is measured).

To start with, we must define what have become known as 'conventional' and 'non-conventional' cash flows.[18] A conventional project cash flow is one where a cash outflow, or a series of cash outflows, is followed by a cash inflow or series of cash inflows. The essence of the definition is that in a conventional cash flow, there is only one change in sign $(+, -)$ between the time periods. Examples of three conventional cash flows are given below:

Year	0	1	2	3	4
Project					
C6	-1000	$+400$	$+500$	$+800$	$+50$
C7	-1000	-500	-600	$+1500$	$+2000$
C8	-500	-600	$+2000$	—	—

The one change of sign for Project C6 comes between time 0 and time 1, for Project C7 it comes between time 2 and time 3, and for Project C8 it comes between time 1 and time 2. In each project cash flow there is only one sign change. Such projects will only have one IRR (there is an exception to this, to which we shall return), and so no problems arise for the IRR decision rule.

Non-conventional cash flows can therefore be defined as those which involve more than one change in sign, such as shown below:

Year	0	1	2	3	4	
Project						
C9	-100	$+20$	-50	$+80$	$+170$	3 changes of sign
D1	-100	$+60$	$+80$	-20		2 changes of sign

Such projects are likely to have more than one IRR and, as a general 'rule of thumb', a project will have as many IRRs as its cash flow has changes in sign. Non-conventional cash flows can make life very difficult for the IRR decision rule. For example, Project D2's NPV profile is illustrated in Figure 4.7. This project has three IRRs: 10%, 15% and 18%. In itself, this is not too disturbing if the cut-off rate is either less than 10% or greater than 18%, because the IRR rule still manages to give unambiguous (and operationally correct) decision advice. But if the cut-off rate is (say) 12%, the IRR decision can only give – at best – highly ambiguous advice (which may be incorrect). In such circumstances, the NPV rule would have no difficulty in giving the correct advice, to reject the project because it has a negative NPV.

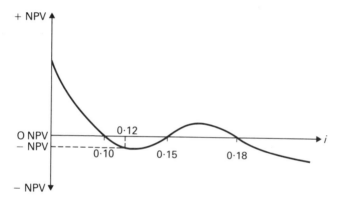

Figure 4.7   NVP profile, Project D2

Other problems with the IRR rule Figure 4.8 illustrates another problematical situation for the IRR rule where there is only a single IRR for Project D3, but at no rate of discount does the project yield a positive NPV. If, in this example, the discount rate were 10%, the NPV rule would correctly reject the project. However, the IRR rule would accept it because its IRR (20%) is greater than the cut-off rate.

Figure 4.9 illustrates an NPV profile which causes the IRR decision rule to break down completely because no internal rate of return exists![19]

In conclusion The conclusion of this analysis appears strongly to favour the NPV decision rule for investment appraisal. At best the IRR method might be used as a support and as a communication device on the basis of management's familiarity with rates of return rather than net present values, for the decision advice given by the

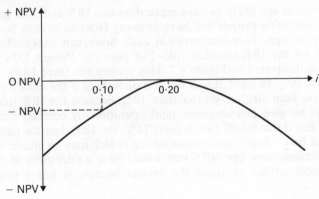

Figure 4.8   NVP profile, Project D3

NPV rule 20. However, it must be remembered that at this stage relatively few of the assumptions of the basic model have been relaxed. We shall have to wait and see how the NPV decision rule fares when more crucial assumptions are dropped.

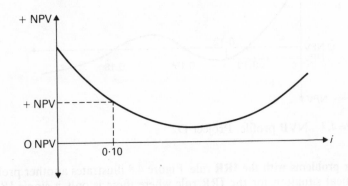

Figure 4.9   NVP profile, Project D4

Appendix: Compounding and discounting

Tables A to F can be found on pp. 255–7.

1 Compound interest factors The amount to which a sum of £1 accumulates when placed on deposit for N years at a constant annual rate of interest of i is given by:

$$(1 + i)^N$$

Thus, £500 placed on deposit for 6 years at an annual rate of interest of 12%, accumulates to:

$$£500(1 + 0.12)^6 = £986.91$$

Similarly, if £200 is placed on deposit for 3 years at 10% and 2 years at 8%, then the accumulated sum at the end of 5 years is:

$$£200(1 + 0.10)^3(1 + 0.08)^2 = £310.50$$

Table A provides compound interest factors for various values of N and i.

2 Present value factors The value now (i.e., the present value) of £1 arising in N years' time when the rate of discount (interest) is i is given by:

$$1/(1 + i)^N \quad \text{or} \quad (1 + i)^{-N}, \text{ denoted as } V_i^N$$

Thus, £500 arising in 6 years' time, when the annual rate of discount is 12%, has a present value of:

$$£500(1 + 0.12)^{-6} = £253.32$$

Similarly, £200 arising in 5 years, where the annual rate of discount is 10% for 3 years and 8% for 2 years, has a present value of:

$$£200(1 + 0.1)^{-3}(1 + 0.08)^{-2} = £128.83$$

Table B provides present value factors for various values of N and i.

3 Annuities An annuity can be defined as a constant amount of cash which arises for a given number of consecutive years. Three main types of annuity can be specified:

(a) an annuity due, where the first sum arises immediately;
(b) an immediate annuity, where the first sum arises in one year's time;
(c) a deferred annuity, where the first sum arises in two or more years' time.

Examples of the cash flows of 4 year £100 annuities of each type are given below:

Year		0	1	2	3	4	5
(a)	Annuity Due	£100	£100	£100	£100		
(b)	Immediate Annuity		£100	£100	£100	£100	
(c)	One-Year Deferred Annuity			£100	£100	£100	£100

4 Terminal value of an annuity The amount to which an annuity of £1 per year for N years accumulates when the annual rate of interest is i takes the form of a geometric progression, which simplifies to:

$$\frac{(1 + i)^N - 1}{i}, \text{ denoted as } S_{N|i}$$

Thus the 'terminal value' of a four-year £100 immediate annuity (the amount to which it accumulates to at the end of its life), where the rate of interest is 15%, is:

$$£100 \cdot \frac{(1 + 0.15)^4 - 1}{0.15} = £499.34$$

Table C provides terminal value of an annuity factors for various values of N and i.

5 Present value of an annuity The present value of an *immediate* annuity of £1 per year for N years, where the rate of discount is i, is given by:

$$\frac{1 - (1 + i)^{-N}}{i}, \text{ denoted as } A_{N|i}$$

Thus the present value of a four-year £100 immediate annuity, where the rate of discount is 15%, is:

$$£100 \cdot \frac{1 - (1 + 0.15)^{-4}}{0.15} = £285.50$$

The present value of a four-year £100 annuity due, where the rate of discount is 15%, is:

$$£100 + £100 \cdot \frac{1 - (1 + 0.15)^{-3}}{0.15} = £328.32$$

Whilst the present value of a four-year £100 annuity, deferred for (say) two years (so that the first sum arises at year 3), at a rate of discount is 15%, is:

$$£100 \cdot \frac{1 - (1 + 0.15)^{4}}{0.15} (1 + 0.15)^{-2} = £215.88$$

Table D provides factors for the present values of £1 immediate annuities for various values of N and i.

6 Sinking fund factors The annual value of an annuity which lasts for N years, where the prevailing rate of interest is i, and which has a terminal value of £1, is given by:

$$\frac{i}{(1 + i)^N - 1}, \text{ denoted as } S_{N|i}^{-1}$$

Thus the annual value of a four-year annuity which has a terminal value of £100, where the interest rate is 15%, is:

$$£100 \cdot \frac{0.15}{(1 + 0.15)^4 - 1} = £20.03 \text{ per year}$$

In other words, a four-year £20.03 annuity would have a terminal value of £100 when the annual interest rate is 15%. Table E provides these factors for annuities with terminal values of £1, for various values of i and N.

7 Annual equivalent factors The annual value of an *immediate* annuity which lasts for N years, where the prevailing rate of discount is i, and which has a present value of £1, is given by:

$$\frac{i}{1 - (1 + i)^{-N}}, \text{ denoted as } A_{N|i}^{-1}$$

Thus the annual value of an immediate annuity which lasts for 5 years, where the rate of discount is 8%, and which has a present value of £2,000, is:

$$£2000 \cdot \frac{0 \cdot 08}{1 - (1 + 0 \cdot 08)^{-5}} = £500 \cdot 91$$

If this was a five-year annuity, deferred for (say) 3 years, then its annual value would be:

$$£2000 \cdot \frac{0 \cdot 08}{1 - (1 + 0 \cdot 08)^{-5}} (1 + 0 \cdot 08)^3 = £631 \cdot 00$$

In other words, a £631 five-year annuity, deferred for three years, would have a present value of £2,000 if the annual rate of discount was 8%. Table F provides these factors for immediate annuities with a present value of £1, for various values of i and N.

8 Perpetuities An annuity that continues indefinitely is termed a perpetuity. As it never terminates it cannot have a terminal value. The present value of an *immediate* annuity of £1, which continues indefinitely, where the annual rate of discount is i, is given by:

$$\frac{1}{i}$$

Thus a perpetuity of £150 per year, where the rate of discount is 15%, is:

$$£150 \cdot \frac{1}{0 \cdot 15} = \frac{£150}{0 \cdot 15} = £1000$$

Selected references

A. Alchien, 'The Rate of Interest, Fisher's Rate of Return over Costs, and Keynes' Internal Rate of Return', *American Economic Review*, December 1955.

H. Bierman and S. Smidt, 'Capital Budgeting and the Problem of Reinvesting Cash Proceeds', *Journal of Business*, 1957.

S. Davidson and D. F. Drake, 'Capital Budgeting and the "Best" Tax Depreciation Method', *Journal of Business*, October 1961.

C. L. Dudley, 'A Note on Reinvestment Assumption in Choosing between Net Present Value and Internal Rate of Return', *Journal of Finance*, September 1972.

R. A. Fawthrop, 'Underlying Problems of Discounted Cash Flow', *Accounting and Business Research*, Summer 1971.

W. W. Haynes and M. B. Solomon, 'A Misplaced Emphasis in Capital Budgeting', *Quarterly Review of Economics and Business*, February 1962.

C. G. Hoskins, 'Benefit Cost Ratios versus Net Present Value: Revisited', *Journal of Business Finance and Accounting*, Summer 1974.

W. H. Jean, 'Terminal Value or Present Value in Capital Budgeting Programmes', *Journal of Financial and Quantitative Analysis*, January 1971.

P. F. King, 'Is the Emphasis of Capital Budgeting Theory Misplaced', *Journal of Business Finance and Accounting*, Spring 1975.

B. A. Kolb, 'Problems and Pitfalls in Capital Budgeting', *Financial Analyst Journal*, November–December 1968.

D. Longbottom and L. Wiper, 'Necessary Conditions for the Existence of Multiple Rates in the Use of the Internal Rate of Return', *Journal of Business Finance and Accounting*, Winter 1978.

E. M. Lerner and A. Rappaport, 'Limit DCF in Capital Budgeting', *Harvard Business Review*, September–October 1968.

R. Ma, P. Pandey and M. Scott, 'Discounted Cash Equivalents', *Abacus*, December 1978.

J. C. T. Mao, 'The Internal Rate of Return as a Ranking Criterion', *Engineering Economist*, Winter 1966.

E. F. Renshaw, 'A Note on the Arithmetic of Capital Budgeting Decisions', *Journal of Business*, July 1957.

M. Sarnat and H. Levy, 'The Relationship of Rules of Thumb to the Internal Rate of Return', *Journal of Finance*, June 1969.

E. Solomon, 'The Arithmetic of Capital Budgeting Decisions', *Journal of Business*, April 1956.

G. Terborgh, *Dynamic Equipment Policy*, New York, McGraw-Hill, 1949.

M. H. Weingartner, 'The Excess Present Value Index – A Theoretical Basis and Critique', *Journal of Accounting Research*, Autumn 1963.

M. H. Weingartner, 'Some New Views on the Payback Period and Capital Budgeting Decisions', *Management Science*, August 1969.

J. F. Wright, 'The Marginal Efficiency of Capital', *Economic Journal*, December 1959.

5 The Cost of Company Capital

5.1 The cost of equity capital

Introduction Up to this point, much of our analysis has been based on the two period investment–consumption model. Under the rather unrealistic assumptions of this model, we saw the superiority of the two DCF methods of investment appraisal over the more traditional, 'rule of thumb' appraisal methods. However, we also saw that when the assumptions of a two period investment time horizon and of project cash flow independence were relaxed, the IRR criterion became enmeshed in a number of problems. On the other hand, the NPV decision rule remained optimally operational, with little difficulty.

We are now going to turn away, for the time being, from the world of the investment–consumption model in order to examine one very essential real-world problem: given that the NPV criteria *may*[1] be able to produce satisfactory investment advice in practice, and given that we can satisfactorily draw up a schedule of the future cash flows of a project, then what discount rate should be used to reduce this cash flow to its net present value?

We know that in the world of the investment–consumption model, in which we assumed the existence of a perfect capital market and a certain future, the correct discount rate to be used for calculating NPV was the market interest rate: a single, unique figure which was both the borrowing and lending rate. But in practice, this is not the case. There is a myriad of different interest rates (because the future is uncertain), and at each level of interest rate there are a borrowing rate and a lending rate (which is lower because capital markets contain imperfections such as transaction costs). In this chapter, we are going to keep the assumptions of perfect capital markets (although we shall also examine the implications of some capital market imperfections), but we shall relax the assumption that the future is known with certainty. Therefore, with perfect capital markets but an uncertain future, we have instead of just a single market rate of interest, a whole range of different interest rates (but each one is both a borrowing and a lending rate). The reason for this multiplicity is as follows.

Investment and uncertainty With the introduction of uncertainty,[2] we have to take a closer look at what we have termed financial investment opportunities. In fact the distinction between financial and physical investments is almost entirely artificial, as far as decision making is concerned. A physical investment could be defined as involving cash (i.e., consumption power) being spent in order to combine and operate productive resources (the factors of production) so as to generate a saleable output (of either goods or services), which can be exchanged for cash. A financial investment still involves an outlay of cash – it is lent on the capital markets – but now a *third party* undertakes the physical investment. Individuals or companies borrow money through the medium of the capital markets in order to undertake physical investments, with the hope that the investment will produce a sufficient cash return, in the future, to allow a surplus to remain once the borrowed funds (capital plus interest) have been repaid. (Obviously, this is a highly simplified view of the distinction between physical and financial investments, but it is essentially correct.)

In a world of certainty, the future return on a physical investment is known with certainty. Therefore, no one would borrow money on the capital market unless they had found a project which would yield a return at least sufficient to repay interest and borrowed capital.[3] Thus in such circumstances, there is no uncertainty for the borrower (he would not borrow unless he had the certain knowledge that the physical investment would enable the debt to be repaid) and therefore there is also no uncertainty for the lender. (Let us ignore the possibility of dishonesty.) However, once we introduce the fact that the future is uncertain, then borrower and lender can only *expect* (they cannot know for certain), that the physical investment undertaken will yield sufficient return to repay capital and interest.

The outcome of some physical investments (and hence the return generated) is likely to be more uncertain, or risky, than others. This is really the great difference between certainty and uncertainty: certainty is uniform, uncertainty varies widely in degree. To reflect this fact, a lender of money through the capital markets will usually have to be compensated for lending money for investment in physical projects with high expected levels of risk. This compensation takes the form of a higher rate of interest charged on the lent capital. Thus the more risky, or uncertain, the outcome of the physical investment which the borrowed money is to be applied, the greater the investment rate, and vice versa. And so, the greater the uncertainty about the future outcome of a physical investment opportunity, the greater must be the *expected* return on the project for it to be undertaken. For this reason, there are likely to be a whole variety of different interest rates on the capital markets, reflecting the different levels of risk of the physical investments for which the capital is to be lent. Therefore in such circumstances it would appear that the correct discount rate for a company to use in investment appraisal is the rate which corresponds to the perfect capital market interest rate appropriate to the project's level of perceived risk.

It is important to realize that this relationship between risk and expected returns is based on the fundamental (and probably realistic) assumption that, in general, investors dislike uncertainty: they are said to be 'risk averse'. Therefore, if they are to agree to accept risk, they must be rewarded or compensated with an increased level of expected return.

The required return on equity capital There are many ways in which investors can lend money on the capital market. One is to buy the ordinary shares issued by a company (either directly from the company or from a third party) so that the company, rather than the investor personally, undertakes the physical investments. An essential characteristic of an investment in ordinary shares or 'equity capital', which differentiates it from most other forms of capital market lending, is that the loan never comes to maturity, i.e. the loan is permanent and is never repaid.[4] However, ordinary shares are negotiable: the permanent loan to a company can be sold on to another investor. These transactions form the bulk of stock exchange dealings. Because of this characteristic of equity capital, the investors making such loans to a company are held to be the legal owners of the company.

To find what is the expected interest rate or expected return required by ordinary shareholders on their capital, we have to return to our discussion on the objective of financial management decision making. The objective, we said, could be stated as the maximization of the (current) market value of the company's ordinary share capital, which was a surrogate for maximizing the (cash) dividend flow to shareholders through time (which in itself was a surrogate for wealth maximization), because it is this dividend flow which gives a share its market value. However, we also know that cash flows which arise at different points in time cannot be directly compared but must first be converted to values at one point in time (usually, the present time is chosen). Thus the market value of an ordinary share represents the sum of its *expected* future dividend flow, discounted to present value. But to get such a value, what interest rate should be used for the discounting process? It is the expected return required by ordinary shareholders.

An example Suppose that an ordinary share in a particular company is generally expected by all investors to produce a 10p dividend at the end of each year for ever (i.e., in perpetuity). If the share has a market value of 80p, this represents the sum of the expected future discounted dividend stream:

$$80p = 10p \ V_i^1 + 10p \ V_i^2 + 10p \ V_i^3 \ldots + 10p \ V_i^\infty$$

as this is a perpetuity, the sum reduces to:

$$80p = \frac{10p}{i} \quad \text{and so} \quad i = \frac{10p}{80p} = 0 \cdot 125 \text{ or } 12 \cdot 5\%$$

Therefore i, the rate of discount being used to give the share its market value, is $12\frac{1}{2}\%$. It is this interest/discount rate which reduces the sum of the future expected dividend flow to a present value of 80p.[5] Therefore $12\frac{1}{2}\%$ must be the expected return which is being required by ordinary shareholders in this company, taking into consideration the riskiness of the future expected dividend flow (which, in turn, depends upon the riskiness of the expected returns from the physical investments which the company has undertaken).

If equity capital were the only source of investment funds used by this company, and the shareholders required a minimum expected return of $12\frac{1}{2}\%$ on their investment, then $12\frac{1}{2}\%$ would be the discount rate used in the company's NPV calculations: it represents the minimum acceptable expected rate of return which it should achieve on each of its physical investments. The reason for this is that shareholders have implicitly specified $12\frac{1}{2}\%$ through the market price of the shares, by comparing the returns which they could earn elsewhere on their capital for accepting a similar level of risk. Thus the inference is that, as shareholders can invest their money elsewhere to earn $12\frac{1}{2}\%$, the company must ensure that any physical investment it undertakes earns at least this return. If such physical investments are unobtainable, then the cash should be returned to shareholders (say in the form of dividends).

Therefore the discount rate which reduces the sum of a share's expected future dividend flow to a present value equal to its market price is called the 'cost of equity capital'. It is in fact an opportunity cost, and it is the minimum expected return required by shareholders from the investment of their funds by the company's management. Hence it is also the rate of discount to be used in NPV calculations, but it is *only* the appropriate rate for appraising physical investment projects which have the same level of risk as the company's *existing* risk (i.e., the risk of the company's existing cash flows). This is a very important proviso, but it is obvious from the foregoing analysis. Any rate of return is only relative to a specific risk level, and so a company's cost of equity capital is a required rate of return relative to its existing level of risk. Therefore, this will be appropriate to use as a discount rate for project evaluation only if the project has a similar level of risk as the company. If the project has a different level of risk, the company's existing cost of capital is not the appropriate discount rate. A discussion of just what would be the appropriate rate will have to wait until the later chapter on risk (Chapter 11).

Expected return, dividends, market price Before proceeding to consider further how the required expected return on equity is to be estimated, let us examine the nature of the relationship between expected return, dividends and market price. In order to do so we shall be taking a simplified but generally correct view of the workings of stock markets.

With the company in the example above, shareholders required a minimum expected return (or yield) of $12\frac{1}{2}\%$. On the basis of an expected annual dividend per share of 10p in perpetuity, this produced a market value of 80p per share. Now, in the following analysis, the riskiness of the expected future dividend flow will remain unchanged. Suppose something happens which leads investors, in general, to believe that the company will now pay an annual dividend per share in perpetuity of 12p, instead of 10p. At the market price of 80p the share now yields a return of $12p/80p = 0.15$. This 15% return is above the required return (of $12\frac{1}{2}\%$) for this level of risk, and so investors will start to buy the company's shares. Stock exchanges work through a supply and demand market mechanism, and therefore this increased demand for the company's ordinary shares will force up the market price. Suppose, in response to this increased demand, the market price rises to 85p per share. It is still yielding an excessively high return: $12p/85p = 0.141$, and so demand will continue. In fact the price of the share should rise until its yield equates with the required yield of $12\frac{1}{2}\%$. So the market price will settle at $12p/0.125 = 96p$ per share. (Any *further* increase in share price will cause the share to have too low an expected return, investors will wish to sell, and so the reverse process will start, with the share price falling until it produces the required yield of $12\frac{1}{2}\%$.)

The foregoing example illustrates the positive relationship between the dividend expectations of a share and its market price. Increases or decreases in the expected dividend flow will cause a respective rise or fall in market value, with the lynch-pin of the mechanism being the required yield. Similarly, if an event occurs which causes investors to change the level of a share's required rate of return (either because a company's expected future dividend flow is viewed, for some reason, as becoming more or less risky than before, or because alternative investments have become more or less attractive in terms of their risk-return), then a consequent change in market price will occur until the revised required yield has established itself. There is an inverse relationship between required return and market price.

The individual investor has to decide whether to buy, hold or sell a particular share. It is not the individual shareholder's actions but those of the market as a whole (i.e., all investors collectively) which determines a share's expected yield. Therefore the individual investor has to estimate a share's future expected dividend flow and from this, together with the share's market price, he will be able to derive its expected yield or return. What action he then takes (buy, sell or hold) depends upon his own personal attitude to risk and the return he requires for bearing varying amounts of it. If he believes that the share's expected yield is *at least* sufficient compensation for the risk that owning the share involves he will buy; if *just* sufficient he will hold; if *less than* sufficient he will sell. The individual shareholder's actions will not have much direct effect on the market price, but if investors in general have a similar attitude to the required 'risk-expected return' trade-off, then they are all likely to undertake similar action and the share's market price will adjust accordingly.

However, not only are individual investors interested in estimating a share's expected return, but so too is the management of the company concerned. Its interest arises from the fact that the share's expected yield represents the minimum return that the company must earn on any investment project it undertakes, i.e., it reflects the discount rate that should be used in project appraisal. But before we turn to examine how this expected yield may actually be found, let us review our progress to this point.

We have been concerned with the yield that is produced on equity capital, with the idea that this indicates the minimum acceptable return that management must achieve on any investment it undertakes. But, from the shareholder's viewpoint, an ordinary share's yield is no more than a convenient way to express – in an encapsulated form – the relationship between current market price and future expectations of dividend flow. Thus we are implicitly postulating that a share's stock market value is based on the summation of the future expected dividend flow, discounted to present value by the expected return. This is the dividend valuation model of stock market share prices.

The dividend valuation model The dividend valuation model is obviously a rather naive and incomplete model of share price behaviour, because prices are likely to be affected by a variety of other factors. However, in essence, it is likely to be valid and it fits in well with the general assertion made earlier in this book: values are applied to objects (including ordinary shares) in order to allow decisions to be made about them, and an object's current value, on the assumption of a rational, economic man, is based on the net stream of future benefits it will produce (or, rather more correctly, that it is *expected* to produce). In addition, we have already recognized the importance of cash and cash flow in economic wealth-maximizing decisions, and the dividend valuation model, being a cash flow valuation model, is therefore in close accord with this reasoning.

On the assumption that the future flow of annual dividends is expected to be a perpetuity[6] (i.e., it will remain at a constant level for all future periods), then the dividend valuation model can be expressed in general terms as:

$$E = \frac{d}{K_e}$$

where E is the market value of the equity capital (either of an individual ordinary share or the total equity value of the company), d is the constant expected annual dividend (again, and depending upon how E is defined, d is either the expected dividend per share or the total equity dividend payout) and K_e is the average expected annual return that is required by ordinary shareholders. The model can also be rearranged so as to define the required equity return: $K_e = d/E$.

The value of E There are a number of additional points to be made in connection with this model. The first concerns the value of E that is to be used. Looking at share prices in the pages of the financial press, it can be seen that shares are normally given two prices: a bid (buying) price and an offer (selling) price. The former will be greater than the latter, with the difference being known as the 'jobber's turn'[7]. However, we are retaining the assumption of a perfect capital market and one of the sub-assumptions of this is that there are no transaction costs involved in buying and selling shares. As the jobber's turn is a type of transaction cost, this assumption allows us neatly to side-step the problem and instead, assume that there is no difference between the bid and offer price.[8]

The second point to be made concerns the fact that market prices of ordinary shares can sometimes be quoted either 'cum div', or 'ex div'. A 'cum div' market price applies to a share just prior to its dividend being paid, whilst an 'ex div' price applies to a share just after its dividend has been paid. Suppose a company is generally expected to pay a 10p per share dividend in perpetuity and shareholders require an expected return of 10%. The dividend valuation model can be used to estimate the equity's market value: $E = 10p/0.10 = 100p$. This is the ex div market value of the equity (i.e., it is the market value of the share at that point in the company's year when the *next* 10p dividend is due to be paid in approximately 12 months), because the model is based on the summation of an *immediate* annuity.[9]

Assuming that there are no changes in investors' expectations and that all expectations are fulfilled, a share's market price will follow a 'dog-tooth' pattern over time. Using the example above, the share's market price will rise steadily over the year from the ex div market price of 100p until, just prior to the payment of the next dividend, it will have a price of 110p (100p plus the forthcoming dividend of 10p). This latter figure is the share's cum div price. Once the dividend has been paid, the market price falls back to the ex div price of 100p and so restarts the slow rise over the year to its cum div value. The diagram below illustrates this highly simplified, but basically correct, account of a share's market price movements over time in a perfect market with unchanging and fulfilled expectations about the future:

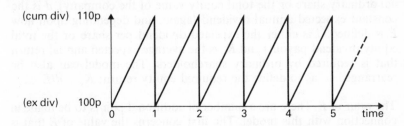

As the simple dividend valuation model employs ex div market prices, so cum div prices have to be adjusted accordingly. For example, if a share was expected to yield a constant annual dividend of 22p and it had a current market price of £1·59½ cum div, then its equivalent ex div price would be the cum div price less the expected forthcoming dividend: $159\frac{1}{2}p - 22p = 137\frac{1}{2}p$. The share's required return would thus be: $22p/137\frac{1}{2}p = 0·16$.[9] From now on we shall use E to represent the ex div market price of equity.[10]

The dividend growth model Up to this point, the dividend valuation model has been developed under the assumption of expectations of constant dividends through time.[11] This may well be a realistic assumption because there are several companies which have been observed to pay (approximately) constant dividends per share over relatively long periods. However, a more commonly sought pattern of dividends (sought by both shareholders and management) is that of steady *growth* over time. The basic dividend valuation model can be easily adapted to allow for such a pattern based on the assumption that dividends *grow* at a constant annual rate, in perpetuity. Table 5.1 shows how the dividend growth model can be derived as:

$$E = \frac{d_1}{K_e - g} \quad \text{if } K_e > g$$

where g is the expected constant annual dividend growth rate and d_1 is the dividend expected in twelve months' time, (i.e.

$d_1 = d_0[1 + g]$).[12] The model can be easily rearranged to give the expected return on equity:

$$K_e = \frac{d_1}{E} + g \quad \text{or} \quad K_e = \frac{d_0(1 + g)}{E} + g$$

Thus if a company's equity has an ex div market price per share of 70p, a dividend of 10p has just been paid and a constant annual dividend growth rate of 5% is expected, then:

$$K_e = \frac{10(1 + 0 \cdot 05)}{70} + 0 \cdot 05 = 0 \cdot 2 \text{ or } \underline{20\%}$$

The estimation of g We have examined the dividend valuation model on the basis of two alternative assumptions of the future expected dividend pattern: constant dividends in perpetuity, and dividends growing at a constant rate in perpetuity. Obviously, these are only very general simplifications of real-world dividend patterns, and the model can be fairly easily adjusted to reflect more complex and realistic patterns. But for our purposes, no point is served in making the assumed future dividend pattern more complex, because no further insights are gained thereby.

There are two main approaches to estimating g – the constant expected dividend growth rate – in practice. One is to take the average *past* rate of growth of dividends and assume that this rate will continue unchanged in the future. If need be, this rate can be adjusted to take account of any additional information that leads to the belief that the past growth rate will not be approximately reflected in the future growth rate.

The other approach, originally put forward by the American economist Myron Gordon, examines the basis of dividend growth and attempts to derive a future growth rate rather than just to extrapolate a past growth rate. Gordon started from the idea that a growing stream of future dividends arises from a growing level of investment by the company in profitable projects, and it will therefore be this rate of investment which will partially determine the rate of dividend growth. The other determinant of dividend growth must be the rate of return yielded by these projects. On this basis, and by making a number of limiting assumptions, a simple model can be constructed for deriving the value of the dividend growth rate. The necessary assumptions are as follows:

1 An all-equity company.
2 Retained net cash earnings (after the deduction of depreciation and tax) is the only source of investment capital.
3 A constant proportion of net cash earnings is retained each year for reinvestment.

4 Projects financed through retained cash earnings produce a constant annual return.

On this basis, if b is the constant proportion of earnings retained each year and r is the average rate of return produced by the projects undertaken by the firm, then the future dividend growth rate can be estimated as: $r \cdot b$. Thus the dividend growth model then becomes:

$$E = \frac{d_0(1 + rb)}{K_e - rb}$$

Notice that this particular version of the model is only applicable to companies which have an all-equity capital structure, because if debt capital is involved (a case examined in the next section), then it causes problems in keeping r and b, and hence g, constant. Obviously Gordon's variant of the dividend growth model is very naive, but it may well be a self-fulfilling predictor of share market values if investors generally believe that g can be estimated as rb and so partly base their market actions on such calculations.

Taxation and the calculation of K_e. Up to this point we have ignored the part played by taxation by assuming a tax-free world. However, from the viewpoint of the minimum acceptable return that management must achieve from their physical investments, taxation on dividends may play an important part. There are two possible effects which must be taken into account. First of all, tax may actually reduce the amount of cash dividend received by the shareholder (in much the same way as tax reduces a gross salary). In such circumstances, from the company's viewpoint in examining projects, what is of importance is the quantity of cash paid out as dividends, rather than the quantity of cash dividends (after tax) actually received by the shareholders. Secondly, if the company can arrange its affairs (principally in relation to its dividend policy) so as to reduce the amount of tax paid by shareholders, then company management should evaluate the net effects of doing so on shareholder wealth.

The latter point is examined directly in the chapter on dividend policy (Chapter 10), but the former is of immediate interest in the context of the cost of capital because tax can affect the rate of discount to be used by a company in investment appraisal (to be applied to the after-corporation tax cash flows of a project). However, the exact effect of tax on the cost of equity capital may well depend upon the intricacy of the actual tax régime. To avoid becoming involved in the finer detail, we shall examine the general effects of certain simple examples of tax régime.

If a taxation régime existed in which dividends were allowable as an expense chargeable against corporation/profit tax liability (i.e., in circumstances where governments wished positively to encourage non-retention of annual net cash earnings), then the required return given by the dividend valuation model would have to be adjusted before it could be used as a rate for evaluating investment proposals. In such circumstances, assuming that a constant dividend is paid in perpetuity and the rate of corporation tax (T) is also expected to remain constant, then the required expected return on equity capital – from management's viewpoint – becomes: $K_{e_{at}} = d(1 - T)/E$. For example, if a company's taxable profit before allowing for dividends was £5,000 and the corporation tax rate was 40%, then the amount of tax payable would be: £5,000 × 0·40 = £2,000. If the company wished to pay dividends of £1,000 and this were allowable against tax liability, then the tax payable would be reduced to: (£5,000 − £1,000)0·4 = £1,600. Therefore, of the £1,000 dividend paid, £400 would be provided through the reduced corporation tax liability, and so effectively the company would have to pay only the remaining £600. In general terms, in such circumstances, the dividends actually payable by the company are: $d(1 - T)$. It is for this reason that the dividend valuation model is adjusted as shown.

Similarly, but with the additional assumption that corporation tax is payable at the time of the dividend payment, the dividend growth model can be adjusted thus:

$$K_{e_{at}} = \frac{d_0(1 - T)(1 + g)}{E} + g$$

Currently, the UK has an imputation system operating as far as corporation tax is concerned. Dividends are not allowable against corporation tax liability and their only effect in terms of K_e can be seen as bringing forward the payment of part of the company's corporation tax liability. This portion of the company's overall tax liability is known as 'advance corporation tax' (ACT). With a constant annual dividend (not greater than the taxable profit) and unchanging tax rate in perpetuity, the net effect of such a tax régime on the value of K_e from the company's viewpoint is zero. Each year's constant amount of ACT liability is exactly offset against the allowance for the amount of ACT paid in the previous year. So, in such circumstances, the 'before tax' K_e is the same as the 'after tax' K_e. (This is obviously a slight approximation because increases in equity capital, still paying a constant dividend per share, will produce 'once-and-for-all' distortions in the equality of the ACT offset.)

With dividends expected to grow at a constant rate in perpetuity, and assuming that the mainstream corporation tax liability (i.e., total tax liability, minus ACT) is paid twelve months in arrears, the dividend growth model requires the following adjustment:

$$K_{e_{at}} = \frac{d_0(1 + g) + \lambda(d_1 - d_0)}{E} + g \qquad \text{given } \lambda = \frac{\rho}{1 - \rho}$$

where ρ represents the standard rate of personal income tax and d_0, d_1 represent the net dividend (i.e., net of ACT – the actual cash dividends paid to shareholders) at times 0 and 1 respectively. This adjustment is required because, through dividends being increased at an expected annual rate g, the payment of a small proportion of corporation tax is permanently brought forward in time. The expression $\lambda(d_1 - d_0)$ can alternatively be represented as the ACT attached to the company's current dividend, multiplied by the expected dividend growth rate.[13] Table 5.2 gives a small numerical example to illustrate the mechanics. However, the reader may like to derive the general form of the adjusted model using the same approach as in Table 5.1. It is important to understand that the ACT element has been

Table 5.1

$$E = \frac{d_1}{(1 + K_e)} + \frac{d_1(1 + g)}{(1 + K_e)^2} + \frac{d_1(1 + g)^2}{(1 + K_e)^3} \cdots + \frac{d_1(1 + g)^{n-1}}{(1 + K_e)^n} \quad (1)$$

multiplying each side by $(1 + g)/(1 + K_e)$ gives,

$$\frac{E(1 + g)}{(1 + K_e)} = \frac{d_1(1 + g)}{(1 + K_e)^2} + \frac{d_1(1 + g^2)}{(1 + K_e)^3} \cdots + \frac{d_1(1 + g)^n}{(1 + K_e)^{n+1}} \quad (2)$$

subtracting equation (2) from equation (1) gives,

$$E - \frac{E(1 + g)}{(1 + K_e)} = \frac{d_1}{(1 + K_e)} - \frac{d_1(1 + g)^n}{(1 + K_e)^{n+1}} \quad (3)$$

as long as $K_e > g$ then, as n approaches infinity so $d(1 + g)^n/(1 + K_e)^{n+1}$ approaches zero and therefore,

$$E - \frac{E(1 + g)}{(1 + K_e)} = \frac{d_1}{(1 + K_e)} \quad (4)$$

multiplying equation (4) by $(1 + K_e)$ gives,

$$E(1 + K_e) - E(1 + g) = d_1 \quad (5)$$

$$E(K_e - g) = d_1$$

$$\therefore E = \frac{d_1}{K_e - g} \quad (6)$$

where E = ex div market value, g = constant annual growth rate in dividends and d_1 = the dividend expected in (approximately) 12 months time. In the notation of our time scale, $d_1 \equiv d_0(1 + g)$ i.e. where d_0 is the dividend that has just been paid by the company. In which case:

$$E = \frac{d_0(1 + g)}{K_e - g}$$

added to the numerator (even though it is of no direct interest to the basic rate taxpayer) if the cost of equity capital to the company's management is to be set at a high enough level to ensure that the shareholders receive the return they require. For example, in Table 5.2 the management must earn a return on equity of slightly over 12% (0·12078) in order to provide the 12% return expected by the shareholders.

The cost of retained earnings One of the most important sources of corporate long-term investment capital is retained earnings, i.e., that part of net cash flow generated by a company's past investment projects which, at the time it arises, is retained within the firm rather than being distributed to shareholders as part of the dividend flow. Because retained earnings arise from sources internal to the company,

Table 5.2

With the current imputation system in the UK, for the basic rate taxpayer who receives relatively little income in the form of dividends (unearned income) there is effectively no tax on dividends. However, from the company's viewpoint, dividend payments have the effect of bringing forward (by one year under the assumption below) the payment of part of the total corporation tax liability. This advanced corporation tax is calculated as the amount of tax that would have been payable on the dividends paid, if they were taxed at the basic rate of income tax.

As an example, suppose a company has a constant annual taxable profit of 100. Corporation tax is levied at 40%, assumed payable 12 months in arrears. The company propose to pay a net dividend this year of 10, increasing at a compound annual rate of 10%. Income tax is at 30% and there is an imputation system. The current market value of the company's equity is 550 ex div.

Unadjusted to allow for the effects of corporation tax, the dividend growth model yields:

$$K_e = \frac{10(1 + 0\cdot1)}{550} + 0\cdot1 = 0\cdot12$$

However, this is only an approximation. Taking account of tax:

$$K_{e_{at}} = \frac{10(1 + 0\cdot1) + \tfrac{3}{7}(11 - 10)}{550} + 0\cdot1 = 0\cdot12078$$

The reason why the corporation tax regime has this effect of increasing the required expected return can be seen as follows:

Year	0	1	2	3
Net dividend (10% growth rate)	10	11	12·10	13·31
ACT (3/7th of div.)	4·29	4·71	5·19	5·70
Gross dividend	14·29	15·71	17·29	19·01
Corporation Tax liability	40	40	40	40
− ACT paid in previous year	3·90[a]	4·29[b]	4·71	5·19
Corporation Tax payable	36·10	35·71	35·29	34·81
+ ACT payable	4·29	4·71	5·19	5·70
Total CT payable	40·39	40·42	40·48	40·51
Extra CT payable (i.e. > 40)	0·39	0·42	0·48	0·51
Dividend	10·0	11·00	12·10	13·31
Cash out-flow from dividends	10·39	11·42	12·58	13·82

[a] This is calculated on the assumption that the dividend at time − 1 was:

$$\frac{100}{110} \times 10 = 9 \cdot 1 \text{ (approx).}$$

[b] The ACT payable on the dividend of 10 is given by: $10 \times 3/7 = 4 \cdot 29$

Therefore, as a result of a policy of increasing dividends by 10%, a small proportion of corporation tax is brought forward in time and this also increases at 10% per annum; but in terms of the required expected return, this is raised slightly to allow for this tax effect.

rather than externally (such as a new equity issue), there is a temptation to believe that this source of capital is somehow 'costless'. In fact, both from a legal and an economic standpoint, retained earnings belong to the ordinary shareholders of a company and so the 'cost' of retained earnings, or the minimum expected return that their use in investment projects should generate, is exactly the same as the expected return required by shareholders on new equity. Retained earnings form part of the equity capital of a company and their cost is therefore a reflection of this fact. This has already been implicitly taken into account in that the market value of equity was used in the specification of K_e, and the market value reflects both the nominal value of a company's equity capital and the retained earnings. (In practice retained earnings are a slightly cheaper source of capital than a new issue of equity because of the issue costs incurred with the latter).

5.2. The cost of debt capital

Introduction We have seen that the minimum required expected return on equity represents the 'cost' to a company of using that source of investment capital. Management should ensure that, when using shareholder's funds to undertake investment projects, at least this expected return is generated. In this section we now turn to examine, in a similar way, the cost of using the major alternative source of investment funds: debenture capital.

A debenture can be defined as a loan made to a company which is secured against the assets (usually the land and/or buildings) of the company. Debenture capital differs from ordinary share capital in two fundamental ways. Firstly, subscribers to debenture capital do not become part-owners of the company but are merely (secured) creditors, because they are only lending money to the company for a fixed period.[14] On the elapse of this period, the loan is repaid: the debenture is said to be redeemed. In contrast, equity capital represents a permanent loan which is never repaid except in very special circumstances (such as company liquidation). Secondly, the holders or suppliers of debenture capital receive a contractually *fixed* annual percentage return on their loan (which is specified when the debentures are issued and is known as the 'coupon' rate).[15] Again, this contrasts with the situation of the suppliers of equity capital whose annual return – the dividend – is variable and the exact level of which is at the discretion of the directors.

In addition to these two fundamental differences between debenture and equity capital, debentures are ranked ahead of equity for payment of the annual return. In other words, interest on debenture capital must be paid in full before any dividend may be paid to the suppliers of equity. Thus, if there is any shortfall in company earnings in any year, it is the ordinary shareholders who are more likely to suffer than the debenture holders.

A debenture therefore represents a loan with a contractually fixed rate of return, a contractually fixed time of repayment and preferential payment treatment over equity capital. In an uncertain world, all three factors combine to make the debenture capital of any given company a substantially less risky investment for a supplier of capital than that company's ordinary share capital. As debentures can be viewed as less risky than ordinary shares, it follows that the required expected return on a company's debentures[16] will be less than that required on its equity capital. In a *certain* world, debentures and equity capital would logically require the same return from any given company; but with the introduction of uncertainty the required returns differ.

In the next chapter we shall examine how companies handle the investment decision process in situations where blocks of capital from different sources (i.e., debt and equity) and hence having different required returns, are combined in order to undertake projects. But, before doing so, we must first investigate how the required expected return on debenture capital can be determined.

The interest valuation model Debentures are traded (i.e., bought and sold) in markets which are very similar to those for trading in ordinary shares, and we shall use the principles upon which the dividend valuation model was based in order to develop a debenture valuation model. Therefore we shall postulate that the market value of a debenture is determined by the summation of the future cash flows it will produce, discounted to present value. These future cash flows consist of the expected future interest flow and (if it is a redeemable debenture) its redemption value.

In the UK debentures are normally issued in blocks of £100, and attached to each such debenture (which is usually drawn up in the form of a trust deed) are details of its coupon rate, the date of redemption and the value of the debenture at which it will be redeemed. (Normally debentures are redeemed at par, i.e. £100, but sometimes a redemption value above par will be promised as an additional inducement to investors to purchase the debenture.) As debentures are traded in supply and demand markets, its market price will depend upon its level of demand in the market. In turn, this level of demand will largely depend upon the difference between the current *market* interest rate for an investment with a similar level of risk to the debenture, and the debenture's own *coupon* rate. Thus, if a debenture has a coupon rate which is below the current market interest rate, then its market value will be below its £100 par value, and vice versa.

For example, let us consider an irredeemable (or undated) debenture whose coupon rate is 5%, whilst the current market rate of interest (at the debenture's risk level) is 8%. The debenture is expected to produce a flow of interest payments of £5 per year, in perpetuity, and when this stream is discounted at the current market rate of interest and summed, its present value is £5/0·08 = £62·50. This represents the debenture's current market value. Its market value is only £62·50, against a par value of £100, because this is the amount that would purchase other debentures producing £5 of interest per year: £62·50 × 0·08 = £5. On a similar analysis, if the market rate of interest fell to 4%, then the market value of the debenture would rise to £5/0·04 = £125.

The marginal cost of debenture capital It is at this point that an important fact emerges. We are concerned with finding the 'cost' to a company of the various types of capital it might use to finance an investment project, in order to use this cost as the discount or cut-off rate in the appraisal process. For such a use we might easily believe that the debenture's coupon rate, rather than the current market interest rate (assuming they differ), reflects the cost to the firm of using this source of capital. However, such a belief would be incorrect.[17] Investment decisions must be evaluated 'at the margin' and so the current market interest rate rather than the debenture's coupon rate would be the correct discount factor to use. An example can easily show the logic of this approach. Suppose a company undertook an issue of debentures some time ago at a coupon rate of 5%, and the current market interest rate (for a similar risk level) is

Table 5.3

Project cash flows

Year	0	1	2	3	4
	$-1,000$	$+290$	$+290$	$+290$	$+290$

At a 5% discount rate:

$$\text{NPV} = -1,000 + 290A_{4|0.05} = +\pounds 28\cdot 34$$

At an 8% discount rate:

$$\text{NPV} = -1,000 + 290A_{4|0.08} = -\pounds 39\cdot 48$$

As the project has a negative NPV at the market rate of discount, it should not be undertaken. The £1,000 required outlay could be better employed deposited on the money market at 8% where it could produce the following flows:

Year	0	1	2	3	4
	$-1,000$	$+301\cdot 92$	$+301\cdot 92$	$+301\cdot 92$	$+301\cdot 92$

Compare this flow with that expected from the project.

now 8%. The company has discounted the flows of an investment opportunity which requires an outlay of £1,000 and which produces cash inflows as shown in Table 5.3. It proposes to use part of the proceeds of the 5% debenture issues to finance the investment and so discounts the project's cash flows at 5%. This produces a positive NPV of £28·34 and therefore the company undertakes the investment. If we recall our analysis of the logic of the NPV decision rule, we shall see why such a discount rate is incorrect. In discounting a project's cash flows to produce a positive or negative NPV, an implicit comparison is automatically being made between the returns from investing in the project and the returns that could be achieved by investing the project's outlay on the capital market. Hence we use the market interest rate as the discount rate. Therefore, discounting the project in Table 5.3 by 5% means that an incorrect comparison is being carried out: in fact, as an alternative to the project, an interest rate of 8% can be earned for the same level of risk. We can see that when discounting the project at 8% it yields a negative NPV, indicating rejection – a better return could be earned by investing the £1,000 on the capital markets.

The cost of irredeemable debenture capital   Thus, the general debenture valuation model for irredeemable debenture capital is:

$$D = \frac{I}{K_d}$$

where I is the amount of annual interest paid on the debenture in perpetuity, K_d is current market interest rate (at the given risk level) or alternatively the cost of the debenture capital and D is the 'ex interest' market value of the debenture. (Debenture market values follow a dog-tooth pattern similar to that of ordinary share values. Just as we only dealt with ex-dividend equity market values, so similarly the debenture valuation model only deals with ex-interest debenture market values.) The model can be switched around to produce the cost of irredeemable debentures as:

$$K_d = \frac{I}{D}$$

For example, if a company has issued irredeemable debentures at a coupon rate of $7\frac{1}{2}\%$ and each debenture currently has a market value of £93·75 (ex-int), then the company's cost of debt capital can be estimated as: $K_d = £7·50/£93·75 = 0·08$ or 8%. We can conclude from this that, for an investment of the debenture's risk level, the current market interest rate is also 8%.

Because we are dealing with an uncertain world, just as we talked in terms of K_e being the minimum required *expected* return to equity, so we should talk in terms of the *expected* return to debenture holders. Although a company's debentures are less risky than their ordinary shares, they are not riskless. Sometimes debentures can be very risky investments, for instance in cases where there is a substantial probability that the issuing company will be unable to meet the future interest and redemption payments (if the debenture is redeemable). In calculating the cost of debenture capital by means of the formula $K_d = I/D$, we are calculating what is called the debenture's 'yield to maturity'. This is the maximum yield (as opposed to the expected yield), that the debenture will produce at its current market price, as it assumes that all future contractual payments attached to the debenture will be met by the issuing company. However, working on the normal assumption of viewing companies as 'going concerns', then K_d, or the yield to maturity, is likely to be a fairly accurate estimate of the cost of debt capital for investment appraisal purposes (i.e., the marginal cost of debt capital). If the going concern concept is not thought applicable to a particular company, its marginal cost of debenture capital should be based on the alternative cash flow which its debentures are *expected* to yield.

The cost of redeemable debentures The cost (or, more accurately, yield to maturity) of redeemable debentures is estimated by finding the internal rate of return of the debenture cash flow.[18] This can be easily approximated by the linear interpolation method introduced in the previous chapter. For example, suppose a company had, some years ago, issued 5% debentures. These debentures currently stand in the market at £96 ex int and are due for redemption in seven years' time, at par. The cash flows, whose IRR we wish to estimate, are as follows:

Year
0   + 96·00
1-6   − 5·00
7   − 105·00   i.e., £100 redemption plus £5 interest.

The internal rate of this cash flow is approximately 5·7%, which represents the debenture's yield to maturity and which can be used as an estimate of its marginal cost.

The impact of taxation The company requires knowledge of the marginal cost of debenture capital for investment appraisal purposes and so, from this viewpoint, the expected return which the *supplier* of debenture capital receives is not the main focus of attention. The point of importance is the cash flow which the *company* must secure in order to service the debentures. In this respect, taxation has an important effect when the tax régime allows companies to offset debenture interest (but *not* redemption payments), against corporation tax liability. Therefore, as far as company investment appraisal is concerned, it is the *after-tax* cost of debenture capital which is important.

So far, we have ignored taxation in the calculation of K_d, and so we have, in effect, been calculating a before-tax cost of debenture capital: $K_{d_{bt}}$. Where T represents the current corporation tax rate (which is assumed to remain constant), the after-tax cost of irredeemable debentures can be found as:

$$K_{d_{at}} = \frac{I(1 - T)}{D} \qquad \text{or} \qquad K_{d_{at}} = K_{d_{bt}}(1 - T).$$

For redeemable debentures $K_{d_{at}}$ can be found by solving the IRR for the following cash flow:

$$D - I . (1 - T) . A_{n|K_{d_{at}}} - R . V^n_{K_{d_{at}}} = 0$$

where R is the debenture's redemption value and n represents the number of years until redemption.

This adjustment must be made to K_d, as the following example shows. If a company issues debentures with a 10% coupon rate and pays corporation tax at 40%, then the company does not actually pay £10 interest per debenture per year (although the debenture holder actually receives £10 of interest per year). As debenture interest is allowable against corporation tax, the company only pays £10(1 − 0·4) = £6. The balance of interest of £4 can be viewed as being paid by the Inland Revenue. This obviously causes the *effective* marginal cost of debentures (to the company) to fall substantially below the before-tax rate.

There are two further points worth noting. First, the after-tax K_d is only applicable on the assumption that a company has sufficient tax liability to take advantage of tax relief on debenture interest, and secondly, the $K_{d_{at}}$ computation is an approximation because the fact that corporation tax (and hence the reduction in corporation tax which comes about through offsetting debenture interest) is paid in arrears, is not being taken into account in the discounting. The calculation could be adjusted to allow for this, but such exactness is probably not really justified, especially as K_d is, in itself, only an estimate of the *expected* K_d.

Implicit and explicit costs of debenture capital It is important to remember that financial decisions are principally made on behalf of and for the benefit of ordinary shareholders, the legal owners of a company. As far as debenture holders are concerned, management only wish to fulfil their contractual obligations of interest and redemption payments. In this respect, we have only considered the *explicit* cost of debenture capital, but there is also an implicit opportunity cost which company management must take into account. This implicit cost of debentures arises from risk considerations and directly affects the ordinary shareholders. We shall examine it in detail later in the chapter on capital structure, but it is as well to be aware at this stage that debentures do involve an additional cost.

Costs of miscellaneous long-term capital There are a wide variety of sources of long-term investment capital, the costs of which we have not mentioned. Examples include long-term bank loans, preference shares and convertible debentures. The costs of all of these can be found using the principles of valuation derived earlier. Thus the cost of long-term bank loans, which can play an important part in the company's capital structure, can be ascertained by the same approach as is used with debenture capital. The cost of preference share capital can also be calculated in a way analogous to debentures, except that preference share dividends are not usually allowable against corporation tax.

The cost of preference shares and debentures that are convertible into ordinary shares may be slightly more problematical. Essentially, the holder of either a convertible preference share or a convertible debenture acquires debt capital (i.e., paying a fixed rate of interest), with an option – at a later date – to convert the debt capital into ordinary shares or to have the debt redeemed. The option to convert into ordinary shares is usually at a specified, predetermined price per share, and the owners of such convertibles are allowed to choose the time of conversion, within limits set down by the issuing company. It is these variable elements – the time of conversion, the proportion of investors converting into ordinary shares and the subsequent dividend flow received by these shares – which make the calculation of the cost more difficult. An example may help to clarify the computational difficulties. A company has £1 million of 6% convertible debentures. It is assumed that, at the earliest conversion point, which is in ten years' time, 90% of the debenture holders will convert (at par) to ordinary shares at 20p per share. The remaining 10% will accept redemption of their debentures at par. The current dividend per share is 3p and it is expected to grow at a constant rate of 2% in perpetuity. The current cost of equity capital is 12% and the corporation tax rate is 45%. Neither is expected to change. The after-tax expected cost of the convertible debentures can be found from the IRR (estimated via linear interpolation) of the following cash flow:

$$+1{,}000{,}000 - 60{,}000(1 - 0{\cdot}45)A_{10|K_d} - 100{,}000V_{K_d}^{10}$$

$$- \left[\frac{4{,}500{,}000[0{\cdot}03(1 + {\cdot}02)^{11}]}{0{\cdot}12 - 0{\cdot}02} \right] . \ V_{K_d}^{10} = 0$$

Discounting the cash flow at 10% yields:

$$+1{,}000{,}000 - 60{,}000(1 - 0{\cdot}45)A_{10|0{\cdot}10} - 100{,}000V_{0{\cdot}10}^{10}$$

$$- \left[\frac{4{,}500{,}000[0{\cdot}03(1 + 0{\cdot}02)^{11}]}{0{\cdot}12 - 0{\cdot}02} \right] . \ V_{0{\cdot}10}^{10}$$

$$= +1{,}000{,}000 - 202{,}771 - 38{,}554 - 647{,}156 = +111{,}519 \text{ NPV}$$

and discounting at 5% yields:

$$+1{,}000{,}000 - 60{,}000(1 - 0{\cdot}45)A_{10|0{\cdot}05} - 100{,}000V_{0{\cdot}05}^{10}$$

$$- \left[\frac{4{,}500{,}000[0{\cdot}03(1 + 0{\cdot}02)^{11}]}{0{\cdot}12 - 0{\cdot}02} \right] . \ V_{0{\cdot}05}^{10}$$

$$= +1{,}000{,}000 - 254{,}817 - 61{,}391 - 1{,}030{,}487 = -346{,}695 \text{ NPV}$$

By linear interpolation, the company's after-tax cost of convertible debt capital is approximately:

$$0{\cdot}05 + \left[\frac{346{,}695}{346{,}695 + 111{,}519} . \ (0{\cdot}10 - 0{\cdot}05) \right] = 0{\cdot}088 \text{ or } 8{\cdot}8\%$$

Selected references

F. D. Arditti and H. Levy, 'Pre-tax and Post-tax Discount Rates', *Journal of Business Finance*, Winter 1971.

E. F. Brigham and J. L. Pappas, 'Duration of Growth, Change in Growth Rates, and Corporate Share Prices', *Financial Analyst's Journal*, May–June 1966.

A. Chen, 'Recent Developments in the Cost of Debt Capital', *Journal of Finance*, June 1978.

S. Davidson and D. F. Drake, 'Capital Budgeting and the "Best" Tax Depreciation Method', *Journal of Business*, October 1961.

D. Durand, 'Growth Stocks and the St Petersburg Paradox', *Journal of Finance*, September 1957.

M. J. Gordon, 'Dividends, Earnings and Stock Prices', *Review of Economics and Statistics*, May 1959.

M. J. Gordon, 'The Investment, Financing and Valuation of the Corporation', Homewood, Illinois, Richard D. Irwin, 1962.

M. J. Gordon and L. I. Gould, 'The Cost of Equity Capital with Personal Income Taxes and Flotation Costs', *Journal of Finance*, September 1978.

M. J. Gordon and L. I. Gould, 'The Cost of Equity Capital: A Reconsideration', *Journal of Finance*, June 1978.

R. C. Higgins, 'Dividend Policy and Increasing Discount Rates: a Clarification', *Journal of Financial and Quantitative Analysis*, June 1972.

J. Lintner, 'Dividends, Earnings, Leverage, Stock Prices and the Supply of Capital to Corporations', *Review of Economics and Statistics*, August 1962.

D. Vickers, 'Profitability and Reinvestment Rates: a Note on the Gordon Paradox', *Journal of Business*, July 1966.

J. E. Walters, 'Dividend Policies and Common Stock Prices', *Journal of Finance*, March 1956.

P. F. Wendt, 'Current Growth Stock Valuation Methods', *Financial Analyst's Journal*, March–April 1965.

6 The Cost of Capital in Investment Appraisal

6.1 The weighted average cost of capital

In the previous chapter we examined the costs, or – more accurately – the opportunity costs, which are incurred by companies when using the various types of long-term capital to finance investment projects. We now come to the main point of this analysis by posing the question: What cost of capital should a company use as the discount rate in its NPV project appraisal calculations (or what cut-off rate should it use with the IRR decision rule)?

All-equity companies The (long-term) capital structures of companies can be separated into two types. Companies can have either a capital structure which consists entirely of equity capital, or a mixed capital structure where debt (i.e., fixed interest) capital and equity capital are held in varying proportions. The latter structure is the more common in practice (especially amongst stock exchange quoted companies) but the former provides us with a much less complex situation, and so initially we shall examine the question of the investment appraisal discount rate in terms of an all-equity company.

If a company has an all-equity capital structure and intends to remain as such (at least up to the horizon of its current planning) then, under a number of limiting assumptions, we can state that its current cost of equity capital is what should be used as the discount rate for investment appraisal. This rate, the expected return required by the ordinary shareholders, should be used because it represents the minimum acceptable return for a project undertaken by the company, in opportunity cost terms. The rate reflects the opportunity cost of the shareholders' capital, and so this capital should be applied only to projects which yield this return as a minimum. This condition applies whether the project is being financed by a new equity issue, by funds from an equity issue made in the past, or by using retained net earnings. In all cases, the investment capital represents shareholders' funds, and the company should only use such funds if each project to which they are applied earns at least this minimum return. Use of the NPV decision rule, with the cost of equity capital as the discount rate, will ensure that this is the case.

There are two important limiting assumptions to this advice, as well as the continuing assumption of a perfect capital market. The first is that the company is assumed to be evaluating projects which, if they were accepted, would not cause any significant change[1] in the company's overall level of risk[1] (and that the level has not been changed by any external events). That is, the acceptance of the project would not cause investors generally to view the company's expected future cash flows as having changed in their level of uncertainty. The reason for this assumption is obvious. The market-derived cost of equity capital is the required return relevant *only* to the company's existing level of risk and so would be an inappropriate rate to apply to a project which had a different level of risk. The second limiting assumption is that the project being appraised is small, relative to the overall size of the company, i.e., the project represents a marginal investment. Again, the reason for this assumption is obvious. The company's cost of equity capital is a marginal cost; it refers to the minimum expected return required by the marginal or incremental investor and therefore is only appropriate for the evaluation of marginal changes in the company's total investment. If one or other, or both, of these assumptions are violated by a particular investment proposal, then the appropriate discount rate to use is the cost of equity capital by which the stock market evaluates the company's ordinary shares, *once the project is undertaken*. The estimation of such a rate clearly poses a number of difficulties. We shall return later to this particular aspect of project evaluation.

Finally, the advice to use the company's existing cost of equity capital – under the limiting assumptions – will later have to be modified slightly, when we temporarily relax one of the characteristics of a perfect capital market: zero capital market transaction costs. But let us now turn to the much more realistic situation of the mixed capital structure company.

Mixed capital structure companies Where a company's capital structure is composed of both debt and equity capital, with their differing opportunity costs, what discount rate should be used for investment appraisal purposes? The short answer to this question, which we shall expand upon and attempt to justify, is that a weighted average of the costs of all the individual components of the capital structure should be used. On the surface this can appear to be strange advice. For example, assume a company possesses a capital structure of which (measured in current stock market values) half is equity with a cost of (say) 20% and half is debt with a cost of (say) 10%.[2] Using the proportion of each type of capital in the overall structure as the weights, we find that the company's weighted average cost of capital (which we shall call K_o) is given by: $(0.5 \times 0.2 + 0.5 \times 0.1) = 0.15$. Now, suppose an investment opportunity is perceived by the company which requires a cash outlay of £1m and the company proposes to raise the capital through a debenture issue at the current market rate of interest of 10%. The cost – in the everyday sense of the word – of the capital put into the project would be 10% and so it would appear logical to use this as the discount rate: if the project yields a return greater than 10% (i.e., it has a positive NPV at a 10% discount rate), the company must find the project beneficial.

In contrast to this, we have stated that the company's weighted average cost of capital should be the discount rate used for project evaluation: 15%.[3] But why should the company require a minimum return of 15%, when it appears that the project would be worth while as long as it yields a return in excess of 10%? For instance, if the project were found to have a yield (i.e., an IRR) of 14%, evaluating it using K_o as the discount rate would lead to its rejection even though it appears to produce a return 4% above its cost. To use K_o as the discount rate looks nonsensical. For another view of things, suppose the same company has another investment opportunity which it is proposed to finance through an issue of equity capital (where cost is 20%). If the project yields a return of 17% (say), it would have a positive NPV when discounted by K_o and so would be accepted. Once again, the use of K_o appears to lead to a nonsensical decision: acceptance of a project which does not even generate sufficient return to cover the cost of the capital outlay required.

The reason for these apparent anomalies arises principally from the assumption that the company intends to retain its existing capital structure mix of fixed interest and equity capital. (Just *why* a company should wish to do so will be dealt with in a separate chapter on the capital structure/financing decision. However, for the moment, let us accept that management believe that the company's existing capital structure is somehow 'ideal' and so wish to retain it.) This does not mean that, in the case of the example used above, because the company's current capital structure represents a 50 : 50 mix of debt and equity the £1 million required to undertake the proposed project should be raised from between these two sources in similar proportions. Although we have so far ignored them, there are relatively substantial issue costs attached to the raising of (external) capital, which exhibit considerable economies of scale (i.e., the greater the amount of capital raised from a single source, the lower will be the percentage of issue costs). In order to take advantage of these scale economies, the capital structure mix of companies is likely, in the short run, to fluctuate around the existing or desired structure, as first (say) debt capital is raised for one project and then equity capital for the next. So the assumption underlying the use of the weighted average cost of capital is that, although there will be minor fluctuations in the short run, in the medium/longer term a company's capital structure will remain stable.

It is neither practical nor especially sensible, to identify a particular source of investment cash physically with a particular project. Once cash enters a company, it enters the general 'pool' of capital within that company, and it is out of this pool that investment funds are drawn, in order to be applied to particular investment projects. Not unnaturally, the cost involved in using funds out of this pool of capital is the weighted average of all the individual capital inputs. Therefore, on the assumption that a company's capital structure (and hence the make-up of its capital pool) remains stable in the medium/longer term, it is the weighted average of these capital costs that must be the minimum acceptable return from any investment project. Neither the cost of what appears to be the individual source of capital used, nor the K_o of the short-term capital structure fluctuation are appropriate for designating a minimum acceptable return in opportunity cost terms.

The arguments for the use of the weighted average cost of capital as the investment appraisal discount rate are not perfect, and they are made under a number of assumptions which may or may not be borne out in practice. We have already noted these when examining the all-equity company case: unchanging capital structure, unchanging company risk, marginal projects. But if we return to the example we used previously, we can see that using K_o does produce the correct investment decision advice. The first project should indeed be rejected, for two reasons: first, and this is the crux of the K_o argument, because it cannot generate the expected return required in the medium/longer term. Second, its desirability should not be evaluated by comparison with the capital cost of an individual source. The particular source chosen is a decision taken, not in relation to the proposed project, but to the (chance) situation of the relationship between the company's existing capital structure and its desired/longer term capital structure (i.e., the short term imbalance: if it has too much equity to debt, then debt capital will be used to finance the project, and vice versa). On a similar reasoning, the second project is correctly accepted by using K_o as the evaluating discount rate. By using the weighted average cost of capital, under the assumptions specified, management is likely to get consistently correct investment decision advice whatever the source of financing used for a particular project. If the individual costs of capital were used instead, investment decision advice would partially depend upon the financing decision and would produce inconsistent advice. For example, with the projects referred to above, reversing the proposed financing methods would lead to a reversing of the investment decision advice.

Changes in the capital structure The use of a company's existing K_o in investment appraisal was made on the basis of two major assumptions. The first is that the investment opportunity being appraised would not, if accepted, alter the existing riskiness of the company. We will deal, in a later chapter, with the problems that occur when a company wishes to appraise investments which do not have this property. The second assumption is that the company's existing capital structure will remain unchanged. (The third assumption, that the project is marginal, really arises out of the first two.)

However, if a company is consciously changing its existing capital structure, then problems may arise in determining the discount rate to be used for investment appraisal purposes. Ideally, and on the assumption that the company's move to its new capital structure will be relatively rapid, the correct discount rate to use would be the weighted average cost of capital that *will* exist once the new/desired capital structure is attained. If instead, the capital structure change is likely to occur over a considerable period, then estimates should be made of the likely effects on K_o and these rates should be used for investment appraisal. For example, if a company's current K_o is 18% and capital structure changes in three years' time are designed to reduce this to 15%, then a project with the following cash flows should be evaluated accordingly:

Year	Cash flow	×	Discount factor	= Present value
0	− 1000		1	− 1000
1	+ 100		$V_{0.18}^1$	+ 84·75
2	+ 200		$V_{0.18}^2$	+ 143·64
3	+ 400		$V_{0.18}^3$	+ 243·45
4	+ 800		$V_{0.18}^3 \cdot V_{0.15}^1$	+ 423·40
5	+ 1200		$V_{0.19}^3 \cdot V_{0.15}^2$	+ 552·26
			Net present value	+ 447·50

The Calculation of K_o Let us now turn to examine how the weighted average cost of capital (WACC) is calculated and how a company's capital structure is 'measured'. The two questions are to some extent interlinked, but we shall start with the calculation of K_o.

A company's weighted average cost of capital is derived (or imputed) in a way analogous to other costs of company capital, because it is the lynch-pin of the relationship between the expected *total* future net cash flow of the company (i.e., dividends plus interest) and the current *total* market value of the company (i.e., debt capital plus equity). That is to say, using as a basis the logic which underpins the dividend valuation model, a company's total market value must be based on the sum of the expected future net cash flow, discounted to present value. This cash flow can be split into two separate streams: interest payments (and loan capital repayments) and dividend payments. Thus a company's WACC can be found by solving the following equation for K_o (i.e., finding the IRR of the cash flow):

$$+E + D - \sum_{t=0}^{\infty} \frac{dt}{(1 + K_o)}t - \sum_{t=0}^{\infty} \frac{It}{(1 + K_o)}t = 0$$

where E and D are the current, total market values of equity and debt capital, and dt and It are the total expected dividend and interest payments in time t.

Just as our calculations of both K_E and K_D were average costs of capital, so too is the overall cost of capital K_o. On the assumption of a constant dividend flow in perpetuity and irredeemable debentures (and hence constant interest flows in perpetuity), the expression for K_o simplifies to:

$$+E + D - \frac{d}{K_o} - \frac{I}{K_o} = 0$$

multiplying both sides by K_o and rearranging, gives:

$$+E \cdot K_o + D \cdot K_o - d - I = 0$$

$$K_o(E + D) = d + I$$

$$K_o = \frac{d + I}{E + D}$$

On the basis that, under such cash flow assumptions, $E = d/K_E$ and so $d = E \cdot K_E$, and similarly $I = D \cdot K_D$:

$$K_o = \frac{E \cdot K_E + D \cdot K_D}{E + D} \quad or \quad K_o = \frac{E}{E + D} \cdot K_E + \frac{D}{E + D} \cdot K_D$$

So here we can see why the discount rate to be used in project appraisal is the weighted average cost of capital and that the weights to be applied to the individual costs of capital are the market values of each capital source, as a proportion of the company's total market value.

There are two points of note here. Firstly, it is often a disputed point about just what weights should be used to calculate K_o. The argument is divided between the use of market values and book (i.e., balance sheet) values of debt and equity. We have seen in the above analysis that, following the logic of our fundamental valuation principles, it is market values that should be used as weights. The reasoning should by now be familiar. We are using the WACC in order to give decision advice, and so what is required is a marginal, opportunity cost weighted average, which is just what market value weights provide. Book value weights of debt and equity capital are just historical artifacts, which have often been adjusted on an arbitrary basis. The proponents of the use of book value weights raise two main arguments. First, market values are constantly fluctuating and so a company's WACC will likewise fluctuate, which causes problems for its use as an investment appraisal discount rate. This is true, but in calculating or estimating values for K_E and K_D, we have already discussed how we could tackle the problem of fluctuating market prices. The problem is relatively simple to overcome and a similar approach can be used for K_o. Second, it is argued that in terms of the minimum required return to be earned by a company, what is important are the expectations of the different suppliers of capital, but as market prices of debt and equity capital result from a whole range of different market forces besides the capital supplier's expectations, they are not necessarily the appropriate weights to use.[1] In one sense, there is some validity in this argument because market prices will not always be correct, in the sense of being in equilibrium. But it is probably safe to say that, especially in the longer run, these extraneous influences are likely to be relatively small and can be safely ignored. Even if this argument against market values were accepted, it in no way justifies the use of book value weights.

Turning briefly to the second question posed in this section, how a company's capital structure is to be measured, it should be clear from the foregoing analysis that market values of capital should be utilized in measuring or expressing a company's capital structure because they are the relevant factor. We shall describe a company's capital structure by the term 'gearing' ratio,[4] and we shall normally define it as the ratio of the total market value of a company's fixed interest capital to the total market value of its equity: D/E. We shall expand upon the significance of a company's gearing ratio in the chapter concerned with investment financing.

A summary of the use of K_o It is important to remember that a company's weighted average cost of capital is used for investment appraisal purposes because it represents the opportunity cost which is incurred by undertaking the expenditure of capital on an investment project. Given a perfect capital market, the market 'costs' of the individual sources of capital do reflect their opportunity costs. Therefore, on the assumption that a company's existing capital structure will remain unchanged, an average of these individual opportunity costs – weighted by their proportion in the company's total capital structure – will adequately reflect the overall opportunity cost of cash to that company. In addition, we know that this rationale only applies to the use of K_o for appraising marginal projects, the acceptance of which will not alter the company's existing level of risk.

Under all these assumptions, and ignoring the possible effects of many other real-world imperfections such as inflation and substantial changes in the national economy, a single estimate of a company's WACC is suitable to represent the opportunity cost of capital at each point of time over a project's life, i.e., it is acceptable to assume that the opportunity cost of cash will remain a constant over the life of an evaluated project.

Capital issue costs One of the components of the perfect capital market concept is that of zero transaction costs. In the context of this chapter, this specifically means that there are no costs incurred by a company in the act of raising capital from external sources. In practice, this assumption is manifestly false. Issuing house fees and commission, underwriting fees, printing and stationery costs and very substantial clerical costs are likely to be involved in the raising of new capital, be it fixed interest or equity. The point to be examined here is the effect on the foregoing analysis of issue costs.

Up to this stage we have regarded the cost to a company of using capital as an opportunity cost derived purely[5] from the capital markets, but the presence of issue costs effectively increases this cost of capital. In this respect, debentures cause little problem if it can be assumed that issue costs account for a constant proportion of debt capital raised. For example, if a company's irredeemable 10% debentures currently stand at par in the market, issue costs account for 3% (say) of a capital issue and corporation tax is at 45%, then the cost of debt capital could be calculated at:

$$\frac{10(1 - 0.45)}{100(1 - 0.03)} = 0.0567 \quad \text{or} \quad \underline{5.67\%}$$

as opposed to a cost of 5.5% when issue costs are ignored; however, 5.67% does represent the actual marginal cost of debt capital for the company. In terms of our general notation, where c represents the percentage issue costs:

$$K_{d_{at}} = \frac{I(1 - T)}{D(1 - c)}$$

for the case of irredeemable debentures. Similar amendments also apply to the redeemable debenture case.

The real problem arises with equity capital. It is easy to see that issue costs will slightly increase the cost of equity capital, in much the same way as they did for debt capital. But this only applies to externally raised equity because 'internally raised' equity (i.e., retained earnings) does not incur issue costs. So far, we have avoided having to take account of retained earnings explicitly in the calculation of the WACC by using the market value of equity as the weight for K_E, which represents the combined value of externally raised equity and retained earnings. If we now accept that these two sources of capital have slightly different costs when issue costs are taken into consideration, then we need to split the market value of equity into two parts: one to act as the weight for externally raised equity (and its slightly higher cost) and the other to act as the weight for retained earnings. The problem is that there is no very satisfactory way in which the market value of the equity can be divided up for this purpose. For example, the ratio of the nominal value of equity and the share premium account to the value of the revenue reserves could be taken as the basis of the division, but such values have a fairly arbitrary nature anyway, and there is also a problem when revenue reserves have been capitalized through a bonus issue.

As there is no logically correct way in which the market value of equity could be split up in practice, perhaps the most satisfactory solution (although alternative solutions could be envisaged) is to simply adjust our present calculation of K_E to allow for issue costs and ignore the fact that retained earnings have a slightly lower total cost, on the basis that externally raised equity more fully represents *marginal* equity capital. Therefore, assuming that a constant dividend stream in perpetuity is expected,[6] the calculation of K_E becomes:

$$K_E = \frac{d}{E} \cdot \frac{1}{(1-c)}$$ where c represents the issue cost percentage.

This rather pragmatic solution leads to the greatest degree of error in the calculation of a suitable discount rate for investment appraisal in the case of an all-equity company with a very high level of earnings retention. However, in this worst possible case the opportunity cost of funds will be only marginally exaggerated. For example, if equity issue costs represented 5% of capital raised, a company whose K_E before issue costs is 15% would have this figure raised only by something like $\frac{3}{4}$%.

An alternative approach is to leave the costs of capital unadjusted but instead to add the issue costs into the cash flow of the project involved. There appears no reason why this approach should produce better decision advice and, in addition, it transgresses the arguments used against the use of the cost of an individual capital source as the discount rate and may move away from the opportunity cost meaning of K_o.

In conclusion In conclusion, we can say that the procedure emerging from our discussion about the calculation of the costs of the various types of capital and the amalgamation of these costs into an overall cost of capital suitable for use in investment appraisal is dependent upon a large number of assumptions about the real world. We shall continue to examine the effects for investment appraisal of the relaxation of these assumptions. The next chapter examines how the theory of investment appraisal, as we have developed it so far, can be applied to one of the practical problems of the real world: that of inflation.

Selected references

F. D. Arditti, 'The Weighted Average Cost of Capital: Some Questions on its Definition, Interpretation and Use', *Journal of Finance*, September 1973.

M. J. Brennan, 'A New Look at the Weighted Average Cost of Capital', *Journal of Business Finance*, 1973.

M. J. Gordon and E. Shapiro, 'Capital Equipment Analysis: The Required Rate of Profit', *Management Science*, October 1956.

M. J. Gordon and P. J. Halpern, 'Cost of Capital for a Division of a Firm', *Journal of Finance*, September 1974.

L. W. Haley and L. D. Schall, 'Problems with the Concept of the Cost of Capital', *Journal of Financial and Quantitative Analysis*, December 1978.

S. M. Keane, 'The Tax Deductibility of Interest Payments and the Weighted Average Cost of Capital – a Reply', *Journal of Business Finance and Accounting*, Spring 1979.

S. M. Keane, 'The Cost of Capital as a Financial Decision Tool', *Journal of Business Finance and Accounting*, Autumn 1978.

M. A. King, 'Taxation and the Cost of Capital', *Review of Economics and Statistics*, January 1974.

S. C. Myers, 'Interactions of Corporate Financing and Investment Decisions – Implications for Capital Budgeting', *Journal of Finance*, March 1974.

A. Robichek and J. McDonald, 'The Cost of Capital Concept: Potential Use and Misuse', *Financial Executive*, June 1965.

R. C. Stapleton and C. M. Burke, 'Taxes, the Cost of Capital and the Theory of Investment: a Generalisation to the Imputation Systems of Dividend Taxation', *Economic Journal*, December 1975.

7 Investment Appraisal and Inflation

7.1 Allowing for inflation

Introduction Up to this stage in the analysis there has been an implicit assumption that, within our world of managerial investment decision making, market prices have been generally stable. This is not to say that we have excluded the possibility of any price changes, but that we have assumed that there are no general price movements within the economy, either upwards – inflation – or downwards – deflation.

In this section we shall relax this implicit assumption and examine how the existence of general price movements affects investment appraisal and decision making, and how appraisal techniques can be adapted – if need be – to cope with such circumstances. These effects will be examined mainly by analysing the inflation case, but the approach and conclusion will also apply by analogy to the case of deflation.

Inflation as a forecasting problem Inflation can be simply defined as a situation where prices in an economy are, in general, rising over time.[1] Its presence (or expected presence) is likely to cause problems in appraisal of an investment opportunity in two main ways. The first is that it will make the estimation of a project's expected net cash flow more difficult because, in addition to all the other cash flow components which have to be estimated, management will also have to estimate the expected future rates of inflation, i.e., the rates at which the prices of the project's individual inputs and its output are likely to rise. The second problem is, in one sense, an extension of the first. The expected rates of return required by the company's suppliers of capital can be viewed as the price of that capital and so its price, in the presence of general inflation, is likely to rise along with most other prices in the economy. These expected rates of return are combined in the company's weighted average cost of capital and then used (under certain restrictive assumptions which we have outlined in the previous chapter), to discount the project's net cash flows to present value. Management have the added task of estimating the effects of inflation on the project appraisal discount rate.

The effects of inflation on market costs of capital can most easily be seen by way of an example. In a situation of zero inflation, we know that suppliers of capital make a trade-off between consumption now and consumption at some future point in time. In order to be persuaded to forgo consumption now (but invest instead) they have to be rewarded with increased consumption at the later time point. Perhaps for a particular investor, for a particular amount of forgone consumption and involving an investment with a particular level of risk, an annual rate of interest of 5% would be sufficient reward, i.e., to forgo, say, £100 now, he would require £105 in a year's time. The investor is prepared to forgo £100 *of consumption* now for £105 *of consumption* in twelve months' time. Now if inflation suddenly becomes present in the economy, the £105 in cash received in twelve months' time will not purchase an additional 5% of consumption over what was forgone a year previously. In the face of inflation, because interest rules are in *monetary* terms and because the investment–consumption decision is taken in essentially *consumption* terms, if our individual requires a consumption interest rate of 5%, the money interest rate required will be greater than 5% to counteract the effects of inflation. Just what monetary interest rate will be required depends upon the rate of inflation. If the economy is suffering an annual rate of general inflation of 10%, then to replace £100 of forgone consumption now will require £100 $(1 + 0.1) = £110$ in cash, in twelve months' time. In order to be persuaded to forgo £100 of consumption now, our investor requires an extra 5% of consumption in twelve months' time. Therefore, in cash terms, he will require £110 $(1 + 0.05) = £115.50$, this represents an annual money interest rate of: $(1 + 0.10)(1 + 0.05) - 1 = 0.155$ or 15.5%. In terms of a company's investment appraisal, management would have to first of all estimate the future annual inflation rate at 10% before it could calculate that this particular source of capital would require an expected money return of 15.5%.

Therefore we can conclude that, as far as investment appraisal is concerned, the presence of inflation causes a problem because a further element is required to be estimated; but the actual technique remains unaffected. The project's expected net cash (money) flows are discounted by the appropriate (money) discount rate/cost of capital, and the investment decision advice is based on the sign of the resulting NPV.

An alternative approach An alternative course of action to that outlined above (but one which results in an identical NPV figure being produced for any given project) is to take the net cash flow of a project expressed in *current purchasing power* (CPP) terms and discount this to present value using the money cost of capital, *deflated* to allow for the effects of inflation. To illustrate this alternative approach, we can utilize much of the information given in the example above.

If inflation is generally expected to remain constant in an economy at 10% per annum and a company's money cost of capital (i.e., the costs of capital derived from the usual valuation models and based on expected cash flows – of dividends and interest – and on market values of ordinary shares and debentures) is 15·5%; then what can be termed the 'real' or CPP rate of discount can be calculated by deflating the market/money cost of capital to allow for the inflationary element which it contains. We already know, from the data used in the example above, that this 'real' rate of discount is 5%. From this knowledge we can see how to derive the real discount rate from the market/money rate and the inflation rate. This is shown in Table 7.1.

Table 7.1

Let the market/money rate of interest $= m$
Let the real rate of interest $\quad = r$
Let the general rate of inflation $\quad = i$

Then $(1 + r)(1 + i) - 1 = m$. If $r = 0.05$ and $i = 0.10$, then:
$$m = (1 + 0.05)(1 + 0.10) - 1 = 0.155$$

Therefore, as $(1 + r)(1 + i) = 1 + m$
then $r = \dfrac{(1 + m)}{(1 + i)} - 1$

If $m = 0.155$ and $i = 0.10$, then:
$$r = \frac{(1 + 0.155)}{(1 + 0.10)} - 1 = 0.05$$

When referring to inflation, then, it is important to emphasize that we are dealing with a phenomenon which consists of a *general* upward movement in prices, and so an annual rate of inflation is thereby necessarily just some sort of average of this general movement (for instance, we could take the percentage increase in the Retail Price Index). It is assumed that the rate of inflation that the company uses in order to deflate the market cost of capital/discount rate, so as to convert it into a rate expressed in 'real' (i.e., consumption power) terms rather than money terms, is equal to the rate of inflation which the market incorporates into the money cost of capital.

An example An example can be used to show how the two approaches to allowing for inflation operate so as to produce identical results. Suppose a company is considering a project which requires an outlay of £1,000 now. The project yields a cash inflow of £600 in twelve months' time, and this inflow increases at a compound rate of 10% per annum until the end of year 4 when the project comes to the end of its life and is sold as scrap for £50. In addition, there are annual running costs, of £200 in the first year and increasing in line with the general level of inflation, which is expected to remain constant at 8% per annum. The company's (money) cost of capital, which is appropriate to this project, is 14%.

Table 7.2 shows the project's net cash flows being calculated and discounted to present value using the company's cost of capital of 14%. The alternative approach, in which the project's money cash flows are deflated by the general rate of inflation so as to convert

Table 7.2

Year	Capital Cash Flow	Project Revenue Cash Flow		Running Costs Cash Flow		Net Money C/F
0	−1000					−1000
1		+600		−200		+400
2		$600(1 + 0.1)$	= +660	$200(1 + 0.08)$	= −216	+444
3		$600(1 + 0.1)^2$	= +726	$200(1 + 0.08)^2$	= −233.28	+492.72
4	+50	$600(1 + 0.1)^3$	= +798.6	$200(1 + 0.08)^3$	= −251.94	+546.66

Year	Net Money C/F	×	Market Discount Rate	=	Present Value C/F
0	−1000			=	−1000
1	+400	.	$V_{0.14}^{1}$	=	+350.88
2	+444	.	$V_{0.14}^{2}$	=	+341.64
3	+492.72	.	$V_{0.14}^{3}$	=	+332.57
4	+546.66	.	$V_{0.14}^{4}$	=	+323.68
				Net present value	+348.77

Table 7.3

Year	Net Money C/F	×	Discount Inflation Rate	=	C.P.P. Cash Flows	×	Discount 'Real' Interest Rate	=	P.V. Cash Flows
0	−1000	.	1	=	−1000	.	1	=	−1000
1	+400	.	$V_{0.08}^{1}$	=	+370.37	.	$V_{0.055}^{1}$	=	+350.88
2	+444	.	$V_{0.08}^{2}$	=	+380.66	.	$V_{0.055}^{2}$	=	+341.64
3	+492.72	.	$V_{0.08}^{3}$	=	+391.14	.	$V_{0.055}^{3}$	=	+332.57
4	+546.66	.	$V_{0.08}^{4}$	=	+401.79	.	$V_{0.055}^{4}$	=	+323.68
							Net present value		+348.77

them into current purchasing power cash flows, and are then discounted to present value using the 'real' discount, is shown in Table 7.3. The 'real' discount rate in this example can be calculated as:

$$r = \frac{(1 + 0 \cdot 14)}{(1 + 0 \cdot 08)} - 1 = 0 \cdot 0\dot{5}\dot{5}$$

The same net present value is achieved using either approach for reasons that can be shown if we take the net money cash flow of £492·72 in year 3 as an example. Discounting this sum to present value using the market discount rate produces a present value of £332·57. A similar present value sum is also achieved if the year 3 money cash flow is first converted into a current purchasing power sum of £391·14 and then discounted to present value at the 'real' discount rate. Thus:

$$\frac{1}{(1 + 0 \cdot 14)^3} = \frac{1}{(1 + 0 \cdot 08)^3} \cdot \frac{1}{(1 + 0 \cdot 0\dot{5}\dot{5})^3}$$

In other words, the second approach to the handling of inflation does, in two stages, what the first approach does in one. Contained within the market/money cost of capital or discount rate is the underlying 'real' rate, plus an allowance for inflation. The second approach explicitly splits the evaluation process into its two component parts.

In conclusion, we can state that this example has helped to show that the presence or expectation of general and specific price level changes certainly does cause problems for a company's investment appraisal in that it introduces an extra element of uncertainty into the situation and so causes problems with forecasting. But the cause of the problem is essentially *only* one of forecasting, and the underlying theoretical structure of investment appraisal is left unscathed.

Selected references

M. Bromwich, 'Inflation and the Capital Budgeting Process', *Journal of Business Finance*, Autumn 1969.

B. Carsberg and A. Hope, *Business Investment Decisions under Inflation: Theory and Practice*, Institute of Chartered Accountants in England and Wales, 1976.

I. Friend, Y. Landskroner and E. Losq, 'The Demand for Risky Assets under Uncertain Inflation', *Journal of Finance*, December 1976.

F. M. Wilkes, 'Inflation and Capital Budgeting Decisions', *Journal of Business Finance*, Autumn 1972.

8 Capital Market Imperfections

8.1 A definition of capital rationing

Introduction In Chapter 3 we set up a two-period investment–consumption model to use as a guide to effective financial investment appraisal. The model was a crude and unrealistic simplification of the real world, but it was used so that the underlying principles of investment decisions could be examined without becoming embroiled in elaborate complications (such as the existence of taxation, inflation and an uncertain future). In addition, a time horizon of only two periods was used so that the conclusions could be presented graphically rather than algebraically.

Under the very limiting assumptions of that model, we saw how the two DCF techniques of investment appraisal both gave optimal advice on investment decisions. From then on, we started to relax these assumptions, one by one, to see what the effect would be on the advice given by the two appraisal methods. Up to this point, we have dropped the assumptions of project cash flow independence, of a two-period time horizon and (to a very limited extent) of certainty. The result has been that the NPV method has emerged *relatively* unscathed, whilst the IRR method has been considerably less successful. However, even at this early stage, when none of the more important initial assumptions has been relaxed, we find that we must accept that optimal investment decisions are unlikely to be consistently achieved in practice and instead we are able to conclude only that following the NPV decision rule is *likely* to give correct advice on investment decisions.

In previous chapters, as part of the process of relaxing the assumptions of the initial model, we examined the effects of two real-world complications that were originally assumed away: inflation and taxation. One problem here that was not mentioned was that, because individuals and companies often have to bear different marginal rates of taxation (in the UK private individuals and companies have completely different tax systems as well as tax rates), the presence of tax often interferes with the operation of one of the model's most crucial assumptions, that of a perfect capital market. For instance, part of this concept assumes that, for a given level of risk, all investors will receive the same return. Clearly this may not be the case in cash terms, if individuals can be taxed at differing rates and therefore receive different returns on their investments. This is, quite simply, problematical – as we have already seen in discussing the concept of the cost of capital – and we shall return to this aspect when examining the dividend policy decision and again when we come to look formally at allowing for the presence of uncertainty.

In this chapter we are going to examine the effects of relaxing another of the assumptions which is contained within the overall concept of a perfect capital market: that all individuals and companies are able to borrow unlimited amounts of cash from the capital markets, within their ability to repay. When either individuals and/or companies are *constrained* by the quantities of cash which are available to them for borrowing, then there exists a capital market imperfection, which is normally termed 'capital rationing'.

Capital rationing as a managerial problem A great deal of attention, in both the applied and theoretical literature, has been paid to the problem of capital rationing but, even so, there is no general agreement on what precisely is meant by the term, and this has resulted in a great deal of confusion. In an effort to avoid adding to this, it is important that we explicitly state from the outset what we shall take to be the meaning of capital rationing.

From the viewpoint of the making of investment decisions by financial management within companies, capital rationing is a *managerial* problem. It is, most certainly, a theoretical problem for our decision making model but, more importantly, it is also a practical problem. Up to this point, we have followed the NPV investment appraisal rule because it is most likely to indicate (in a practical sense) consistently good investment decisions. In its basic form the NPV decision rule is: accept all projects whose cash flows, when discounted by the appropriate cost of capital/discount rate, and summated, have a zero or positive net present value. The reason for their acceptance is that such projects will be yielding a return which is either equal to or greater than the minimum return required or expected by the owners of the company (and defined by the rate of discount). This minimum return is viewed in opportunity cost terms and must be earned (at a minimum) by a company because the suppliers of the investment capital can obtain that level of return (for the same level of risk) by investing their capital elsewhere. Implicit in this decision rule is the idea that as long as a company's management can find investment opportunities that yield at least this return, then capital will be available to finance the investment. Thus, if an investment is undertaken, its cost is the opportunity (or return) forgone in not investing that capital elsewhere. Here is the great advantage of a supply-and-demand capital market, in that it acts as an automatic mechanism which discloses this opportunity cost in terms of the market rate of interest.

We shall define capital rationing as a situation where capital investment funds are *not* freely available, but are limited in supply. Management has therefore to 'ration out' this limited amount of investment cash amongst the available investment projects. The reasons why such capital rationing may occur in practice are many and varied, but in the context of our analysis they are only of passing interest. The point that we wish to examine is, given a situation of capital rationing, how does it affect the efficiency of the investment decision advice given by the appraisal techniques and can these appraisal techniques be adapted to operate successfully in such situations?

Hard and soft capital rationing Two types or classes of capital rationing are usually specified: 'hard' capital rationing (which has received the lion's share of attention in the literature but which is probably of little importance in practice, as far as investment decisions in companies are concerned), and 'soft' capital rationing. Hard capital rationing describes the situation where forces external to the company, usually either the capital market itself or the government (which may or may not act through the capital market), will not supply unlimited amounts of investment capital to a company, even though the company has identified investment opportunities which would be able to produce the required return.[1] Soft capital rationing arises from forces internal to a company, such as a capital budget which limits the amount of capital available for investment. In certain situations and in certain cases, the distinction between hard and soft capital rationing and between the various different causes of hard rationing may be important for the analysis. Where they are, such a distinction shall be made, but for the moment we shall concentrate on the problems which capital rationing 'per se' causes for investment appraisal.

An example In a situation where capital rationing is non-existent (and hence we are assuming a perfect capital market), investment decision making involves a choice between the investment funds being applied to the particular investment under consideration or being applied to the capital market, because this alternative reflects the opportunity cost of undertaking the investment. With the introduction of capital rationing, choice is still involved, but the alternative to the application of capital to a proposed investment project is not *necessarily* the capital market, but may instead be another investment project. In other words, the opportunity cost of undertaking a particular investment is now not necessarily reflected in the capital market interest rate, but may be a higher value, represented by the return yielded by another project which could not be undertaken by the company because the supply of capital is limited. An example can help illustrate the point. Suppose a company has discovered two (independent) projects, A and B. Each requires £500 of investment capital, and Project A yields a return[2] of 12%, whilst B yields a return of 15%. We assume that each project is equally risky. If the company's cost of capital were 10% and funds were unlimited, both projects would be accepted because both would have positive NPVs. The acceptance procedure, using the NPV method, would involve the comparison of the return given by each project *in turn* with the return available on the capital market. However, if instead capital rationing exists, and the company's investment funds are limited to a total of £500, then a different decision process is required. The company must now choose, *not* between each project and the capital market return, but first between the two projects themselves and then, once it is decided which is the best project, compare its return with the alternative given by the capital market. Thus in a non-rationing situation the company would be making two decisions: accept/reject Project A, accept/reject Project B; whilst in a rationing situation they would be making one, two-stage decision: select Project A or B, then accept/reject the selected project.

8.2 One-period capital rationing

It appears at first sight that capital rationing involves little more than another type of the 'mutually exclusive projects' decision, which we dealt with in Chapter 4. In fact, as we shall see, the existence of capital rationing produces a much more difficult decision problem. Most readers will be familiar with the idea of a budget as a means of planning and control[3] and so, for the sake of presenting a clear argument, we shall assume that for each decision period (say, a year), management have a capital budget within which to keep, i.e., total capital expenditure must not exceed some stated upper limit: the capital budget or (to avoid terminology confusion) the capital constraint. Therefore we shall assume a soft rationing situation, but the conclusions we derive will be equally applicable to hard rationing.

Let us begin with the most simple and straightforward capital rationing problem. A situation where capital is rationed in the present period (i.e., t_0) but will be freely available in future periods – a rather unlikely situation in practice – or one where the collection of investment projects the company wishes to appraise involve capital outlays *only* in the current period (i.e., the capital outlay required for the project does not extend over more than one period).[4] In addition, it is assumed that projects are infinitely divisible, so that fractions of projects may be undertaken, and that they exhibit constant returns to scale. In such a situation, only a slight modification to the standard NPV decision rule is required. Each investment opportunity should have its expected future cash flows discounted to net present value by the company's discount rate.[5] This NPV is then expressed as a ratio of the capital outlay which the project requires in the rationed period. This ratio is often termed the 'benefit–cost ratio'. All projects which have a positive or zero value for this ratio would normally be accepted in a non-rationed situation. However, because capital rationing exists and a choice has to be made between the alternative projects, they should be ranked in order of decreasing benefit–cost ratio. Starting with the project with the largest (positive) ratio and working down the rankings, as many projects as possible (with positive or zero ratios) should be accepted, until all the available capital is allocated.

An example of benefit–cost ratios The following example shows this decision method in operation, using the assumption that capital rationing will only exist in the current period (year 0), all the projects are independent and divisible, and none can be delayed. In a non-rationing situation all the projects in Table 8.1 would be accepted, except for Project F which has a negative NPV when discounted at the company's cost of capital.[6] In order to undertake them all, the company would require £460 of capital now (year 0) and this would produce a total NPV of £283·09. Therefore acceptance of Projects A to E when communicated to investors would, in theory at least, cause the total stock market value of the company to rise by this amount.[7]

Table 8.1

Year	0	1	2	3	4	NPV 10% Discount Rate	Benefit–Cost Ratio
Project							
A	−100	+20	+40	+60	+80	= +50·96	$\frac{50\cdot96}{100}$ = + ·51
B	−150	−50	+100	+100	+140	= +57·94	$\frac{57\cdot94}{150}$ = + ·39
C	−60	+20	+40	+40	—	= +21·29	$\frac{21\cdot29}{60}$ = + ·35
D	−100	+60	+60	+100	—	= +79·26	$\frac{79\cdot26}{100}$ = + ·79
E	−50	+20	+40	+60	+40	= +73·64	$\frac{73\cdot64}{50}$ = + 1·47
F	−100	+30	+30	+30	+30	= − 4·91	$\frac{-4\cdot91}{100}$ = − ·05

However, suppose that capital rationing exists in year 0 (but not in years 1 to 4) and as a result the company has only £300 of investment capital available. Which projects should be selected to be undertaken? Table 8.2 ranks the projects in decreasing order of benefit–cost ratio and shows that the £300 of capital should be applied to Projects E, D, A and one third of Project B. This gives the company for its £300 capital outlay, a total positive NPV of: £73·64 + £79·26 + £50·96 + £19·31 = £223·17. Therefore, because investment capital is scarce, the market value of the company's ordinary share value will only rise by £223·17 as a result of the investment decisions made, rather than by £283·09. Thus, we can see that, as far as shareholders are concerned, there is a definite cost to capital rationing. In this case, because of the presence of capital rationing, the total market value of the company's equity capital will be approximately £60 below the value it would have otherwise attained.

Table 8.2

Project	Benefit–cost ratio
A	+0·51
B	+0·39
C	+0·35
D	+0·79
E	+1·47
F	−0·05

Project	Benefit–cost ranking	Outlay yr. 0	
E	1	50	
D	2	100	ACCEPT: E, D, A, ⅓B
A	3	100	
B	4	150	
C	5	60	
*F	—	100	

* Note that in this simple type of rationing situation, Project F would never be accepted because it has a negative benefit–cost ratio.

However, given the situation specified, the process of selecting projects on the basis of their benefit–cost ratios ensures that the company will maximize the total amount of positive NPV gained from the available projects, assuming limited investment capital. This is because the terms in which the benefit–cost ratio focuses attention on the size of a project's NPV are not absolute but *relative* to the scarce resource required to undertake it. In other words, projects are ranked in order of preference, in terms of the NPV they produce, for every unit (i.e., £1) of the limited investment capital which they require. In the example used above, Project A is preferred to Project B because it produces 51p of (positive) NPV for every £1 of the scarce investment capital applied to its undertaking, whilst Probject B only produces 39p of NPV per £1 of investment outlay.

The opportunity cost of capital It is interesting, as well as serving to introduce more complex capital rationing situations, to examine the opportunity cost of capital in the example used above. In a binding capital rationing situation, that is, where the capital constraint causes a company to reject projects which have positive NPVs, the opportunity cost of capital to a company is no longer represented by the market interest rate (or its weighted average cost of capital), but is the rate of return which the company earns on its marginal investment project. The company's marginal project can be defined in the following way: when faced with capital rationing, the company ranks the available investment opportunities in an order of preference and undertakes the projects in decreasing order of preference, continuing to do so until the available investment capital is fully used up. The project in which the last (i.e., marginal) £1 of capital is invested in is termed the marginal investment, and the return which that particular project yields on every £1 invested in it represents the company's marginal return. In the example above, the company's marginal investment was Project B and its return or IRR of (approximately) 21% represents the company's marginal return. (This is rather an oversimplification and the point will have to be more carefully developed later. However, it serves a useful purpose in giving a general insight into the concept of a company's marginal return.)

As such, the company's marginal return represents its opportunity cost of capital, and any additional project evaluated by the company should be evaluated in terms of this opportunity cost return, rather than the company's weighted average cost of capital. This is because, given that investment capital is limited, acceptance of any additional project would mean the *displacement* of another project, and the displaced project would be the company's marginal project. Thus, to be worthy of acceptance, any additional project would have to yield a return in excess of that produced by the project it would displace i.e., it would have to yield a return in excess of its opportunity cost.[8]

Divisibility assumption The benefit–cost ranking approach to the situation of single-period capital rationing depends heavily on the assumption that investment projects are divisible (i.e., that fractions of projects can be undertaken, such as one third of Project B in the example above) and that they are independent. Where these assumptions do not hold, benefit–cost ratios do not work and instead, the investment selection decision has to be undertaken by examining the total NPV values of all the feasible alternative combinations of investment opportunities, where collective capital outlay falls within the capital outlay limit. (In fact, the benefit–cost approach is just a short-cut way of doing this when projects are divisible.) Again, using the example above, if none of the investment projects were divisible, the combination of accepting Projects B, D and E would produce the greatest amount of NPV, keeping within the £300 capital expenditure limit.

8.3 Multi-period capital rationing

Introduction The problem of investment decision making in the face of capital rationing which extends over more than one period is both complex and, at present, not completely resolved. The complexity of the problem has not been helped by general confusion and differences in the literature over what is meant by the term capital rationing and by the range of differing assumptions that have been made, both explicitly and implicitly. The main source of confusion over capital rationing, as far as the theory of corporate investment decision making is concerned, has occurred through a failure to isolate the problem from general capital market theory. As a result, a number of paradoxical problems have arisen.

In attempting to outline a normative theory of investment decision making, we shall try to be both as practical and as realistic as possible. In doing so, we will assume that hard (or external) capital rationing, both for individuals and companies, is likely to be only a relatively short-run phenomenon which may well arise, in practice, out of poor forward planning. Concentrating for the time being on the company, this assumption can be justified as follows. It is certainly true to say that unlimited amounts of investment capital are not immediately available to companies, because capital raising operations, for both debt and equity, can take some time to arrange. Thus there is a very definite limit to capital supplies in the very short run. However, as long as a company plans its future operations carefully and well ahead of time and its management appears competent, it is unlikely that it will be unable to raise the capital it requires for any planned project which is expected to be 'profitable', i.e., it is unlikely that it will run into any serious, externally imposed capital rationing. By this we are not stating that hard capital rationing is impossible but that, by way of justifying our earlier assumption, in the majority of cases, for most of the time, it is an unlikely phenomenon.

Soft capital rationing If we make the assumption that externally imposed constraints on the supply of capital to a company are unlikely to be anything but relatively short-term phenomena, we are left with the task of examining the effects of internally imposed or soft capital rationing on the investment decision making process. We can define soft capital rationing as a capital expenditure constraint which is imposed on a company by its own internal management rather than by external capital markets, and which limits the amount of capital investment funds available in any particular time period. This capital limit will normally be imposed by a capital expenditure budget of which, in a well-managed company, there are likely to be two: a short-term capital budget for the immediate twelve months ahead and a medium-term capital budget which covers the next three to five years ahead.[9] Both budgets are likely to impose relatively inflexible capital constraints upon management.

When looking at how the NPV appraisal method could be adapted to deal with the single-period rationing problem, we saw that when the capital constraint was binding (i.e., there was insufficient capital available to invest in all projects with positive NPVs), companies would have to forgo undertaking some projects which they would have otherwise undertaken. Such a situation is understandable when imposed from outside the company, but it seems ludicrous when imposed from within the company. Why should a company wish to constrain itself in this way? The reason is that companies require to plan for the future and to monitor, control and evaluate the implementation of these plans so that future planning and control can be further improved upon. A capital budget is just one part of these plans and of the controlling process. It requires the imposition of a ceiling on capital expenditure, because capital investment is not a simple operation but one which takes time and a range of resources. For example, the decision to invest in a particular project does not consist simply of the evaluation and appraisal process. Capital may have to be raised for the project (an operation which cannot be carried out instantaneously), the company must have the trained manpower available to implement the project and monitor its performance (again, not an instantaneous process), and even the evaluation and decision procedure itself is likely to have its own manpower and resource constraints, as is the whole of the company's organizational structure. Thus, in order to plan carefully and to control efficiently, limits may quite properly have to be imposed – in the short and medium terms – on the level of capital investment expenditure that a company allows itself to undertake.[10]

The existence of capital budgets within companies is likely to mean that management is faced with the problem of decision making in a situation of multi-period capital rationing (i.e., where capital rationing extends over a number of future periods). In such circumstances, the simple benefit–cost ratio technique cannot be used to place investment opportunities in an order of preference. This is because, in the single-period rationing case, the problem was to allocate investment capital amongst competing projects in the face of a *single* constraint, in order to maximize the total amount of positive NPV gained; whilst in the multi-period case, this allocation procedure has to be carried out simultaneously under more than one constraint, each period's rationing being a separate constraint. To assist in this simultaneous allocation problem, we employ the mathematical programming optimizing technique of linear programming (LP). It is assumed that the reader is familiar with the basic mechanics of this technique, which can be found in any introductory book on operational research methods.

The opportunity cost of capital dilemma The presence of multi-period capital rationing does not alter the objective of financial management decision making: the maximization of shareholder wealth. This, we know, can be achieved through making investment decisions so as to maximize the total amount of positive NPV generated. The NPV figure gains its significance from the fact that it represents the result of netting out project cash flows and comparing this net cash flow with the opportunity cost, which is embodied in the perfect capital market discount rate. In examining how investment resources can be allocated to projects in a situation of multi-period capital rationing, we will assume that the *suppliers* of capital to a company do not themselves suffer any form of capital rationing. It is only the company which is faced with capital rationing, and it is self-imposed, rather than market imposed. This assumption releases the analysis from one of the major aspects of the multi-period rationing problem: the choice of discount rate. We know that the discount rate used in NPV calculation represents the opportunity cost of cash which, in a perfect capital market, is reflected in the market rate of interest (or our weighted average cost of capital). Once a perfect capital market no longer exists, then the market interest rate no longer necessarily reflects the opportunity cost of capital. In such circumstances, as we saw when looking at the single-period rationing problem, the opportunity cost of investment capital is represented by the return gained from the marginal project in the rationed period. Therefore, in a multi-period rationing situation, the appropriate discount rate for any period is given by the return on the marginal project in that particular period. This is the dilemma. The company requires to know the opportunity cost of cash in each period to use as the discount rate, in order to make the correct project selection. Each period's opportunity cost of cash is represented by the return on the marginal project in that particular period, but this marginal project can only be identified *after* the correct project selection has been made. In other words, in order to make the correct investment project selection, the opportunity cost of capital in each rationed period needs to be known, but this can only be known once the correct selection of projects has been made. Thus, we are firmly on the horns of a dilemma, unless we assume that the company's capital suppliers face perfect capital markets and it is the company alone which faces capital rationing. In such circumstances, the market interest rate or the company's weighted average cost of capital[11] still represents the opportunity cost of capital to shareholders and so can be used as the discount rate to aid project selection.

The LP solution to capital rationing An example is the best means of showing how, in multi-period capital rationing (which is self-imposed by the company), linear programming can help to allocate scarce investment capital to projects so as to maximize the total amount of positive NPV:

A company has found the following independent investment opportunities (all figures in £000s):

Project	Year	0	1	2	3	4	5
A		− 100	− 50	− 25	+ 100	+ 100	+ 100
B		− 50	− 70	+ 100	+ 100		
C		—	− 100	− 30	+ 150	+ 200	
D		− 10	− 20	+ 50	− 100	+ 100	+ 100
E		− 100	− 100	+ 200	+ 100	+ 50	
F		—	—	− 200	+ 300	+ 100	+ 100

We shall assume that none of these projects can have the timing of its cash flow brought forward or delayed and none can be undertaken more than once. In addition, we shall assume that selection of any one single project, or any combination of projects, will not change the company's existing level of risk, which is reflected in its current weighted average cost of capital of 10%. This rate is expected to remain constant over the next five periods and can be assumed to reflect the capital suppliers' opportunity cost.

Calculating the NPVs of the projects, using a 10% discount rate, we can see that the company would normally undertake them all, because each has a positive NPV:

Project	£ NPV
A	+ 39,409
B	+ 44,140
C	+133,597
D	+ 68,402
E	+ 83,662
F	+190,499

but in order to do so, would require the expenditure of £260,000, £340,000, £255,000 and £100,000 of investment capital in the next four periods (years 0–3) respectively.

Suppose that the company has an internally imposed capital constraint, such that capital expenditure in any one period must not exceed £150,000. Clearly, in these circumstances the company cannot undertake all six projects, and so which should be selected to be undertaken and which should be rejected?

There are a number of ways in which this problem could be formulated into a linear programme, but each alternative formulation would produce a solution giving exactly the same selection of investment projects to undertake. One approach, which fits directly into our NPV approach, is to take as the LP's objective function the maximization of the total amount of NPV which the company can generate over the next four periods, given the imposed constraints. Thus, taking a, b, c ... f to represent the proportion of Projects A, B, C ... F undertaken:

Objective function:

$$39,409a + 44,140b + 133,597c + 68,402d + 83,662e + 190,499f \text{ MAX}$$

Constraints:

$$100,000a + 50,000b + 10,000d + 100,000e \qquad \gtrless 150,000 \ (t_0)$$
$$50,000a + 70,000b + 100,000c + 20,000d + 100,000e \gtrless 150,000 \ (t_1)$$
$$25,000a + 30,000c + 200,000f \qquad \gtrless 150,000 \ (t_2)$$
$$100,000d \qquad \gtrless 150,000 \ (t_3)$$

a, b, c, d ≥ 0, ≤ 1

Solving this linear programme on the computer gave the following selection of projects: the whole of both Projects C and D should be undertaken, together with 0·3 of Project E and 0·6 of Project F; Projects A and B should not be undertaken.[12] This selection results in a total NPV of +£341,397 being generated, which is the maximum possible total sum, given the circumstances specified.

The assumptions behind LP In using linear programming to solve this type of capital rationing problem, there are a number of assumptions and limitations involved, one of which we have already touched upon: the specification of the rate of discount to be used. In addition, the technique assumes that all the relationships expressed in the model are linear (for example, all the projects are assumed to exhibit constant returns to scale) and that the variables are infinitely divisible. There is also an assumption that the project cash flows are known with certainty because, as yet, no way has been found of satisfactorily adjusting the technique to take account of risk. The first of these three assumptions does not necessarily cause too much trouble because, where there are non-linear relationships involved, they can often be adequately described in the LP formulation as a number of linear approximations. Similarly, the second assumption also may not be too troublesome, especially if the LP is being applied to the solution of the capital rationing problem within a company operating in a process industry (e.g., oil or chemicals), because the output is (approximately) infinitely divisible. (Integer programming – another type of allocation technique – avoids this assumption, but in doing so involves a number of new, and often more difficult, problems.) However, what really is a serious practical drawback to the use of LP in capital rationing situations, is the inability of the technique to handle risk. There have been some attempts to allow for uncertainty[13] but by and large they represent mathematical solutions to mathematical, rather than practical problems.

The dual values In the example we used above, where the objective was to maximize the total amount of positive NPV generated, the solution involved the company undertaking Projects C and D completely, together with 30% of Project E and 60% of Project F. The reader will see that this solution results in the utilization of only £40,000 of the £150,000 available for investment in year 0 and of only £100,000 of the £150,000 available in year 3. Therefore, although the company's capital expenditure is constrained in these two periods, the constraints are 'non-binding', i.e. they do not bind or constrain the company in its efforts to achieve its objective. For this reason, there is no *additional* opportunity cost of the cash used for capital expenditure in these two periods (i.e., there is no opportunity cost incurred in addition to that opportunity cost already allowed for in the discounting process used to convert the project cash flows to NPVs), because the company does not forgo any of its investment project opportunities as a result of these two constraints.

The situation is different in respect of the year 1 and year 2 capital expenditure constraints. In these periods, the linear programme's project selection results in the £150,000 available (in years 1 and 2) being fully utilized and therefore the constraints are said to be 'binding': their existence limits the company's freedom of action in pursuit of its objective of NPV maximization because it limits the amount of investment the company can undertake.[14] As a result, there is an additional opportunity cost attached to the use of investment cash in each of these two periods. These additional opportunity costs are represented by the 'dual' values produced by the linear programme. In the example used above, the LP solution produced the following dual values for the four capital expenditure constraints:

Period	Dual value
0	0
1	£0·837
2	£0·952
3	0

The dual values which are produced from a LP with a maximizing objective function represent the increase (decrease) in the total value of the objective function that would arise if a binding constraint were marginally (i.e., by one unit) slackened (tightened). Thus, in the example, the investment capital constraints result in the company achieving a total NPV value (i.e., the objective function value) of £341,397. If £150,001 were available for investment in year 1 (keeping the £150,000 limit in force in each of the three other periods), then the value of the objective function would rise by £0·837 to £341,397·837. In this very simple example, this increase in the objective function would be achieved by increasing the level of investment in Project E (the marginal project in year 1) from 30% of E to 30·001%.[15] Also, because the use of LP assumes linear relationships, a reduction in the amount of capital available in year 1 to £149,999 would result in the value of the objective function falling by £0·837. A similar analysis can be made in terms of the year 2 capital constraint dual value of £0·952, which is caused by a 0·0005% change in the level of investment in Project F. Because the capital constraints in years 0 and 3 are non-binding, their dual values are both zero: a marginal change in either constraint will leave both the original project selection and the value of the objective function unaltered.

There are a number of points to be made here. The first is that the example is a highly simplified one and the practical application of the use of LP to solve capital rationing problems is far more complex and problematical. We have only outlined the approach and specified the main theoretical difficulties. Second, if we accept that Projects E and F are the marginal projects in years 1 and 2 respectively (i.e., investment levels in these two projects change in response to marginal changes in available investment capital in these two years), it is important to realize that the relative IRRs of these two projects do *not* produce their dual values, because the IRR represents a project's average return over the whole of its life, whilst the dual value refers to a project's marginal return in just the period specified. A third point of importance is that dual values apply only to incremental/marginal changes in binding constraint values. To identify the effect of any non-marginal change – i.e., a substantial change – the LP has to be reformulated accordingly and re-solved. Finally, dual values apply only to *individual* marginal changes in binding constraints, i.e., they operate under a *ceteris paribus* assumption that all other variables in the formulation remain unchanged. Thus, in the example used, if an extra £1 of investment capital is available in years 1 *and* 2, the resulting change in the value of the objective function is not necessarily the sum of the two individual dual values. Therefore we can see that dual values can be informative in that they represent part of the opportunity cost of investment capital, but their usefulness is relatively limited because of their marginal nature.

8.4 Lend–borrow interest differentials

Introduction We have been examining the investment decision in the face of one particular capital market imperfection, that of soft capital rationing. Let us now turn to examine another common imperfection: the existence of a gap between the borrowing and the lending interest rate at any given risk level, caused by the presence of market transaction costs, where the borrowing rate is somewhat higher than the lending rate. Perhaps the best way to lay bare the problem here is to make use of the two period investment–consumption diagram.

Identification of the opportunity cost In the basic model we saw that, because of the so-called 'Separation Theorem', it made little difference to the appraisal of physical investment opportunities whether a company had one or several owners and, if it had several owners, whether their utility curve sets were similar or dissimilar; in fact the company did not even require a knowledge of its owners' utility curve sets. In the face of a perfect capital market, a company would invest in physical investment opportunities until the return from the marginal project equated with the market rate of interest (i.e., it would invest in all projects which had positive or zero NPVs). This investment decision rule determined the two-period dividend flow pattern which the individual shareholder could adjust, if he wished, by using the capital market. The company used the market interest rate as the investment appraisal discount rate because it reflected the opportunity cost of capital/cash to the shareholders.

Let us now start with the simple case of a single shareholder company and a perfect capital market except that transaction costs result in the borrowing interest rate being higher than the lending interest rate. In such a case the separation theorem (i.e., separation between management investment decisions and shareholder consumption decisions) breaks down, as there is no longer a single opportunity cost of cash because there are now two market interest rates. Figure 8.1 illustrates this situation with the steeper of the two financial investment lines (BC) representing the borrowing rate and the other (DF) representing the lending rate. In these circumstances the shareholder's utility curve may be tangential at any point along the boundary BCDF. We can specify three separate cases:

1 If a point of tangency occurs on the BC segment then, in time t_0, the company should undertake physical investments up to point C, and then the shareholder should add to his received dividend by borrowing on the capital market. For the company to locate itself correctly at point C on the physical investment line, the market borrowing rate should be used as the NPV discount rate because it would represent the opportunity cost of cash. The borrowing rate

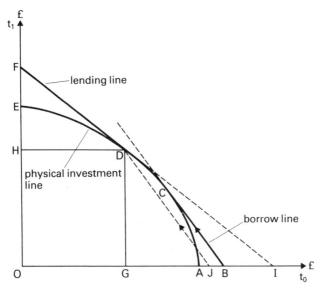

Figure 8.1   Capital market imperfection: differing lend–borrow rates

reflects the opportunity cost in these circumstances because the shape and location of the shareholder's utility curve set is such that preference emphasis is placed on consumption at time t_0. Thus, if cash is to be invested rather than consumed at time t_0, the investment should earn a return at least equal to the borrowing rate, because the shareholder will be borrowing to replace (at least in part) the investment outlay undertaken.

2 If a point of tangency occurs along segment DF, then the company should locate itself at point D on the physical investment line and the shareholder should then lend out some part of his received dividend on the capital market. In this case, the company can ensure optimally locating at point D by undertaking all physical investments which produce positive or zero NPVs when discounted at the market lending rate. This rate represents the shareholder's opportunity cost of cash for reasons analogous to those cited in the previous case, except that his utility curve set is now shaped so as to bias preference towards consumption at time t_1. Thus the company should undertake physical investments as long as they earn a return which is at least equal to that which the shareholder could earn by lending on the capital market.

3 If the point of tangency between the shareholder's utility curve set and the boundary curve BCDF occurs along the segment CD, then

this also represents the optimal point of location for the company on its physical investment line. In such circumstances, the opportunity cost of cash is represented by the slope of the shareholder's utility curve at the point of tangency (his marginal rate of time preference) and it is also represented by the return on the marginal investment at the point of tangency on the physical investment line. Therefore, this is the rate of discount which the company should use in its investment appraisal, to ensure that it locates itself at the optimal point on the physical investment line.

In practical terms, the company management is unlikely to be aware of the location of its shareholder's utility curve set in relation to the boundary BCDF and so will not know whether to use the borrowing rate (case 1), the lending rate (case 2) or some intermediate rate between the borrowing and lending rates (case 3) as the investment appraisal discount rate. (Indeed, with case 3 there exists a dilemma similar to that already discussed in the case of hard capital rationing.) However, even if the company were aware of its single shareholder's utility map and so could optimally locate on the physical investment line, in the more realistic case where there are several shareholders, their utility curve sets are unlikely to be the same, which may well lead to a direct conflict over the value at which the discount rate should be set in order to reflect the opportunity cost of cash.

Quite simply, then, the real-world solution to the problem is indeterminate, and all that a company can hope to do is to use a single discount rate both consistently and publicly, so that it attracts shareholders whose opportunity cost of cash approximates to this rate.

Three further points There are three further points worth noticing in this analysis. First, if the company uses the lending rate for discounting and so locates at point D in Figure 8.1, the total net *present* value of the company's investments (given by AI) does not have any real meaning in the sense that the dividend flow produced of OG at time t_0 and OH at time t_1 cannot be converted by the shareholder into a cash flow of zero at t_1 and OI at t_0. Such a dividend flow can only have a present value of OJ. This presents an interesting problem in terms of management's objective function, which we have stated as the maximization of the ordinary share's stock market valuation. To do this – and assuming the stock market valuation is based on the present value summation of the future expected dividend flow – it could be argued that the company should use the borrowing rate as the discount rate, because this is the only meaningful way a 'present value' could be stated, but then in this example, maximization of the market value of the company's equity capital would not bring maximum benefit to the shareholders, in terms of assisting them to obtain the highest possible utility curve.

A second point is that, given the company selects a discount rate between the market borrowing and lending rates (inclusively) and it makes an incorrect selection (or alternatively the selection is incorrect as far as some shareholders are concerned), the smaller the gap between the borrowing and lending rate, the less serious (in terms of lost utility) will be the mistake.

Finally it is interesting to speculate upon the situation of a company which was either totally ignorant of its shareholders' utility curve sets or had shareholders with widely different utility maps. In these circumstances, and still using a two-period analysis, the most conservative action for the company to take would be to use the borrowing rate for discounting when evaluating projects. If that is the correct rate (i.e., case 1) then there is no problem. If either the lending rate or some intermediate rate is correct, then, although shareholders will not maximize their utility, the utility level achieved will *always* be higher than if the company did not undertake any investment at all. If either the lending rate or an intermediate rate is chosen to evaluate investment possibilities and this chosen rate proves to be incorrect, then shareholders *may* find themselves at a *lower* utility level than if the company had undertaken no investment at all, but instead had liquidated[16] itself at time t_0. Taking immediate corporate liquidation as the ultimate alternative, investing in projects with positive NPVs when discounted at the borrowing rate will always raise shareholders' utility level. The use of a discount rate above the borrowing rate may reduce the utility level to below that achieved through immediate liquidation.

In conclusion There are an almost infinite number of variations on the capital rationing theme, and it is not the purpose of this book to examine the problem in depth, but just to outline some of the main areas of difficulty for investment appraisal and to indicate to the reader that at present many of the difficulties have yet to be satisfactorily resolved.

In the first section of the next chapter, we look at yet another aspect of capital market imperfection, that of differing corporate and personal interest rates. This analysis is then used to introduce the second major financial decision area: the financing decision.

Selected references

F. D. Arditti, R. C. Grinold and H. Levy, 'The Investment–Consumption Decision under Capital Rationing: an Efficiency Analysis', *Review of Economic Studies*, July 1973.

W. J. Baumol and R. E. Quandt, 'Investment and Discount Rates under Capital Rationing – a Programming Approach', *Economic Journal*, June 1965.

R. H. Bernard, 'Mathematical Programming Models for Capital Budgeting – a Survey, Generalisation and Critique', *Journal of Financial and Quantitative Analysis*, June 1969.

K. N. Bhaskar, 'Linear Programming and Capital Budgeting: a Reappraisal', *Journal of Business Finance and Accounting*, Autumn 1976.

R. J. Dean, J. Leather and J. W. Bennett, *FIRM: a Computer Model for Financial Planning*, Institute of Chartered Accountants in England and Wales, 1975.

H. R. Fogler, 'Ranking Techniques and Capital Budgeting', *Accounting Review*, January 1972.

C. W. Haley and L. D. Schall, 'A Note on Investment Policy with Imperfect Capital Markets', *Journal of Finance*, November 1972.

J. S. Hughes and W. G. Lewellen, 'Programming Solutions to Capital Rationing Problems', *Journal of Business Finance and Accounting*, Spring 1974.

J. H. Lorie and L. J. Savage, 'Three Problems in Rationing Capital', *Journal of Business*, October 1955.

H. M. Weingartner, *Mathematical Programming and the Analysis of Capital Budgeting Problems*. Englewood Cliffs, N.J., Prentice-Hall, 1963.

H. M. Weingartner, 'Capital Rationing: n Authors in Search of a Plot', *Journal of Finance*, December 1977.

9 Financing the Investment

9.1 Differing corporate and private interest rates

Financing via debenture capital Through the two-period investment–consumption model, we developed the important Separation Theorem without which the theory of managerial investment decision making loses much of its operational relevance. The essence of the theorem is that investment and consumption decisions can be effectively separated and analysed in isolation. Thus company managements can make decisions about physical investment opportunities without reference to the utility maps of individual owners/shareholders. On receipt of the dividend from the company, each shareholder then decides, with reference to his own utility map, whether or not to use the capital market to borrow or lend money. In this way, the theory of investment decision making is able neatly to side-step one of the great stumbling-blocks of the practical application of economic theory: the identification of individuals' utility maps and the need to make an interpersonal comparison of utility, when the preferences of individuals differ.

The reader may well have wondered at the ease with which the Separation Theorem conclusion gave way to a seemingly different analysis. The theorem would appear to suggest that companies need be financed only by equity share capital and retained cash earnings (or retained dividends), and that money market borrowing and lending at fixed interest rates can be left to individual shareholders, in their personal manipulation of the pattern of their received dividend flows. But, having dealt with the conclusion of this theorem, the analysis then turned to examine the costs of a *variety* of sources of company finance and the way in which these costs may be combined into a weighted average, to be used as a discount rate for investment appraisal. Therefore, the idea of using debenture capital to finance a company was introduced without either giving any reason *why* a company should raise fixed interest capital (when the Separation Theorem tells us that this decision can be left to the individual shareholder) or analysing the alterations it makes, if any, to the conclusions of the investment–consumption model. In fact, under the initial assumptions of the two-period model, the answers to both questions are relatively straightforward. There is really no reason why a company should borrow money on a perfect capital market (i.e., raise debenture capital), because individual shareholders are perfectly capable of taking such action if they wish. But, even where a company does raise debenture capital, it does not really disturb the conclusions of the model because the debentures can be viewed as just another investment undertaken by management,[1] which can be fitted into the physical investment line with little difficulty. However, in the real world, companies raise debenture capital as well as equity capital for many reasons, principal among which is the disturbance in the capital market caused by taxation: companies can offset interest payments against taxation whereas individuals normally cannot. Therefore, assuming that a company and an individual are seen as equally risky by the capital markets, the company can effectively borrow at a lower rate of interest (after tax) than can individual shareholders. So let us now analyse this situation, in terms of the two-period investment–consumption model, where the company's cost of borrowing on the capital market is less than that of the individual shareholder.

Debt capital in the perfect market case First of all, assuming the existence of a perfect capital market in which individuals and companies borrow at effectively the same rate of interest, and under an assumption of certainty, let us examine in what circumstances a company may raise debt capital, i.e., borrow. Figure 9.1A shows the physical investment opportunities discovered by a company which have been ranked in order of decreasing rate of return. Under our previous analysis, we know that in order to help maximize shareholder wealth, the company will move along its physical investment line (PIL) until a point of tangency is reached with the financial investment line (FIL). This tangency occurs at point Q. Moving to Figure 9.1B, where the vertical axis is superimposed on the previous figure, this shows that the shareholders' current resources in the company, OA, are not sufficient to achieve the point of optimality on the physical investment line. Resources to the value of AB are required. To reach this point of optimality, the company is faced with two possible alternatives: it can either request its shareholders to subscribe additional equity capital (thus causing the vertical axis to shift to the left so as to intersect the horizontal axis at point B, rather than at point O); or the company can itself borrow amount OB on the capital market and repay CD (capital plus interest) at time t_1. With this latter course of action, the current/present value of the company's equity capital would be OE, whereas its current value would only have been OF if the company had simply done no more than invest up to point R. This gain of EF in the current value of the company would also arise if the company, instead, undertook the former course of action and asked its shareholders to subscribe an amount OB of new equity. The resulting *net* current value of the equity would be BE less OB = OE (i.e., the current value of the total equity, less the amount of newly subscribed equity).

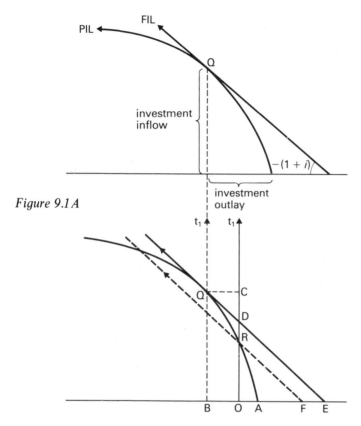

Figure 9.1 A

Figure 9.1 B

The important result from this analysis is that, in a perfect capital market, a company which wishes to maximize its shareholders' wealth should make physical investments until the return on the marginal investment becomes equal to the market interest rate; and it makes no difference to shareholders' wealth how these investments are financed, whether it be by equity capital or debt capital or by some combination of equity and debt. In the example used above, the company can maximize its shareholders' wealth either by using all equity investment capital (i.e., raise OB of additional equity) or by a mixture of both equity and debt (i.e., raise OB on the capital market).

Debt capital in the imperfect market case So much for the perfect market case. Let us now examine the effects of debt capital financing when we have the particular type of capital market imperfection described earlier, which enables companies to borrow on the capital market at lower interest rates than can shareholders. In this analysis we shall assume that the company's interest rate and the individual shareholders' interest rate, represent both the borrowing and the lending rate for each, and we shall continue to assume certainty.

Figure 9.2 sets up a situation similar to that of the previous analysis, except that there are now two points of tangency between the physical investment line and the *two* financial investment lines (one reflecting the company's interest rate and the other the shareholders' interest rate). These two points of tangency are at Y and Z respectively. Just as in the previous analysis, we shall assume that both points represent a capital investment requirement which is in excess of the company's existing resources. Thus both tangency points occur in the graph's north-west quadrant.

In this situation, the company is faced with a number of alternative courses of action, of which we shall initially specify and examine the effects of four:

1 Raise no additional capital.
2 Raise equity capital only.
3 Raise both debt and equity capital.
4 Raise debt capital only.

With the first of these four alternatives, the company would invest the whole of its capital resources (OA) available in time t_0 in physical investments, so as to reach point D on the physical investment line. The effect of this would be to give the company's equity capital a current (present) value of OM. Taking the second alternative of raising additional equity capital only, the maximum amount which the company could raise would be ON, thus allowing the company to move around the physical investment line to point Z. At this point, any further investment – which would necessitate raising further amounts of equity capital – would reduce the gain in the equity's current value; as it is, moving to point Z would cause the current value of the equity (in *net* PV terms) to increase by AB to OB. This represents a further increase in the company's current value, over that gained by the first alternative, of MB. It is important to notice that, with the first alternative (where no additional cash is raised), it would not matter which cost of capital (i.e., the company's interest rate or the shareholders' interest rate) was used to appraise investment opportunities, because both would effectively move the company to point D. However, with the second alternative, the company must use the shareholders' cost of capital as the NPV discount rate to ensure its location at point Z (which in Figure 9.2 equals shareholders' borrow/lend rate).

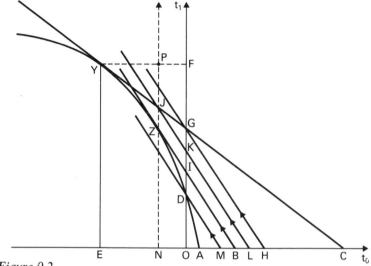

Figure 9.2

The third alternative would be for the company to raise amount ON in new equity capital and amount NE in debt capital. In order to do so, investment opportunities would first be appraised with the shareholders' cost of capital as the discount rate. The total investment capital required for acceptable projects at this discount rate would specify the amount required to be raised in the form of new equity. Those investment opportunities which remained unaccepted would then be appraised by the *company's* cost of capital. The total capital outlay required for the acceptable projects at this lower rate would then specify the amount of debt capital to be raised. The overall effect of raising capital from these two sources and investing them in the accepted opportunities would locate the company at point Y on the physical investment line. This level of investment allows the company to generate cash of amount NP at time t_1, of which PJ represents interest and debt capital repayment and the remainder, NJ, is available for payment of dividend at t_1, which, at the shareholders' discount rate, has a net *present* value (i.e., net of the newly raised equity) of OL. Thus this third alternative raises the company's current value by a further amount: BL.

The fourth alternative requires that all investment opportunities are appraised with the company's cost of capital as the discount rate. The total amount of capital required to undertake the investments appraised as acceptable at this rate (AE), less the existing capital resources of the company (AO), specifies the amount of debt capital to be raised (OE). Once again, the combined effect is to move the company around its physical investment line to point Y and so generate a cash inflow of NP at time t_1. Of this cash inflow, amount FG represents the interest and capital repayment, and the remainder, amount OG, is available for dividends. The present value of this dividend (and hence of the company) is OH. Thus this fourth alternative has resulted in yet a further increase in the company's current value, of amount LH.

The extreme use of debt capital The logical conclusion of the foregoing analysis is fairly obvious, but is fully developed in Figure 9.3, where it is assumed that at time t_0 the company has available capital resources (all equity) of amount OA. Facing the physical investment line of AF and using the shareholders' cost of capital as the investment appraisal discount rate, the company would move to point Z, producing a time t_0 dividend of OD and a time t_1 dividend of OG. The present value of this dividend pattern represents the company's current value of OH. If the company then appraises all the unaccepted projects at its own discount rate and borrows amount CD to undertake those which are acceptable, the company is moved further around the physical investment line to point Y. This would result in the company's equity having an (increased) current value of OJ.

However, to maximize the increase in the company's value from its existing level of OA and hence bring greatest benefit to the shareholders, the company should pay a dividend at time t_0 of virtually *all* of OA (this dividend amount is labelled on Figure 9.3 as OB, where AB represents a minute fraction of the existing equity[2]) and borrow amount BC. This would result in paying lenders an amount in time t_1 of KL, which represents interest and capital repayment, whilst leaving BK as dividend. The combined dividend flow of OB in time t_0 and KB in time t_1 has the effect of maximizing the increase in current value of the company (given the investment opportunities available and the market interest rates) from its existing value of OA to that of ON.

Therefore, when faced with an ability to borrow money at a rate below that charged to individual shareholders, the company should evaluate its physical investment opportunities using the corporate interest rate as the NPV discount rate, and should raise as much of the resulting required investment capital in the form of debt rather than equity (i.e., the company's capital structure should be composed of 99·99% debt capital and 0·01% equity capital). This rather surprising result is extremely important, but it should be emphasized that it has been derived under a number of important assumptions including those of certainty and the non-existence of differential borrowing and lending rates.

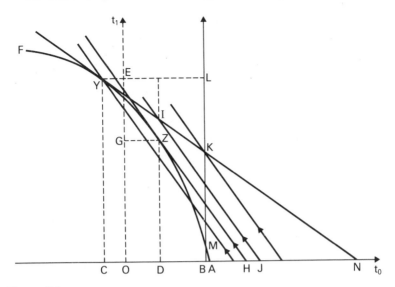

Figure 9.3

The role of the weighted average cost of capital The foregoing analysis has led us to conclude that, in order to locate correctly on the physical investment line, a company should use its own borrowing and lending interest rate as the discount rate for investment appraisal. In the model used, this rate had the appearance of beng the company's after-tax cost of debt capital $(K_{D_{AT}})$, and so how can this be reconciled with our earlier conclusion that a company should use a weighted average of its own and its shareholders' interest rate: the weighted average cost of capital K_o ?

The conclusion that a company's WACC was the appropriate rate to use for investment appraisal was made on the important assumption that the company intended to retain (at least in the medium/longer term) a given, existing capital structure mix of debt and equity. On this basis therefore, the company's financial investment line is not determined by the cost of debt capital but by the weighted average cost of all the types or sources of capital contained within its existing capital structure. Thus, in concluding that the company should use its own market interest rate for discounting/investment appraisal purposes, this rate is its weighted average cost of capital.

9.2 The Modigliani and Miller approach to the capital structure problem

An 'optimal' capital structure? The analysis in the previous section led us to the interesting provisional conclusion that management who wish to maximize their company's shareholders' wealth should gear the company up to such an extent that its capital structure would consist almost entirely (99 + %) of debt capital, with the very minimum of equity capital. This conclusion does not seem to match with practice,[3] where companies' capital structures rarely contain more than 70% debt capital and the average level of gearing is around 35% debt capital and 65% equity capital.

To take a closer look at the problem, let us begin by posing the question: Can any particular ratio of debt to equity in a company's capital structure be said to be optimal in terms of helping to increase the wealth of ordinary shareholders? This is an important question for a number of reasons. First, in advocating the use of the WACC for discounting/appraisal purposes we assumed that a company's capital structure would remain constant. This assumption would obviously gain support if it could be shown that an optimal capital structure does exist for a company, because management would wish to attain and *remain* at that particular gearing ratio. Second, up to this stage we have assumed that management could increase the wealth of ordinary shareholders only by the decisions they made about physical investment projects. If, however, an optimal gearing ratio exists, then it would appear that management could also increase shareholder wealth by manipulating the company's capital structure. Finally, the question has important implications for the approach which we have developed to investment decision making. Hitherto, we have assumed that the question of how a particular investment project is to be financed (the financing decision) can be taken separately from the investment decision itself (as a direct result of the Separation Theorem) and the investment decision has only been examined in isolation. If the financing decision can be shown to be important for the company – in terms of the desired capital structure – then we may have to revise our approach to investment appraisal.

The capital structure argument was first rigorously analysed by two Americans, Franco Modigliani and Merton Miller (universally known in the abbreviated form of M.M.), in a justly famous article that first appeared in 1958. Much of our analysis in this section will be based upon the approach that they took.

A company's total market value We introduced the term 'gearing' or 'leverage' when examining the costs of the various sources of capital which are available to a company, and we defined the term as the ratio of the market value of a company's debt capital to the market value of its equity capital.[4] The distinction between debt and equity was important because, when we rescinded the assumption of certainty, each type of capital bore a different level of risk: debt capital was a less risky investment in a company, for a supplier of capital, than an equity capital investment in that same company. This risk differential resulted from the fact that debt capital interest had first claim on a company's annual net earnings, ahead of equity capital dividends, and in addition, debt capital had repayment preference over equity capital in circumstances of company liquidation. As a result of this risk differential, the suppliers of debt capital to a company would require a lower return than the suppliers of equity, because they bore less risk.

In order to calculate the costs of the different capital sources, various valuation models were constructed, all based on the premise that an object's value is determined by the flow of future net benefits which it produces. Therefore, a company's equity capital derived its value from the future (discounted) flow of dividends which it was expected to produce. Similarly, debt capital was valued on the basis of the summation of the future expected (discounted) interest flow and the redemption payment. From these two valuation models, it follows that the total market value of a company (debt plus equity), V, must be derived from its expected future (discounted) net cash flow – which consists of its future dividend flow and its future interest and redemption flow. It will be helpful, for later analysis, to restate this in terms of the notation used earlier when analysing a company's cost of capital. Table 9.1 gives this restatement (ignoring taxation for the present). From this table, and under the assumption of constant annual dividends in perpetuity and irredeemable debentures, if we let $[E \cdot K_E + D \cdot K_D] = \bar{Y}$, and if we assume for simplicity that none of a company's net cash flow is retained, but is paid out each year as interest and/or dividends, then $\bar{Y}$ is a constant and so a company's total market value is given by: $V = \bar{Y}/K_o$.

Table 9.1

$$E = \sum_t^\infty \frac{dt}{(1 + K_E)^t}, \qquad D = \sum_t^N \frac{It}{(1 + K_D)^t} + \frac{R_N}{(1 + K_D)^N}$$

$$V = \sum_t^\infty \frac{dt}{(1 + K_E)^t} + \sum_t^N \frac{It}{(1 + K_D)^t} + \frac{R_N}{(1 + K_D)^N}$$

Assuming constant annual dividends in perpetuity and irredeemable debentures, this simplifies to:

$$E = \frac{d}{K_E} \qquad\qquad D = \frac{I}{K_D}$$

$$V = \frac{d + I}{K_o} \qquad \text{where } d = E \cdot K_E$$

$$\text{and } I = D \cdot K_D$$

As the current analysis is concerned with the total market value of a company:

d = total annual dividend payout
E = total ex div. market value of the equity capital
I = total annual interest payout
D = total ex int. market value of the debt capital.
R_N = total value of redeemed debentures at time N.

An example The question that we wish to examine is whether or not a company's gearing ratio (i.e., its capital structure) can affect its total market value.[5] From the above it should be clear that changing a company's gearing ratio will affect its total market value (V) only if it causes a change in either the company's annual net cash flow ($\bar{Y}$) and/or its weighted average cost of capital (K_o). A numerical example is perhaps the easiest way to show that a company with a given constant annual net cash flow of $\bar{Y}$ will have an unchanging total market value, whatever its mix of debt and equity capital. But, before doing so, it is necessary to indicate the principal assumptions upon which this analysis and the example are based:

1 At any given level of risk, individuals and companies can all borrow at the same rate of interest, which remains constant regardless of the gearing.
2 There are no costs attached to market transactions, the supply of information or the process of bankruptcy.[6]
3 There is no difference between corporate borrowing and personal borrowing in terms of risk (e.g., there is no limited liability advantage for companies).
4 There is no taxation.

Suppose that there are two companies, A and B, which are identical in every respect except that company A has an all-equity capital structure, whilst company B has a capital structure which consists of (say) 40% debt capital and 60% equity. If both companies have an expected annual net cash flow of £1000 (before interest and dividends) in perpetuity, all of which can be and is paid out in full each year as either dividends (company A) or dividends and interest (company B) then, on the basis of our underlying valuation premise, each company should have exactly the same total market value: they have the same expected annual cash flow both in terms of its size and its riskiness, and so logically they should both have the same total market value. If this total market value was, in each case, £10,000 and the market cost of debt capital (K_D) was 4%, then the facts as set out in Table 9.2 can be deduced.

Table 9.2

	Company A Yrs 1–∞ £	B Yrs 1–∞ £
Market value of equity (E)	= 10,000	6,000
Market value of debt (D)	= —	4,000
Total market value (V)	= 10,000	10,000
Annual interest flow $(D . K_D)$	= —	160
Annual dividend flow	= 1,000	840
Net annual cash flow $(\bar{Y})$	= 1,000	1,000
$K_0 = \bar{Y}/V =$	0·10	0·10
$K_E = d/E =$	0·10	0·14
$K_D = I/D =$	—	0·04

This example does nothing to prove or disprove any hypothesized relationship between changes in a company's gearing ratio and consequential changes in its total market value. The data in Table 9.2 was derived upon the *assumption* that the market values of the two companies were the same, despite different gearing ratios. However, the example does serve two very useful purposes. The first of these is that it can help to highlight the relationship between a company's gearing ratio and its cost of equity capital; but before examining this we must undertake a closer examination of the concept of risk.

Business and financial risk In terms of financial decision theory, we can identify two types of risk, both of which arise from the future being uncertain. The first type of risk is usually called business (or operating) risk and refers to the fact that companies operate in an uncertain world and so the future performance of any company is uncertain and depends – to a ' greater or lesser extent – upon the outcome of a whole range of variable factors: the state of world trade, the condition of the national economy and the individual industry in which the company operates, changes in the tastes and demands of its customers, changes in the industry's technology etc., etc. These represent just a very small selection of the wide range of factors which cause business risk, and some companies (and some investment projects within companies) bear a greater amount of it than others. For instance, a company producing a stable commodity such as bread is likely to suffer from a smaller degree of business risk (i.e., its future performance will be more predictable) than a company operating in an industry such as shipbuilding or advanced electronics, the demand for whose products is much less stable.

In the present analysis, business risk is not of direct importance except for the assumption that a company's business risk level can be measured and that it remains a constant. (The concept of business risk will be more fully explored in a later chapter.) Of more immediate interest is the second type of risk, known as financial risk, which arises directly out of the gearing process and is borne by the equity shareholders in a geared company. This second type of risk is caused through debt capital having priority over equity capital in both the distribution of the company's annual net cash flow (as interest and dividends) and in any final liquidation distribution. As interest payments to debt holders must legally be paid in full by the company before any dividend payments can be made, the greater the proportion of debt capital within a company's capital structure, the greater the probability that the company will have no cash remaining with which to pay a dividend. This risk of a reduced or zero dividend, which is borne by ordinary shareholders, is termed financial risk, and its severity is likely to increase as a company increases its level of gearing. Pictorially, a company's expected annual net cash flow can be portrayed as a probability distribution (see Figure 9.4). In an all-equity company (on the assumption of no retention by the company of this net cash flow), the probability distribution also represents the dividend flow. Gearing up has the effect of imposing a fixed annual charge on this distribution (the interest payments), so shifting the dividend payment probability distribution to the left. The greater the proportion of debt in the capital structure, the further will be the leftward movement and the greater will be the proportion of the dividend probability distribution falling within the negative portion of the horizontal axis. Thus the greater is the risk of a reduced or zero dividend as gearing is increased.

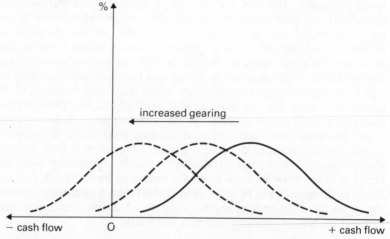

Figure 9.4   The gearing effect on the dividend probability distribution

K_E **and the gearing ratio** In general, investors may be assumed to dislike risk and to try to avoid it as much as possible, and so in situations where they are required to bear an extra amount of risk they are likely to demand an increased return on their investment as a reward, or as compensation, for so doing. Therefore, in the numerical example used above in Table 9.2, the return required by equity shareholders in company B (14%) has a reason for being higher than that in company A (10%). Shareholders in B, the geared company, are bearing some financial risk, unlike the shareholders in A, the all-equity company, and so it is not unreasonable that the shareholders in B might require an extra 4% return on their capital as compensation.

Let us examine more closely the nature of the relationship between the cost of equity capital and the gearing ratio, which we are implicitly assuming to exist when making the explicit assumption that changes in the gearing ratio do not affect a company's total market value. Using the notation introduced earlier, this relationship can be derived as follows:

$$K_o = \frac{E \cdot K_E + D \cdot K_D}{E + D} = \frac{\bar{Y}}{E + D}$$

$$\therefore \quad \bar{Y} = K_o(E + D)$$

$$K_E = \frac{E \cdot K_E}{E} = \frac{\bar{Y} - D \cdot K_D}{E}$$

$$\therefore \quad K_E = \frac{K_o(E + D) - D \cdot K_D}{E} = \frac{E \cdot K_o}{E} + \frac{D \cdot K_o}{E} - \frac{D \cdot K_D}{E}$$

$$\underline{K_E = K_o + \frac{D}{E}(K_o - K_D)}$$

where $\bar{Y}$ represents the company's annual net cash flow, which is assumed to be entirely paid out each year, as dividends and interest. The above indicates that a company's cost of equity capital is equal to its weighted average cost of capital (or, alternatively, the cost of equity capital of an all-equity company of similar business risk) plus the product of its gearing ratio and the difference between its WACC and its cost of debt capital. Thus for company B in Table 9.2:

$$K_{E_B} = 0.10 + \frac{4000}{6000}(0.10 - 0.04)$$

$$\underline{K_{E_B} = 0.10 + [0.66 \times 0.06] = 0.14 \text{ or } 14\%}$$

The point of importance here is that, on the assumption that the total market value of a company remains unaffected by changes in its gearing ratio, the return required by ordinary shareholders (K_E) is equal to the company's WACC – which remains a constant – plus a premium for the financial risk which arises out of gearing. This financial risk premium which is required by shareholders can be expressed as:

$$\frac{D}{E}(K_o - K_D)$$

which is a simple linear (i.e., straight line) function of the gearing ratio if we introduce the additional assumption that the cost of debt capital remains a constant (and so $K_o - K_D$ also remains a constant). These relationships are shown diagrammatically in Figure 9.5.

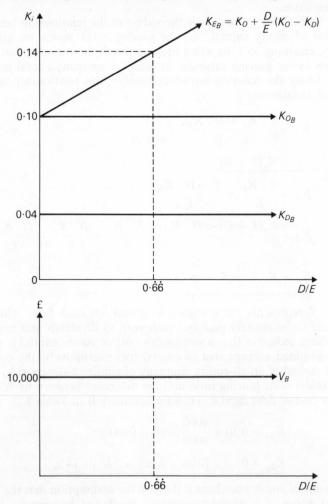

Figure 9.5

The conclusions of this foregoing analysis are based on the initial premise that a company's gearing ratio does not itself determine or affect its total market value; but what reason do we have for believing this initial premise to be correct? By using an example, Modigliani and Miller very neatly demonstrated that if gearing changes *did* affect a company's total market value, they would only be very short-lived because a type of market transaction called *arbitrage* would come into operation to cancel out any such effect. In other words, if a gearing change did affect a company's total market value, arbitragers would quickly act so as to return the company to its original (i.e., pre-gearing change) total market value. We shall continue to use the previous example of companies A and B to demonstrate this market process.

The arbitrage proof Suppose that the situation is as in Table 9.2, except that now the stock market places a higher[7] value on the geared company (B) of, say, £11,000. The ungeared company (A) continues to be valued at £10,000. This higher value is entirely reflected in the market value of B's equity at £7,000,[8] against £6,000 previously. These data, and their implications are presented in Table 9.3. For purposes of illustration we shall assume that company A has issued 20,000 ordinary shares and company B 6,000 ordinary shares.

Table 9.3

	A	B
Annual net cash flow $(\bar{Y})$	£ 1,000	£ 1,000
Market value of debt (D)	—	£ 4,000
Cost of debt capital (K_d)	—	0·04
Annual interest flow $(I = D \cdot K_d)$	—	£ 160
Residual paid as dividends $(\bar{Y} - I)$	£ 1,000	£ 840
Market value of equity (E)	£10,000	£ 7,000
Cost of equity capital $(K_e = \mathrm{Div}/E)$	0·10	0·12
Total market value (V)	£10,000	£11,000
WACC $(K_o = \bar{Y}/V)$	0·10	0·091
Number of ordinary shares	20,000	6,000
Price per share $(E/\text{No. ord. shares})$	50p	$116\frac{2}{3}$p

As these two companies have the same level of business risk, our initial premise would lead us to expect them to have the same weighted average cost of capital (K_o) and – because they have the same expected annual net cash flow – the same total market value (V); but clearly this is not so:

$$V_A = £10,000 \qquad K_{o_A} \doteq 0·10 \qquad V_B = £11,000 \qquad K_{o_B} = 0·091$$

However, we can show that this is simply a short-run disequilibrium in which the ordinary shares in company B (and hence B's total market value) are overvalued. As a result, shareholders in B will undertake arbitrage transactions which will have the effect of equating the weighted average costs of capital of the two companies and also their total market values. Once this point of equality has been reached, arbitrage transactions will no longer bring any benefit (or profit) and so will cease.[9] The purpose and the effect of arbitrage dealings can best be explained by continuing the example.

Suppose an individual owns 1% of company B and so holds 60 ordinary shares. These have a current market value of $60 \times £1\cdot16\frac{2}{3} = £70$ and yield an expected annual dividend of £70 × 0·12 = £8·40. In holding the ordinary shares of a geared company, the shareholder is bearing some financial risk, the amount of which can be 'measured' by the company's gearing ratio of 4 : 7 (£4,000 of debt capital and £7,000 of equity capital). If the individual sells his share-holding in B for £70, this would have the effect of reducing his financial risk to zero. In order to keep his level of financial risk a constant at 4 : 7 (so that we may compare like with like), he can gear *himself* up by personally borrowing £4 ('debt') for every £7 ('equity') of his own cash. As he holds £70 of his own cash, by borrowing £40, he will keep his existing level of financial risk a constant. This money is borrowed at the same rate of interest as company B's cost of debt capital, as a perfect capital market is being assumed. The individual has now got £70 + £40 = £110 with which he can buy ordinary shares in company A. As this company is ungeared, such action will not affect the individual's level of financial risk.

Thus, our individual has sold his shares in company B, borrowed some additional money and invested this loan, plus the proceeds from the share sale, in company A. As both companies have, by assumption, the same level of business risk, our individual's investment is unaltered in these terms. By borrowing money in the same ratio to his share sale proceeds as B's gearing ratio, he also ensures that his financial risk holding also remains a constant. His investment in company A produces an annual dividend of £110 × 0·1 = £11, but out of this, he has annual interest payments of £40 × 0·04 = £1·60. Therefore he is left with a net annual cash flow of £9·40 (i.e., £11 − £1·60), as against only £8·40 from his investment in company B (i.e., £700 × 0·12). The improvement in his annual net cash flow, brought about by undertaking this arbitrage transaction, has been gained without any alteration to his level of either business or financial risk.

Modigliani and Miller argue that other shareholders in company B will similarly realize that their ordinary shares are overvalued by the market and/or company A's equity is undervalued, and so will undertake similar arbitrage transactions, as outlined in the example above, in order to make a financial gain. The resulting sustained selling of

B's equity and buying of A's equity will depress the market price of B's shares and raise that of A. These arbitrage transactions will continue (and so then will the consequent share price movements) until there is no financial advantage to be gained, and this point will be reached when the weighted average costs of capital of the two companies become equal (and, because in this example both companies have the same expected annual net cash flow, where their total market values become equal). For example, such a point is reached when the market price of A's equity rises to 105p per share and B's equity falls to $108\frac{1}{3}$p per share, and their WACCs become equal at 9·52%. Table 9.4 sets out the relevant data and shows that an individual who now holds 1% of B's equity cannot make any financial gain through arbitrage.

Table 9.4

	A	B
$\bar{Y}$	£ 1,000	£ 1,000
D	—	£ 4,000
K_d	—	0·04
I	—	£ 160
$\bar{Y} - I$	£ 1,000	£ 840
E	£10,500	£ 6,500
K_e	0·0952	0·1292
V	£10,500	£10,500
K_o	0·0952	0·0952
Net price per share	105p	108 1/3p

An individual holding 1% of B's shares receives an annual dividend of: £65 × 0·1292 = £8·40. Selling the shares produces £6,500 × 0·1 = £65. Company B has a gearing ratio of 4 : 6·5 and so the individual can borrow £40 at 4% (i.e., K_d) to keep his financial risk level constant. Thus the individual has £65 + £40 = £105 to invest in the shares of company A. This new shareholding produces an annual dividend of £105 × 0·0952 = £10, from which £40 × 0·04 = £1·60 has to be deducted for interest, leaving the investor with a net annual cash flow of £10 − £1·60 = £8·40, which is exactly what he received from his holding in company B.

(Money values have been slightly rounded to take account of the limits placed on the number of decimal places used.)

There are two points of importance in this analysis which should be made clear. First, in the example used, equilibrium is reached when both the total market values and the WACCs of the two companies become equal. However, the equality of market values comes about only through the fact that, in this case, the companies have the same expected annual net cash flow; the point of general importance is that companies with the same level of business risk (and there is *no* requirement that their expected annual net cash flows should be the same) will, in equilibrium, have the same weighted average cost of capital. Secondly, the arbitrage example used above proves that, *under the assumptions made*, changes in a company's gearing, in themselves, leave its market value unaffected, and that the increased return required by ordinary shareholders, as compensation for bearing additional financial risk, is given by the expression: $(K_o - K_D)D/E$.

The practical conclusions of this analysis, as far as investment appraisal is concerned, are as follows. First, in originally advocating the use of the weighted average cost of capital for discounting project cash flows, the advice was based on three restrictive assumptions: that the project acceptance would not change the company's existing level of risk, that the project was small relative to the total size of the company, and that the company's gearing ratio remained unchanged (in the medium/longer run). This analysis, and its conclusions, now removes the need for this third assumption (provided the special Modigliani and Miller assumptions hold) because it shows that the WACC is unaffected by changes in a company's capital structure. Second, its conclusions relegate the financing decision to a position of relatively minor importance (it becomes a decision about convenience), because it is shown to have no bearing on the valuation of the company and so does not affect the wealth of the ordinary shareholders.

The assumptions Having outlined the basic Modigliani and Miller capital structure hypothesis, and before proceeding to examine alternative theories about the relationship between a company's gearing ratio and the cost of its equity capital, let us now take a closer look at the many assumptions upon which the hypothesis is based. In particular, we shall look at the assumptions underlying the arbitrage process which helps to restore the 'M.M. hypothesized' equilibrium to short-run disequilibrium stock market prices and which is held up as proof of their capital structure theory.

'Arbitrage' is, in fact, a technical term to describe a supply and demand market process which prevents perfect substitutes from selling at different prices in the same market. The key phrase here is 'perfect substitutes' and so, for the arbitrage process to act as a proof of the M.M. hypothesis, ordinary shares in an all-equity company must be seen as (or must be able to be made) a perfect substitute for shares in a geared company. We know from the valuation principles, which were defined earlier, that value results from the future flow of net benefits and the certainty (or otherwise) attached to that future flow. Therefore, if we take two companies with the same expected annual cash flow and the same level of business risk, it follows that they should have identical total market values. However, we also know that if one company is all-equity and one company is geared, their ordinary shares are not perfect substitutes for each other, because the shares in the geared company include an additional risk element: financial risk.

If in a disequilibrium situation, the ordinary shares of the geared company were overvalued by the market, shareholders in that company would wish to take advantage of the fact by arbitraging into the all-equity company. In order to make the ordinary shares in the two companies perfect substitutes in terms of the risk borne in holding them, the investors in the geared company must be able to substitute home-made gearing (i.e., personally gear themselves) for corporate gearing. (We saw this process being undertaken in the example used above.) To be able to do so, there must be no difference between the cost and risk of corporate borrowing (and hence gearing) and individual borrowing (gearing). This requires two major assumptions of highly questionable real-world validity: individuals and companies must be able to borrow at the same rate of interest and the facility of limited liability for companies either must not exist, or must also extend to individuals.[10]

In practice, individuals almost invariably have to pay a higher rate of interest on borrowed money than do companies, and in that borrowing their liability is unlimited, whereas companies have the protection of limited liability. Therefore, quite plainly, corporate and individual borrowing differs both in terms of cost and of risk, and so this major requirement of the arbitrage process, as far as share dealings are concerned, appears to be unfulfilled. However, the discrepancy between theory and practice can be resolved to some extent by the fact that for share prices to regain an equilibrium position, not *all* investors have to arbitrage to cause the necessary price changes through the supply and demand market mechanism. There are many limited liability companies with substantial holdings of ordinary shares in other companies, who could themselves undertake arbitrage transactions (and thereby avoid the problems outlined above), and so bring about market equilibrium.

This counter-argument, against the real-world invalidity of the two assumptions required for effective stock market arbitraging, appears reasonably sound – at least in theory – although it should be pointed out that there is some evidence to suggest that many institutional investors do not readily indulge in arbitrage transactions. However, there is another assumption involved in the arbitrage process which in practice does not hold, and so causes frictional problems: the assumption that all market transactions are undertaken at no cost (i.e., no stockbrokers' fees or commissions). In practice, market transactions can be relatively expensive, and such a cost is likely to interfere with the smooth and efficient operation of arbitraging (e.g., the gain that might accrue to an investor from arbitraging may be completely offset by the transaction costs involved, and so these costs could be expected to interfere with the equilibrium producing mechanism). However, it could be claimed that transaction costs will only out-weigh arbitrage gains either in very small share transactions or at the 'fine-tuning' stage, when the amount of disequilibrium remaining (and hence the level of arbitrage gains) is small. Thus, although transaction costs will (as always) interfere with the economic mechanism, the degree of interference may well be relatively unimportant. We shall return to this assumption later, for it contains another, implicit assumption, that bankruptcy costs are zero. But before doing so, we shall examine the effects of two other assumptions within the hypothesis: that the cost of debt capital remains constant whatever the level of gearing, and that there is no taxation.

A rising cost of debt No really satisfactory reconciliation with the conclusions of the M.M. theory exists, once the more realistic view is taken that the cost of debt capital to a company rises as gearing (and hence risk to the suppliers of debt) rises. Logically, as a company gears up, the cost of debt should increase, so that it approaches what would have been the cost of equity capital if the company had remained ungeared because, at the extreme of 99·99 % gearing, the risks borne by the suppliers of debt capital would be virtually the same as the risks borne by equity capital if the company were ungeared. The problem with a rising cost of debt capital is that, for the company's weighted average cost of capital to remain a constant, its cost of equity capital must start to *decline* as the company reaches very high levels of gearing. Figure 9.6 illustrates this rather unlikely situation.

To explain this phenomenon, Modigliani and Miller rather ingeniously reasoned that as a company gears up to very high ratios, ordinary shares become exceptionally risky – so risky that they attract 'gambler' investors who are risk *seekers*, to whom the shares become increasingly attractive as their riskiness rises: hence the expected return on equity (K_E) required by shareholders starts to fall. This explanation for the behaviour of the cost of equity capital at high gearing levels, which is necessary for the M.M. hypothesis to be sustained, is often viewed with considerable scepticism; but their suggestion may sometimes hold. Although the risks involved with ordinary share ownership become substantial at high gearing levels, there is also the chance that shareholders will receive an extremely high level of dividend, and the possible size of this dividend (per share) is likely to increase as the gearing level increases: a typical 'gamble' situation.

Nevertheless, this is a far from satisfactory suggestion when applied to companies in general. Let us conclude (rather lamely), that the problem is likely to become important only at high levels of gearing, and as companies rarely venture into such regions, then perhaps the

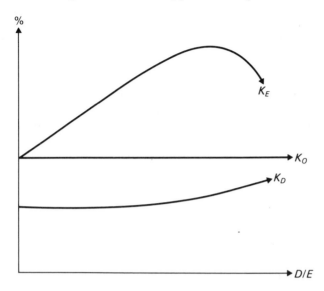

Figure 9.6

case for the M.M. hypothesis can still be said to hold for most normal levels of company gearing, and that there is an equating trade-off between the advantages and disadvantages of gearing up.

Taxation and capital structure The M.M. capital structure hypothesis relies heavily on the assumption of a tax-free world, and the conclusions of their analysis change radically once this assumption is relaxed. In the initial analysis of the capital structure problem (under the set of simplifying assumptions used) we stated that the total market value of a company could be defined as: $V = \bar{Y}/K_o$. Therefore, a company's gearing ratio could only affect its total market value (V) if it affected either the company's expected annual net cash flow $(\bar{Y})$ or its weighted average cost of capital (K_o). With the introduction of a taxation regime which allows debt capital interest to be set off against tax liability, a company will be able to increase its expected annual net cash flow by gearing up.

Table 9.5 shows that a company's expected annual net cash flow arises from the after-tax cash flow, $\bar{X}(1-T)$, plus the product of the annual interest payments and the tax rate: $(D . K_{D_{BT}})T$.[11] Therefore, given a constant rate of corporation tax, $\bar{Y}$ will increase as a company gears up, because the increasing amount of debt capital interest payable enables the company to claim an increasing amount of tax relief, and hence the tax liability declines. In such circumstances, a company would theoretically maximize its total market value by gearing up so that its capital structure consisted of 99·99% debt capital, with the remainder as equity capital. At this gearing level, the company will recoup the maximum possible amount of tax relief from this source. (The reader should recall that a similar conclusion was reached in the final section of the previous chapter, when the two period investment–consumption model was applied to a situation where the cost of corporate borrowing was below the rate at which shareholders could borrow. This situation could be caused in the type of tax regime envisaged here, where interest is allowable against only corporate taxes and not personal taxes, effectively allowing the company to borrow at interest rates below those applying to individual shareholders. Thus the conclusion reached in this analysis should come as no surprise.)

Table 9.5

Let $\bar{X}$ = Before-tax expected annual net cash flow (a constant).
Let $\bar{Y}$ = After-tax expected annual net cash flow.
Let T = Rate of corporation tax (a constant).
Let $K_{D_{BT}}$ = Before-tax cost of debt capital.

Then:
$$\bar{Y} = (\bar{X} - D . K_{D_{BT}})(1 - T) + D . K_{D_{BT}}$$
$$\bar{Y} = \bar{X}(1 - T) - D . K_{D_{BT}}(1 - T) + D . K_{D_{BT}}$$
$$\bar{Y} = \bar{X}(1 - T) + (D . K_{D_{BT}})T.$$

If, as it would be under this type of tax regime, the total market value of a company is an increasing linear function of its gearing ratio, what affect does gearing now have on both a company's cost of equity capital and its weighted average cost of capital? To answer this question, let us once again examine the relationships involved.

The M.M. hypothesis in a taxed world We have two companies which are identical in terms of size and the riskiness of the expected annual *before-tax* cash flow $(\bar{X})$, except that one company is geared whilst the other has an all-equity capital structure. The after tax expected annual cash flow $(\bar{Y})$ of each company, where T is the constant annual rate of corporation tax is as follows:

Ungeared company   Geared company
$\bar{Y}_U = \bar{X}(1 - T)$ $\bar{Y}_G = (\bar{X} - D . K_D)(1 - T) + D . K_D$
                                                $= \bar{X}(1 - T) - D . K_D(1 - T) + D . K_D$
                                                $= \bar{X}(1 - T) + (D . K_D)T$

Thus the geared company has a higher after-tax expected annual cash flow than the ungeared company, the difference being given by: $D . K_D . T$. Obviously, the more highly geared the company, the greater will this difference be.

In terms of market value, that of the all-equity company is given by:

$$V_U = \frac{\bar{X}(1-T)}{K_E} = \frac{\bar{X}(1-T)}{K_o}$$

With the geared company, the expected annual cash flow consists of two elements: $\bar{X}(1-T)$ and $D . K_D . T$. Under our assumptions, the first of these two elements must be valued as it is in the ungeared company: $\bar{X}(1-T)/K_o$; whilst the second element – the tax relief on debt capital interest payments – has the same level of risk as that attached to debt capital itself,[12] and so should logically be capitalized using the cost of debt capital as the discount rate. Thus the total market value of the geared company can be expressed as:

$$V_G = \frac{\bar{X}(1-T)}{K_o} + \frac{D . K_D . T}{K_D} = \frac{\bar{X}(1-T)}{K_o} + D . T$$

From this we can see that the total market value of the geared company is at a premium over that of the all-equity company, which is equivalent to the product of the debt capital's market value and the tax rate $(D . T)$. It therefore follows that the geared company can maximize its total market value by maximizing the amount of debt capital it has in its capital structure.

And what of the cost of equity capital? The shareholder's dividend can be identified as consisting of two elements: the residual cash flow after tax and interest, and the tax relief allowed on the debt capital interest. Thus for the two companies, their total expected annual dividends will be:

$$E . K_{E_U} = \bar{Y}_U = \bar{X}(1-T)$$
$$E . K_{E_G} = \bar{X}(1-T) - D . K_D + D . K_D . T$$

We know from our previous analysis that the relationship between a geared company's cost of equity capital and its gearing ratio is given by:

$$K_E = K_o + \frac{D}{E}(K_o - K_D)$$

where K_o represents the cost of equity capital of an ungeared company which has a level of business risk similar to that of the geared company. So, for ordinary shareholders in the geared company, the first component of their total dividend payment: $\bar{X}(1-T) - D . K_D$, will be capitalized using K_E, as computed above, as the discount rate. The second component of the dividend: $D . K_D . T$, is capitalized using K_D as the discount rate, as it has the same level of risk attached to it as debt capital interest. As K_D will be smaller than K_E, then the *overall* or average cost of equity capital used to capitalize the *complete* annual dividend flow will be lowered as a company gears up. This, in turn, lowers the weighted average cost of capital of the geared company. With increased gearing, the tax relief component of the dividend flow – valued using K_D as the discount rate – becomes an increasingly large and important component of the complete annual dividend flow, and so both the values of K_E, and consequently K_o, are both further depressed.[13]

Table 9.6 illustrates this process, using as an example a company with a constant expected annual cash flow of £1,000 before tax, which faces a corporation tax rate of 40% and a cost of debt capital (before tax) – which is here assumed to remain a constant at all levels of gearing – of 5%. The table computes the various costs of capital and market values for a selection of different capital structures, ranging from an all-equity structure (where K_E is assumed to equal 10%, to act as a starting point) to one which is composed of approximately 97% debt capital and 3% equity capital. Figure 9.7 attempts roughly to sketch the cost of capital relationships in these circumstances.

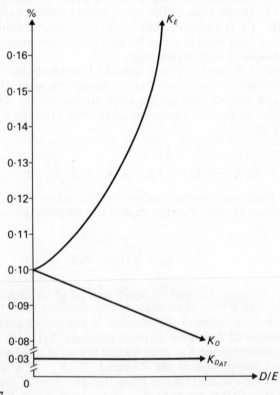

Figure 9.7

Table 9.6

	£	£	£	£	£
$\bar{X}$	1000	1000	1000	1000	1000
$D . K_D$	—	100	300	450	475
$\bar{X} - D . K_D$	1000	900	700	550	525
$E . K_E = (\bar{X} - D . K_D)(1 - T)$	600	540	420	330	315
$D . K_D$	—	100	300	450	475
$\bar{Y}$	600	640	720	780	790
$K_E = E . K_E/E$	0·10	0·1125	0·175	0·55	1·05
$K_o = \bar{Y}/V$	0·10	0·094	0·0857	0·0813	0·0806
K_D	—	0·05	0·05	0·05	0·05
D	—	2000	6000	9000	9500
E	6000	4800	2400	600	300
$V = \bar{X}(1 - T)/K_o + D . T$	6000	6800	8400	9600	9800

A rising cost of debt This analysis suffers from the assumption that the cost of debt capital remains constant at all levels of gearing. This is unlikely to be true in practice. As was argued in the no-tax case, if an all-equity company has an after-tax annual cash flow of $\bar{X}(1 - T)$, which is capitalized (i.e., given a current value) by the stock market using a 10% discount rate – after taking into account the degree of risk it involves – then we know that the company's cost of equity capital and its weighted average cost of capital both equal 10%. Logic tells us that if this same company were 99% geared (i.e., virtually all equity), then the return required by the suppliers of debt capital is also likely to be 10%. This is because, with such a capital structure, the debt holders are now receiving the cash flow distribution that equity holders once received when the company was ungeared. These debt holders are likely to judge the riskiness of this stream in a similar manner to that of the equity holders, and so they will value it at the same capitalization rate of 10%. Thus both the company's cost of debt capital (before tax) and its weighted average cost of capital (before tax) now equal 10%.[14]

Therefore, when a company starts to gear up $K_{D_{BT}}$ is well below K_E (because, at the low-geared stage, the debt interest stream is less risky than the dividend stream) but, as gearing-up continues, $K_{D_{BT}}$ will rise to a level equal to the company's cost of equity capital which held when the company was all equity. Alternatively, we can say that $K_{D_{BT}}$ will rise to a level equal to the K_E of an all equity, equivalent business risk company. The point of interest is the effect that this rising K_D has on the company's weighted average cost of capital. The previous analysis described how the process of gearing-up tends to pull down a company's K_o from its ungeared level, because of the tax relief on interest. We also know that by the time the company is (virtually) fully geared, its weighted average cost of capital will be equal to the all-equity $K_E(1 - T)$. Therefore we can conclude that either the WACC will decline no further than this level or that possibly the WACC will be a U-shaped function which rises up to this level by the time the point of full gearing is reached. Consequently, in this latter case, the company's total market value is likely to be maximized at some capital structure which is less than fully geared; in the former case the point of maximum market value would remain at full gearing. The exact shape of the WACC function depends upon the nature of the rate of increase of K_D with gearing and the rate of corporation tax.

9.3 Alternative approaches to capital structure

Introduction The Modigliani and Miller analysis of the capital structure problem, whether in a taxed or a tax-free world, is based upon a number of assumptions about the environment and the working of the capital markets. On the basis of these assumptions, their analysis produces rigorous conclusions about the nature of the trade-off between financial risk and gearing and about the behaviour of a company's cost of equity capital, its weighted average cost of capital and also its total market value, as the gearing ratio changes. In addition, an important conclusion arising from the discussion, as far as company managements and shareholders are concerned, is that gearing up (i.e., increasing the proportion of debt in a company's capital structure) enhances the market value of the ordinary shares through the tax relief allowable on corporate debt interest. However, the point of greatest academic dispute arises from pushing this conclusion to its logical end: the greatest enhancement to the ordinary shares' market value will be achieved at the greatest possible gearing ratio, 99% + debt capital.

In practice, the gearing ratios of privately owned companies never even approach this sort of level. This leads us to conclude that there is some sort of barrier – which so far has not been considered or accounted for – which prevents companies from gearing up to this extreme point and/or company managements (and shareholders) do not accept the real-world validity of the M.M. analysis and its implications.

The traditional view of capital structure It is often held that the generally accepted wisdom of investors, analysts and company managements alike (hence called the 'traditional' view) is that there are both advantages and disadvantages, as far as the maximization of shareholders' wealth is concerned, to corporate gearing. It is believed that at relatively low levels of gearing the advantages outweigh the disadvantages and so the market value of the company gradually rises, but that after a while the relationship reverses and the disadvantages start to outweigh the advantages, so that further increases in gearing cause the company's market value to decline. Figure 9.8 sketches the various relationships involved in this traditional view of capital structure.

The main advantage of gearing is seen to be that, because corporate debt interest is allowable against taxation, a company is able to raise capital at an effective cost which is substantially below the market rate (i.e., debt capital is held to be 'cheap' capital because of tax relief). The main disadvantage arises from the fact that increased gearing results in an increased level of financial risk being borne by the company's shareholders. This, in turn, leads the shareholders to require a higher expected return on their capital (i.e., an increased K_e), by way of compensation.

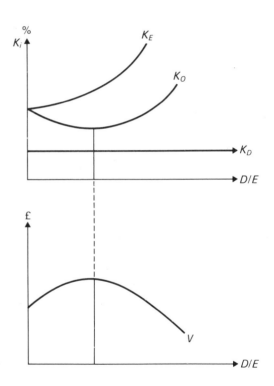

Figure 9.8 The traditional view of capital structure

In contrast to this traditional view of capital structure, the M.M. hypothesis was that, in a tax-free environment, the advantages and disadvantages of gearing exactly offset each other at all gearing ratios; whilst in a taxed world, the advantages consistently outweigh the disadvantages at all levels of gearing. However, the real point of difference between the M.M. and traditional views is the exact nature of the relationship between the cost of equity capital and the gearing ratio. Whereas in the M.M. hypothesis the increased return required by equity capital as compensation for bearing financial risk rises at a *constant* rate as the gearing level increases, the traditional view is that this required expected return rises at an *increasing* rate, i.e., at a rate which is, at relatively low levels of gearing, below that hypothesized by M.M., but which increases above the return required by equity in the M.M. model, at higher gearing ratios.

The traditional view of capital structure is just that: a view or reflection of what is traditionally believed to be the relationship between a company's various costs of capital and the gearing ratio, and it has never rested on a rigorous theoretical model as did the M.M. hypothesis. A number of writers have expressed the traditional view of capital structure in algebraic form, but none has been able to show satisfactorily, in the way in which M.M. used the existence of arbitrage transactions, *why* the cost of equity capital should have a non-linear relationship with the gearing ratio, as argued by the traditionalist view. However, the most notable feature about the traditionalist view of capital structure (which follows on from the assumed nature of the K_E function) is the U-shaped weighted average cost of capital curve and the corresponding inverted-U total market value curve. At low gearing levels, the advantages outweigh the disadvantages, and so K_o is pulled down; and as a result V rises. However, as the company continues to gear up, the advantages are now outweighed by the disadvantages, K_o rises and consequently V falls. This leads firmly to the conclusion that each company has an optimal capital structure which minimizes its weighted average cost of capital and so maximizes its total market value. Company managements must search for this particular gearing ratio (which is likely to vary from company to company and may well vary over time for any one particular company) and so the financing decision is elevated to a position of importance almost on a par with the investment decision itself.

The bankruptcy cost assumption Before any further comment on the traditional view of the capital structure relationships, let us first examine the consequences of relaxing yet another assumption of the M.M. with-tax analysis, by introducing the possibility and associated costs of corporate bankruptcy. The probability of bankruptcy is likely to be (amongst other things) an increasing function of a company's gearing ratio but, as far as the capital structure problem is concerned, the important factor is the substantial cost which may be involved in a company's liquidation or bankruptcy. If a company which was forced into bankruptcy could be liquidated costlessly (i.e., if its assets could be sold off at their 'correct' market values and if there were no legal or administrative costs), then the fact that the probability of bankruptcy is an increasing function of the gearing ratio would not have any adverse effect on the total market value of a company. Unfortunately, in the real world, the costs of bankruptcy are considerable. As well as very substantial administrative and legal costs, the company's specialized assets often have to be disposed of at less than their operational values, because they have lost their going-concern/synergy value and because their sale has to take place hurriedly in an imperfect market. These costs (in whole or in part) will come out of the liquidated pool of funds which is destined to be returned to shareholders. Therefore, bankruptcy involves a company's shareholders in a cost they would otherwise have not incurred and so it is effectively responsible for causing a reduction in their level of wealth.

All shareholders, whether they be shareholders in geared or all-equity companies, face the (hopefully small) probability that their company may be forced into bankruptcy. This fact is just one component of the concept of business risk and, as such, is allowed for in the expected value of the future dividend flow and the required expected return on equity capital. However, the act of gearing up by a company has the effect of positively adding to the probability of its bankruptcy, due to the fact that if a company is unable to meet its fixed debt interest payments, then the debt holders have the legal right to liquidate the company in order to repossess their capital and unpaid interest. Thus, as a company increases its level of gearing, an increasing proportion of its after-tax expected annual cash flow is likely to be paid out as interest but, as the future is uncertain, these annual cash flows are variable and so there is also an increasing probability that the company's after-tax cash flows will not be sufficient to meet these debt interest payments. A succession of such years for a geared company will almost certainly lead to bankruptcy and the incursion of its associated costs.

In our original analysis of the capital structure problem we stated that, on the basis of the valuation model which we used for a company, $V = \bar{Y}/K_o$, changes in the gearing ratio could only affect its total market value if it either affected the value of $\bar{Y}$ and/or the value of K_o. We saw that with the introduction of taxation (and especially tax relief on corporate debt interest), increased gearing lead to a rising value for $\bar{Y}$ and a falling value for K_o. With the additional introduction of bankruptcy and bankruptcy costs, increased gearing will cause an increasing reduction (i.e., a dampening effect) in the value of $\bar{Y}$ – the *expected* future annual cash flow – as the probability, and so the *expected* costs, of bankruptcy grow larger. This is likely to result in a downturn in the total market value function before the point of maximum gearing is reached. Thus a company's total market value is likely to be maximized with a capital structure which has an element of gearing in it, but which consists of something less than 99% debt capital. In other words, after a certain level of gearing has been reached, the advantages of tax relief on debt interest payments are likely to be outweighed by the combined effect of the twin disadvantages of an increasing required return on equity capital and an increasing expected value of bankruptcy costs. Figure 9.9 illustrates what may be a typical set of the relationships involved, although the

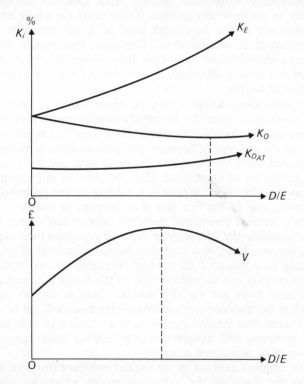

Figure 9.9

gearing ratio at which the company's total market value is maximized now also depends upon the shareholders' perceived probability and the costs of corporate bankruptcy.

Figure 9.9 bears a remarkable resemblance to the traditional capital structure view as represented by Figure 9.8, although the U-shaped weighted average cost of capital curve (caused by a rising cost of debt) may not emerge in practice. However, there is one very important point of difference between the two figures. In the traditional view, the gearing ratio which minimized the WACC also maximized the company's total market value. With the introduction of bankruptcy costs, the gearing ratio at which K_o is minimized will only by chance represent the point of maximization of the company's total market value. The most likely result is for V to be maximized at a lower gearing ratio than that which minimized K_o.

In conclusion In concluding our examination of the capital structure problem, all we can say is that it would appear that the financing decision is of importance, in so far as a company's capital structure can have both beneficial and detrimental effects on its total market value and, consequently, on the market value of the ordinary shares. However, the exact nature of the relationship in real life between a company's gearing level, its total market value and the costs of its various types of capital, remains unclear. What we have seen is that gearing can be a double-edged sword and hence should always be treated with caution: it can bring undoubted benefits to shareholders – through the tax relief generated – but it can also have highly detrimental effects which can ultimately lead to bankruptcy.[15]

Selected references

D. P. Baron, 'Firm Valuation, Corporate Taxes and Default Risk', *Journal of Finance*, December 1975.

W. Baumol and B. G. Malkiel, 'The Firm's Optimal Debt-Equity Combination and the Cost of Capital', *Quarterly Journal of Economics*, November 1967.

N. D. Baxter, 'Leverage, Risk of Ruin, and the Cost of Capital', *Journal of Finance*, September 1967.

H. Bierman, 'Risk and the Addition of Debt to the Capital Structure', *Journal of Financial and Quantitative Analysis*, December 1968.

D. Bodernhorn, 'On the Problem of Capital Budgeting', *Journal of Finance*, December 1969.

R. Brealey, 'A Note on Dividends and Debt under the New Taxation', *Journal of Business Finance*, Spring 1973.

A. H. Chen and E. H. Kim, 'Theories of Corporate Debt Policy: a Synthesis', *Journal of Finance*, May 1979.

J. P. Dickinson and K. Kyuno, 'Corporate Valuation: a Reconciliation of the Miller–Modigliani and Traditional Views', *Journal of Business Finance and Accounting*, Summer 1977.

D. Durand, 'The Cost of Capital, Corporation Finance and the Theory of Investment: Comment', *American Economic Review*, September 1959.

W. Y. Lee and H. H. Barker, 'Bankruptcy Costs and the Firm's Optimal Debt Capacity: a Positive Theory of Capital Structure', *Southern Economic Journal*, April 1977.

M. H. Miller and F. Modigliani, 'Some Estimates of the Cost of Capital to the Electricity Utility Industry', *American Economic Review*, June 1966.

F. Modigliani and M. H. Miller, 'The Cost of Capital, Corporation Finance and the Theory of Investment'. *American Economic Review*, June 1958.

F. Modigliani and M. H. Miller, 'Corporation Income Taxes and the Cost of Capital: a Correction', *American Economic Review*, June 1963.

F. Modigliani and M. H. Miller, 'Reply to Heins and Sprenkle'. *American Economic Review*, September 1969.

S. C. Myers, 'Interactions of Corporate Financing and Investment Decisions – Implications for Capital Budgeting', *Journal of Finance*, March 1974.

E. Schwartz, 'Theory of the Capital Structure of Firms', *Journal of Finance*, March 1959.

E. Schwartz and R. J. Aronson, 'Some Surrogate Evidence in Support of the Concept of Optimal Capital Structure', *Journal of Finance*, March 1967.

J. H. Scott, 'A Theory of Optimal Capital Structure', *Bell Journal of Economics*, Spring 1976.

R. Sherman, 'Financial Aspects of Rate-of-Return Regulation', *Southern Economic Journal*, October 1977.

V. L. Smith, 'Default Risk, Scale and the Homemade Leverage Theorem', *American Economic Review*, March 1972.

E. Solomon (Ed.), *The Management of Corporate Capital*, New York, The Free Press, 1959.

R. C. Stapleton, 'Taxes, the Cost of Capital and the Theory of Investment', *Economic Journal*, December 1972.

R. C. Stapleton and C. M. Burke, 'Taxes, the Cost of Capital and the Theory of Investment: a Generalisation to the Imputation System of Dividend Taxation', *Economic Journal*, December 1975.

G. Stigler, 'Imperfections in the Capital Markets', *Journal of Political Economy*, June 1967.

J. E. Stiglitz, 'A Re-examination of the Modigliani–Miller Theorem', *American Economics Review*, December 1969.

J. E. Stiglitz, 'On the Irrelevance of Corporate Financial Policy', *American Economic Review*, December 1974.

D. Vickers, 'The Cost of Capital and the Structure of the Firm', *Journal of Finance*, November 1970.

G. Warner, 'Bankruptcy Costs: Some Evidence', *Journal of Finance*, May 1977.

J. F. Weston, 'A Test of Cost of Capital Propositions', *Southern Economic Journal*, October 1963.

R. F. Wippern, 'Financial Structure and the Value of the Firm', *Journal of Finance*, December 1966.

D. Wrightsman, 'Tax Shield Valuation and the Capital Structure Decision', *Journal of Finance*, May 1977.

10 The Dividend Decision

10.1 Dividend policy in perfect capital markets

Introduction The dividend decision is the third major category of corporate long-term financial decisions that we shall investigate. It is perhaps the least analysed but most highly involved and controversial of all the three financial decisions, and consequently the theory in this area is the least evolved and complete. The complications and confusions surrounding the dividend decision arise principally because it is the lynch-pin to both the investment decision and the financing decision and, as such, it is difficult to abstract it from these influences so that it may be examined – initially at least – in isolation.

The problem of the dividend decision can be stated in the form of two questions: Does the pattern of the dividend flow through time to shareholders affect the market value of the equity capital? If it does, can a particular pattern of dividends be identified which would maximize the equity's market value? However, the meaning of these two questions can appear ambiguous, and so we shall start by clarifying the nature of our enquiry into the dividend decision.

The fundamental valuation model that we have used tells us that the market value of a company's equity capital is given by the summation of the expected future dividend stream, discounted to present value. In this sense, dividends can clearly be said to affect the market value of a company's ordinary shares – in fact, they are the major determinant. The question that we shall explore is whether or not the *pattern* of the expected dividend flow is a determinant of equity market value, just as is the magnitude of the summated present value of the expected flow.

As far as a company's management is concerned, the problem is one of allocation. How, at the end of each accounting period (for simplicity we shall assume this to be a twelve-month period, although in practice the dividend decision is usually made twice-yearly in the UK and quarterly in the USA), should the company's net after-tax cash flow be allocated amongst the competing ends. There is a possible three-way split to be made: interest payments to the suppliers of debt capital,[1] dividend payments to ordinary shareholders, and retention within the company for application to investment opportunities. It is the capital structure decision (discussed in the previous chapter) which largely determines the level of interest payments, and so we are left with the question as to how the annual net of tax and interest cash flow (we could call it the distributable cash earnings) should be divided up between dividend payments and retention for reinvestment.

Dividends as a residual We can start the analysis by recalling the basic two period investment–consumption model which existed in a world of perfect capital markets, certainty and no taxation. We shall also assume that there are no sources of capital available to management which are external to the company. Figure 10.1 illustrates the model and, in terms of the dividend decision, the company management must decide at time t_0 what proportion of the company's wealth OA (this could be viewed as being equivalent to the distributable cash earnings referred to above) should be invested and what proportion should be paid out as a dividend. We know that for optimality (i.e., for the maximization of shareholder wealth) the company should retain amount AB and distribute amount OB. It is important to realize that the decision on the division of amount OA was taken *only* with reference to the physical investment opportunities available and the perfect capital market rate of interest; the amount OB distributed as dividend to the company owners at time t_0 was purely the cash *residual* that was left after the investment decision had been made. From this, we can derive a rather obvious dividend decision rule,

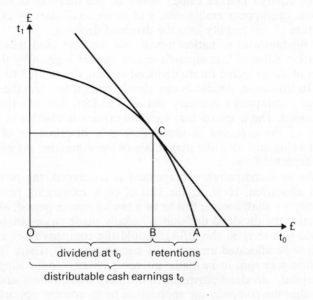

Figure 10.1

which states that the distributable annual cash earnings should be retained within the company for reinvestment, as long as there are investment opportunities available which satisfy the NPV decision rule; once this supply of investment opportunities has been exhausted, (i.e. the company has moved to point C in Figure 10.1) any distributable cash earnings remaining uninvested should be paid out to shareholders as a dividend. This is the so-called 'dividend irrelevancy' hypothesis which was first explicitly formulated by Modigliani and Miller, but the name of the hypothesis is somewhat misleading: dividends themselves are not irrelevant (as we know from the fundamental valuation model) but it is the *pattern* of dividends which is irrelevant. They should be treated purely as a residual which arises once the investment decision is made.

Modigliani and Miller approached the problem from a different, but equivalent, viewpoint which we shall illustrate by means of an example. Suppose an all-equity company normally paid out its entire annual net cash flow as dividends and it has previously made investments which will generate a constant annual net cash flow of £1,000 in perpetuity. The current market value of this company would be the present value sum of the future dividend flow. If the management decided to retain next year's dividend (instead of paying it out to

Table 10.1

	t_1	t_2	t_3		t_n
$E = \sum\limits^{n} \dfrac{dt}{(1 + K_e)^t} =$	$+1,000$	$+1,000$	$+1,000$	$\cdots$	$+1,000$
$NPV_p = \sum\limits^{2} \dfrac{At}{(1 + K_e)^t} =$	$-1,000$	$+1,500$			
$E^* = \sum\limits^{n} \dfrac{d^*t}{(1 + K_e)^t} =$	0	$+2,500$	$+1,000$	$\cdots$	$+1,000$

Where E = current market value of the equity.

d = existing dividend flow.

E^* = post-investment market value of the equity.

d^* = post-investment dividend flow.

NPV_p = net present value of the proposed investment.

$$E^* = E + NPV_p$$

or

$$\sum^{n} \frac{d^*t}{(1 + K_e)^t} = \sum^{n} \frac{dt}{(1 + K_e)^t} + \sum^{2} \frac{At}{(1 + K_e)^t}$$

To undertake the proposed investment: $E^* \geq E$

therefore: $NPV_p \geq 0$

shareholders) and invest it in a project which would produce (say) a £1,500 net cash inflow in the following year, then the *new* market value of the equity would be given by the present valued sum of the revised expected dividend flow. This revised flow can be seen as consisting of two components: the original dividend flow ·and the project's cash flow. The company would undertake the proposed investment in the project only if the resulting new market value of the equity were greater than (or at least equal to) the existing market value. To ensure this, the NPV of the proposed project must be greater than or equal to zero. Table 10.1 sets down the data for this illustration. The conclusion that can be drawn from this example is the same as that which was drawn from the investment–consumption model: shareholder wealth will be maximized only if dividends are treated as a residual of the investment decision.[2]

We can off-set this rather extreme view of the dividend decision with a more traditional view which holds that the pattern of dividend flow is relevant and does affect the market value of ordinary shares. But before examining this alternative argument, it is important to remember that the analysis used so far has been set in a perfect capital market environment in which the future is known with certainty. (This latter assumption can be easily relaxed to one where all investors have the same expectations as to what the uncertain future holds). In addition, we have yet to analyse the dividend decision in situations where investment cash can be raised from a source external to the firm (e.g., by means of a debenture issue) as an alternative to the retention of distributable cash flow. These assumptions will continue to be held as we now turn to examine the traditional view of the dividend decision.

Dividend patterns and the valuation model A company with an all-equity capital structure has made sufficient investments in the past to generate a future annual net cash inflow of $\bar{Y}$, in perpetuity. If a constant proportion, b, of this cash flow is to be reinvested each year in projects which yield an average rate of return of r, whilst the remainder of each year's cash flow is paid out as dividends, then Gordon's version of the basic dividend valuation growth model[3] can be applied to estimate the current market value of the company's equity capital:

$$E = \frac{\bar{Y}(1 - b)(1 + rb)}{K_E - rb}$$

Assuming a given value for $\bar{Y}$ and for K_E, we can see that the value for E produced by the model is dependent on the values given to r and b. It is the effect of different values of b that is of interest, because it is this that reflects the dividend decision: different values of b

produce different dividend flow patterns over time. The effect of the retention proportion on the market value of the equity depends upon the value of r relative to K_E – where $r > K_E$, then E increases as b increases, where $r < K_E$, the reverse relationship holds and where $r = K_E$, then E is unaffected by changes in b. (What is really unaffected in such a situation is the wealth of ordinary shareholders. For example, if $\bar{Y} = £100$ and $K_E = r = 0.20$ then, when $b = 0$, $E = £500$ and when $b = 0.1$, $E = £510$. Shareholder wealth can be seen to be unaffected by changes in b by the fact that when $b = 0$, they received a dividend of £100 and their shares had a market value of £500. Total wealth was therefore £600. When $b = 0.1$, they received a dividend of £90 – £10 being reinvested – and their shares had a market value of £510. Total wealth is unchanged at £90 + £510 = £600.)

At first sight therefore, it may well appear that the dividend decision does affect the market value of the equity (because it determines b), but *how* the dividend decision affects E depends upon the relationship of r to K_E. But in truth, it is not the dividend decision which is causing the market value of the equity to change, but the investment decisions which follow, i.e., it is the investment of the retained earnings which causes fluctuations in the equity market value. We are seeing here, once again, confirmation of the NPV investment appraisal rule: increasing b will lead to an enhancement of equity market value only if the retained cash flows are being invested in projects yielding positive NPVs when discounted by K_E (i.e., when the project's yield or IRR $> K_E$). Retention of distributable cash flow for investment in projects yielding negative NPVs (i.e., $r < K_E$) serves merely to reduce the current market value of the company's equity capital.

Traditional view of the dividend decision Not withstanding the foregoing analysis, the traditional[4] view of the dividend decision is that at any particular point of time £1 of dividends (i.e., distributed cash flow) is somehow more valuable than £1 of retained cash flow – even though the cash flow may have been retained for investment in a project whose IRR/yield $\gg K_E$. Various studies have been undertaken on this phenomenon which suggest that £1 worth of retained earnings may be viewed by investors as being up to four times less valuable than £1 of dividends. An example can easily be used to highlight the traditional view of dividends: If a company's only assets are two £1 notes and it is expected to pay the money out as a dividend, the stock market will put a value of £2 on the company. If it is expected to retain the money, the stock market value may be as low as only 50p. If the company is expected to pay out £1 as dividend and retain the remaining £1, the market value may well be around £1.25.

Proponents of this traditional view use the dividend growth model to support their argument in the following way. So far in this analysis, in using the dividend growth model, we have held K_E constant as b was varied. The traditionalists argue that this cannot be done, because K_E is partly a function of the value of b, because of the presence of risk. The cost of equity capital, as we have calculated it, is really no more than an average of a whole family of discount rates, each of which is related to a cash flow in a specific period. Therefore a company, by retaining a part of its current period cash flow, is replacing a certain cash flow 'now' with an uncertain future cash flow (i.e., the future dividends generated by the investment financed by the cash retention). This increased uncertainty will effectively raise the discount rate used against these future flows and so will cause K_E (the average discount rate) also to rise. Thus increasing the value of b is likely to lead to an increase in the value of K_E, and so equity market values can be said to be affected by dividend policy itself and not simply through the effects of the investment undertaken with the retention, because dividend policy can alter the riskiness of the expected dividend flow. The optimal dividend-retention policy must be that which trades off the beneficial effects of an increasing growth rate (i.e., an increased value for b on the assumption that $r > K_E$), against the detrimental effects of increased risk, so as to maximize the market value of the equity.

The traditional view can be put in an alternative and simpler way. The early payment of dividends may not actually change a company's business risk level, but it can favourably alter an investor's perception of the level of risk. Thus current dividends are viewed as more valuable than retained earnings because the investor's perception of risk is imperfect and this may lead him to undervalue the future dividend stream that the retained earnings will generate.

An arbitrage criticism The arguments of the traditionalists do not really stand up to a close theoretical examination, if the existence of a perfect capital market is assumed. The main counter-argument that can be put forward is that if two companies are identical in every respect except that their dividend-retention ratios differ, and if the market values retained earnings differently from dividends, the market prices of the two companies will be in disequilibrium (i.e., two identical goods will be selling at different prices in the same market). This will allow investors to undertake profitable arbitrage transactions, substituting home-made dividends for corporate dividends by selling part of their shareholding. The following analysis illustrates this substitution in showing the irrelevance of dividend pattern and the opportunities which exist for arbitraging if a traditional view of dividend retention persists in the stock market.

Assume: Perfect capital market
No transaction costs
Certainty
No taxation
Market interest rate constant at 10%

An all-equity company has made previous investments which are sufficient, in total, to generate an annual cash flow of £1,000 in perpetuity. All this cash flow is paid out each year as dividends. Thus the company has a total market value of £1,000/0·10 = £10,000. Each of the company's 1,000 ordinary shares therefore has a market value of £10 and receives an annual dividend of £1.

An investor owns 100 of the company's shares. Thus the market value of his shareholding is £1,000, from which he receives an annual dividend of £100.

The company has just paid the current year's dividend and has informed shareholders that next year's dividend (at time t_1) will be withheld so as to invest in a project that will yield a net cash inflow of £2,000 at time t_2. The project's cash inflow will be paid out, at that time, as an additional dividend. The company's revised dividend flow, and hence its revised market value, at t_0 is as follows:

	t_1	t_2	t_3 $\cdots$
Existing cash flow	+ 1,000	+ 1,000	+ 1,000
Project cash flow	− 1,000	+ 2,000	
Revised dividend flow	0	+ 3,000	+ 1,000

$$E = \sum_{t=0}^{\infty} \frac{dt}{(1 + 0·1)^t} = £10{,}743·80$$

As a result of its intentions, the company's market value has risen by £743·80: the NPV of the project. Our investor's shareholding will have risen in value by £74·38 to £1,074·38. However, suppose he relies upon his £100 per year dividend from the company for consumption purposes and is therefore alarmed at the news that he will receive no dividend next year (t_1). There are two main alternative courses of action he may take to replace the withheld dividend, neither of which will reduce the current level of his shareholding wealth of £1,074·38:[5] he can either sell part of his shareholding to generate sufficient cash to replace the dividend missed at t_1 (i.e. £100), or he can borrow the money at the perfect market rate of interest of 10%. Let us examine the mechanics of this first alternative.

At time t_1, the company's total market value is the sum of the discounted future dividend flow:

	t_1	t_2	t_3	t_4 $\cdots$
Dividend flow	0	$+3{,}000$	$+1{,}000$	$+1{,}000$ $\cdots$

$$E_{t_1} = \sum_{t=1}^{\infty} \frac{dt}{(1 + 0 \cdot 1)^t} = £11{,}818 \cdot 18$$

Therefore each share has an approximate market value of £11·82, and our investor's shareholding is worth £1,181·82. If he now sells sufficient shares to produce £100 in cash as a substitute for his fore-gone dividend, he will sell £100/£11·82 = 8·46 shares.[6] He now only holds 91·54 shares in the company.

At time t_2 the company has £3000 to be distributed as dividend so each share receives a dividend of £3 and our investor receives a total dividend of: 91·54 × £3 = £274·62. Of this, £100 is required for consumption, leaving a balance of £174·62 available to repurchase shares in the company and so recover his original shareholding position. The ex div. market value of the company at time t_2 will be £10,000 (the discounted sum of the future dividend flow) and so the individual share price is £10. Our investor can now buy back the 8·46 shares he previously sold at a cost of £84·60, leaving him with addi-tional cash at time t_2 of £174·62 − £84·60 = £90·02. Thus our share-holder has effectively used 'home-made' dividends as a substitute for the company dividends which the management decided to retain. In doing so, his wealth position remains unchanged as the present value (i.e., at time t_0) of £90·02 at t_2 is £74·38 – the amount by which his shareholding increased in value at time t_0 when the company's deci-sion was announced.

A similar analysis could be undertaken where the investor borrows £100 at t_1 (at the market interest rate), and repays capital and interest at t_2, using his increased dividend payment at that time. The net outcome will be exactly the same as before.

It should be clear from this example that if stock markets valued retained earnings less favourably than dividends, there would be opportunities for profitable arbitrage transactions to take place (with investors either buying shares in companies which are increasing their cash flow retention proportions – as they will be undervalued – or selling shares in companies which are reducing their retention pro-portions – as they are likely to be overvalued). These transactions should rapidly force out correct market valuations. Such an exercise is left to the reader to undertake.

The possibility of external finance Up to this point in our analysis of the dividend decision, we have only considered situations in which the sole source of investment capital has been retained earnings. If we now widen the analysis to include the opportunity for companies to raise exterior finance for investment, what now becomes of the dividend decision?[7] When the possibility of external finance was excluded, the decision rule for company managements wishing to maximize shareholder wealth was to apply each year's cash earnings to investment in projects with positive NPVs. If the source of such projects dried up before all the net cash earnings had been allocated, then the remaining earnings could be paid out as a dividend. Thus the dividend 'policy' was to treat dividends as a residual to the investment decision. Dividends cannot be said to be 'irrelevant'; in such circumstances they are very relevant because, unless they are treated as a residual of the investment decision, they will be preventing 'profitable' investment from being undertaken and so will result in the shareholders' wealth failing to achieve the maximum.

Once the possibility of raising external finance is allowed, dividends no longer need to act as a residual but become truly irrelevant. This is because the payment of a dividend can no longer be held to prevent profitable investment from being undertaken, because the required finance can always be raised externally. However, the raising of external finance in such circumstances – be it either debt or equity – is also likely (but not necessarily) to change a company's gearing ratio, and so the dividend decision can be said to be truly irrelevant only if, at the same time, it is accepted that changes in a company's gearing ratio leave its market value unaffected. If not, then dividend policy may well indirectly affect equity market values. As we are in a tax-free world of perfect capital markets, we can fairly safely assume that the conclusions of the initial M.M. capital structure hypothesis also hold.

It is worthwhile noticing that this interdependence of the two M.M. hypotheses works in both directions: not only does dividend irrelevancy depend on the capital structure hypothesis, but in turn the capital structure hypothesis holds true only if a company's dividend-retention ratio leaves its market value unaffected. For example, suppose that the greater the proportion of cash earnings paid out as dividends, the higher would be the market value of a company's equity capital. In such circumstances capital structure could not be said to be independent of market values because, other things being equal, the smaller the proportion of retained earnings the higher would be the company's market value, and vice versa.

The introduction of the possibility of external finance also leaves the traditional view largely unaffected. Dividend policy still retains its importance on the basis that current dividends are more highly valued than future dividends generated by retained earnings. But in addition, just as the two M.M. hypotheses are in tandem, so too are the traditional views of dividends and capital structure. Therefore a company's dividend policy also gains importance from the fact that it is a partial determinant of the level of retained earnings and so can affect the company's market value through changing the gearing ratio. The exact effects of a company's dividend policy through such influences are not certain, but are dependent on its location on the U-shaped weighted average cost of capital curve.

10.2 Dividend policy in an imperfect market

Consistent dividend policies Once we move away from the assumption of a perfect capital market and a tax-free world, the dividend decision becomes much more problematical. In particular, there are a number of different capital market imperfections which are likely to interfere seriously with the hypothesis of dividend irrelevancy.

The dividend irrelevancy argument has been founded on the perfect capital market approach/separation theorem of our initial two period investment–consumption analysis, in that the pattern of cash flows with which the company provides the shareholder through the dividend policy is irrelevant, because each individual shareholder can adjust this dividend pattern to fit his desired consumption pattern by use of the capital market. It was this characteristic which allowed company managements to avoid the problem of having to identify individual shareholder utility curves, when making investment decisions on their behalf. However, capital market imperfections such as transaction costs (which in practice can be very substantial, especially at the individual shareholder level), differential interest rates, and the presence of absolute capital rationing for the individual shareholder, all interfere with this process. Quite simply, these capital market imperfections mean that an individual cannot *costlessly* adjust his dividend pattern to fit his preferred consumption pattern; indeed the cost of doing so may be relatively high. (In the case of absolute capital rationing for the individual, the cost of some consumption patterns can be seen as infinitely high.) In such circumstances, absolute wealth maximization (i.e., in present value terms) may not be a unique desire of shareholders, with the *pattern* of wealth receipt also becoming important. Thus the company's dividend policy takes on a new dimension: shareholders may positively prefer companies to supply them with a dividend pattern which matches fairly closely with their desired consumption pattern, thereby relieving them of having to adjust this cash flow themselves. In practice companies often do this by following a stable and easily identifiable dividend policy, but whether it is done explicitly for these reasons is open to considerable doubt. As an example, many companies strongly follow a policy in which dividend reduction is anathema and an increased dividend will be declared only if management are convinced that the new dividend level can be at least sustained, if not improved upon, in future years. In this way, shareholders whose own consumption patterns closely follow the dividend pattern of the company will be attracted by the knowledge that they are unlikely to need to resort to the imperfect capital market in order to make dividend/consumption pattern adjustments.

Unfortunately, the fact that an easily identifiable dividend pattern may mean that shareholders avoid the costs of adjustment, does not mean that such advantage is necessarily gained costlessly. Indeed, the cost which is directly saved by the shareholder may be more than offset by the consequential cost to the company (which will, in turn, rebound on to the shareholders). This consequential cost may come about either in that, by paying a dividend, the company is left with insufficient finance to undertake a profitable investment (i.e., one with a positive NPV) and so the investment opportunity is missed, or alternatively, because a dividend has been paid, the company has to raise finance for an investment from an external source which involves the incurrence of issue costs. It may be thought that the dividend decision in this situation resolves into a straightforward cost minimization trade-off, but a problem arises with the identification and quantification of the costs incurred or avoided by the shareholders and the fact that they are unlikely to be the same for each individual shareholder. So we are reduced to concluding that in an imperfect capital market, probably the best approach that a company can hope to take is to follow a consistent dividend policy[8] and hope that the particular policy chosen does not incur too heavy cost penalties, relative to the transaction and opportunity cost savings made by shareholders.

Dividends as information Another capital market imperfection which bears on the dividend decision concerns the need for information in an uncertain world. Capital markets are imperfect in the sense that information is neither costless nor universally available, and so decisions have often to be made by stock market investors on the basis of imperfect and incomplete information.] In such circumstances, a company's dividend declaration – a free and universally available piece of data – is often thought to impart a degree of information and knowledge about its future performance which in fact is largely unjustified. In other words, given that information about a company's future performance prospects is fairly sparse – especially to the individual investor – *any* information that becomes available is seized upon and embodied with a measure of importance which is often far in excess of its real value.

In these terms, the dividend decision once again gains in importance. If the stock market places such an (albeit maybe unjustified) informational content on the dividend decision, then a company will not be acting so as to maximize its shareholders' wealth if it ignores this fact. It is most likely for this reason that many publicly quoted companies follow the dividend policy referred to earlier, where a dividend is reduced or passed completely only in the most dire financial circumstances.

Tax considerations Taxation and especially differential rates of personal income tax, a distinction between income and capital gains, and the fact that a company might have both private and corporate shareholders who are taxed under different tax regimes, form a serious capital market imperfection which interferes with the dividend irrelevancy approach. The major problem with the presence of taxation is that it can interfere with the value equivalence between dividends and retained earnings. As a result, some shareholders may prefer 'home-made' dividends (generated through selling part of their shareholding) because the rate of capital gains tax may be lower than their marginal income tax rate which would be imposed upon company-distributed dividends. In contrast, other shareholders may prefer the company distributed dividends because their marginal income tax rate results in less tax being paid than the combined effect of capital gains tax and transaction costs incurred in the process of providing home-made dividends.

Once again, in the face of different taxation rates and different taxation regimes, we must conclude by saying that if a company follows a widely recognized, consistent dividend policy, then it can be expected to attract that class of shareholders on whom the particular dividend policy chosen has the most favourable (or least harmful) taxation effects. But in so concluding, there still remains the problem of what action the company should take in the face of significant changes in the taxation regime, as far as dividends are concerned. Should it try to adjust its dividend policy so as to bring about the most favourable outcome to its existing shareholders, or should it continue with its existing policy in the hope that new shareholders, to whom the company's dividend policy is now favourable in terms of taxation, will be attracted and so replace some of the existing shareholders? The optimal decision in such circumstances requires an accurate evaluation of the cost trade-off concerned (on the basis that the objective of financial management is to benefit *existing* shareholders) between the cost to the company of changing its dividend policy[9] and the cost to its shareholders of *not* changing its policy. Both costs will be difficult to quantify in precise terms, but both may possibly be substantial and so should not be ignored.

In conclusion This analysis must force us to conclude that when faced with a number of real-world capital market imperfections, the dividend decision is both relevant and important in terms of attempting to maximize shareholders' wealth. However, the identity of the correct dividend decision depends to a great extent upon how the individual shareholders are personally affected by the various market imperfections. It is likely, given a random selection of stock market investors, that the market imperfections with respect to dividends will affect individual shareholders in a number of conflicting ways, thus making a consensus dividend policy an unlikely possibility. The only escape from this dilemma for a company that intends to maximize the wealth of its shareholders is to follow a consistent dividend policy, which then allows the individual shareholder to judge its desirability in relation to his own personal circumstances.

Selected references

W. J. Baumol, On Dividend Policy and Market Imperfections, *Journal of Business*, January 1963.

F. Black and M. Scholes, 'The Effect of Dividend Yield and Dividend Policy on Common Stock Prices and Returns', *Journal of Financial Economics*, May 1976.

M. J. Brennan, 'A Note on Dividend Irrelevance and the Gordon Valuation Model', *Journal of Finance*, December 1971.

J. A. Brittain, *Corporate Dividend Policy*. Washington, D.C., The Brookings Institution, 1966.

D. Durand, 'Growth Stocks and the St Petersburg Paradox', *Journal of Finance*, September 1957.

E. J. Elton and M. J. Gruber, 'Marginal Stockholder Tax Rates and the Clientele Effect', *Review of Economics and Statistics*, February 1970.

E. F. Fama, 'The Effects of a Firm's Investment and Financing Decisions on the Welfare of its Security Holders', *American Economic Review*, June 1978.

T. W. Foster and D. Vickrey, 'The Information Content of Stock Dividend Announcements', *Accounting Review*, April 1978.

I. Friend and M. Puckett, 'Dividends and Stock Prices', *American Economic Review*, September 1964.

M. J. Gordon, 'Dividends, Earnings and Stock Prices', *Review of Economics and Statistics*, May 1959.

M. J. Gordon, *The Investment, Financing and Valuation of the Corporation*, Homewood, Illinois, Richard D. Irwin, 1962.

M. J. Gordon, 'Optional Investment and Financing Policy', *Journal of Finance*, May 1963.

R. C. Higgins, 'Dividend Policy and Increasing Discount Rates: a Clarification', *Journal of Financial and Quantitative Analysis*, June 1972.

J. Y. Kamin and J. Ronen, 'The Effects of Corporate Control on Apparent Profit Performance', *Southern Economic Journal*, July 1978.

S. Keane, 'Dividends and the Resolution of Uncertainty', *Journal of Business Finance and Accounting*, Autumn 1974.

J. Lintner, 'Dividends, Earnings, Leverage, Stock Prices, and the Supply of Capital to Corporations', *Review of Economics and Statistics*, August 1962.

M. H. Miller and F. Modigliani, 'Dividend Policy, Growth and the Valuation of Shares', *Journal of Business*, October 1961.

T. M. Ryan, 'Dividend Policy and Market Valuation in British Industry',

Journal of Business Finance and Accounting, Autumn 1974.

J. Walter, 'Dividend Policies and Common Stock Prices', *Journal of Finance*, March 1956.

F. M. Wilkes, 'Dividend Policy and Investment Appraisal in Imperfect Capital Markets', *Journal of Business Finance and Accounting*, Summer 1977.

11 Dealing with Risk

11.1 Simple solutions to the problem of risk

Introduction Up to this stage in the analysis we have usually 'arranged' things so that many of the effects on financial decision making caused by the uncertainty of the future are negated or neutralized. For example, when justifying the use of the weighted average cost of capital for investment appraisal purposes, we specified the assumption that any investment project undertaken by a company would not result in a change in the company's existing risk level. Indeed, we have even progressed as far as specifying two different types of risk: financial risk and business risk. However all along the consideration of risk has only been brought into the discussion either to exclude it specifically from the analysis (i.e., by assuming the future is known) or to accept that it exists but to assume that it remains at a constant level agreed upon by all concerned.

In this chapter, for the first time, we shall turn to look explicitly at the problem of risk and to examine what it is, how it can be measured, what effects it can have on our analysis of financial decision making to date, and how this analysis should be amended – if at all – to accommodate more fully the presence of risk. We shall start by making a fairly general statement on what is meant by risk and we shall then examine four approaches to 'dealing' with it in investment appraisal: by means of expected values, sensitivity analysis, the use of a risk-adjusted discount rate (RADR), and the use of the properties of a normal distribution.

A definition of risk Risk can be defined in many different ways, none of which can be held to be entirely satisfactory if for no other reason than that the term can be taken to mean different things to different people. In the context of investment decision making (whether it is by a company management or an individual), risk will be regarded as describing the extent to which the actual outcome of a decision *may* diverge from what is *expected*. Thus the greater the possible divergence, the greater the degree of risk and vice versa. When the extent of the possible divergence is zero (in other words the actual outcome *cannot* vary from the expected outcome), risk is zero – the decision is riskless or risk-free because its outcome is known *with certainty*.

In terms of investment decision making, the expected outcome of a decision to invest is the project's expected returns[1] and the possible divergence from this expected outcome can be a return which is *greater* than expected as well as less than expected. As far as the rational investor is concerned who is averse to risk,[2] what is of importance is the possible divergence from the expected outcome of the investment decision which results in a *lower* return – we can term this the 'downside' risk. (Although this is not to say that the risk of a greater than expected return is of no importance. Indeed for the risk-seeking decision maker, this is the more important aspect.)

'Expected' NPVs and risk[3] In an uncertain world, even assuming the presence of perfect capital markets, use of the NPV method of investment appraisal cannot be said necessarily to lead to optimal investment decisions or to the maximization of shareholder wealth. All it can do is to lead to the *expected* maximization of wealth. Hindsight, that is knowledge about the actual outcome of past events, may suggest different advice from that given by the NPV appraisal rule, because the latter is based only upon estimates of the future.

When we examined the rationale and operation of the NPV appraisal method, we paid very little attention to how the estimates of a project's future net cash flows were derived. In practice, management is unlikely to produce a series of 'point' (i.e., single figure) estimates of each year's net cash flow but instead is likely to construct a *range* of estimates. For example, a project may have an initial cost of £1,000 and a life of three years, but the level of the net cash flows may be uncertain, depending, say, on the general state of the industry in which the company operates. Table 11.1 shows a simple example of the estimated annual net cash flows based on three economic states: boom, normal and depression conditions. From these data the project's NPV is calculated in each state and a figure is attached expressing the probability or likelihood of each state actually occurring. These data are combined to produce the arithmetic mean (i.e., average) NPV of the project: the *expected* NPV of the project, given the different estimates and their probabilities of occurrence. It is upon the value (and more importantly, the sign) of this expected net present value (ENPV) that the normal investment appraisal decision rule is applied.

It is important to notice that, as this example shows, management not only has the task of estimating the project's annual net cash flow in each of the different states of the industry, but must also estimate the probability of the occurrence of each state. (Strictly, these are *subjective* probabilities, because they are based upon management's subjective judgement rather than on past observations of similar events.) In addition, it is assumed in the example that whichever state of the industry occurs, the industry will remain fixed in that state over the duration of the project. If this assumption is unrealistic, further adjustments will need to be made to the ENPV calculation, using a 'decision-tree' approach.[5] Table 11.2 recalculates the ENPV of the project, using such an approach, on the assumption that the state of the industry in any year (and hence the project-generated net cash flow for that year) is independent of the state in any prior year.

Table 11.1

Year:		0	1	2	3
State	Boom	−1,000	+550	+700	+980
of	Normal	−1,000	+500	+600	+700
industry	Depression	−1,000	+300	+300	+250

Using (say) a 10% discount rate, the possible NPVs of the project are as follows:

Boom	+£770
Normal	+£480
Depression	−£290

State of industry	Probability of occurrence
Boom	0·20
Normal	0·60
Depression	0·20
	1·00

State of industry	Prob.	NPV	NPV × Prob.
Boom	0·20	+770	+154
Normal	0·60	+480	+288
Depression	0·20	−290	− 58
		Expected[4] NPV	+384

The concept of expected NPV (indeed an expected IRR could be similarly calculated) is useful for project appraisal in an uncertain world because it provides an average value of the proposed project's performance. However it cannot be said to take account of risk (as we have defined it), because all the ENPV calculation provides is a measure of the investment's expected performance, whilst risk is concerned with how far the *actual* performance may diverge from what is expected. Table 11.3 illustrates this point with a very simple example in which there are two projects requiring identical investment outlays, both of which have just a one-year life. Management has tried to forecast each project's net cash flow at the end of year 1 and has attached various subjective probabilities to each possible outcome (in other words they have constructed subjective probability distributions of the year 1 cash flows). The means of these cash flows

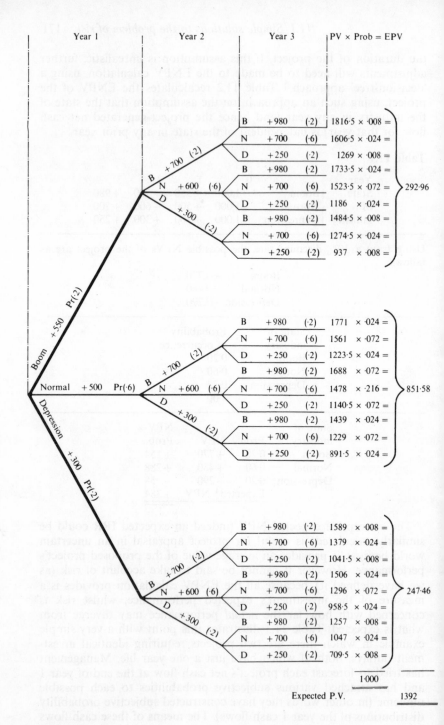

Year 1	Year 2	Year 3			PV × Prob = EPV	
		B	+980	(·2)	1816·5 × ·008 =	
		N	+700	(·6)	1606·5 × ·024 =	
	+700 (·2)	D	+250	(·2)	1269 × ·008 =	
		B	+980	(·2)	1733·5 × ·024 =	
	B N +600 (·6)	N	+700	(·6)	1523·5 × ·072 =	292·96
	D +300 (·2)	D	+250	(·2)	1186 × ·024 =	
		B	+980	(·2)	1484·5 × ·008 =	
		N	+700	(·6)	1274·5 × ·024 =	
		D	+250	(·2)	937 × ·008 =	
Boom +550 Pr(·2)		B	+980	(·2)	1771 × ·024 =	
		N	+700	(·6)	1561 × ·072 =	
	+700 (·2)	D	+250	(·2)	1223·5 × ·024 =	
		B	+980	(·2)	1688 × ·072 =	
Normal +500 Pr(·6)	B N +600 (·6)	N	+700	(·6)	1478 × ·216 =	851·58
	D +300 (·2)	D	+250	(·2)	1140·5 × ·072 =	
		B	+980	(·2)	1439 × ·024 =	
Depression +300 Pr(·2)		N	+700	(·6)	1229 × ·072 =	
		D	+250	(·2)	891·5 × ·024 =	
		B	+980	(·2)	1589 × ·008 =	
		N	+700	(·6)	1379 × ·024 =	
	+700 (·2)	D	+250	(·2)	1041·5 × ·008 =	
		B	+980	(·2)	1506 × ·024 =	
	B N +600 (·6)	N	+700	(·6)	1296 × ·072 =	247·46
	D +300 (·2)	D	+250	(·2)	958·5 × ·024 =	
		B	+980	(·2)	1257 × ·008 =	
		N	+700	(·6)	1047 × ·024 =	
		D	+250	(·2)	709·5 × ·008 =	

1·000

Expected P.V.   1392

Table 11.2   *As the outlay = 1000, the ENPV = +1392 − 1000 = +392*

are calculated to produce each project's expected cash flow, which is then discounted and summed to produce the ENPV*l* However, in this example we can see that although the expected performance (i.e., ENPV) of each project is identical, Project A has much greater scope for divergence from this expectation than has Project B. For instance, the worst possible outcome that could be produced by B is a net cash inflow of only £500 in year 1 (leading to an NPV −£545) whilst Project A could produce a net cash *outflow* in year 1 of £2,500 (leading to an NPV −£3,273). Thus we can conclude that Project A is riskier than Project B, even though they have the same *expected* outcome or expected NPV.

Before turning to look at how risk can be more precisely quantified, let us first examine one approach to taking account of uncertainty which tries to concentrate on the down-side risk aspect of any investment project's estimates: sensitivity analysis.

Table 11.3

Projects A and B both involve initial investment outlays of £1,000 and have lives of one year only. The year-end net cash flows are estimated as follows:

PROJECT A

Estimated yr 1 net cash flow	C/F range mid-point	Subj. Prob.	Mid-point × Prob.
Between −£2,500 and +£499	−£1,000	0·25	−£ 250
Between +£500 and +£3,499	+£2,000	0·50	+£1,000
Between +£3,500 and +£4,499	+£5,000	0·25	+£1,250
	Mean/expected cash flow		+£2,000

PROJECT B

Estimated yr 1 net cash flow	C/F range mid-point	Subj. Prob.	Mid-point × Prob.
Between +£500 and £1,499	+£1,000	0·25	+£ 250
Between +£1,500 and +£2,499	+£2,000	0·50	+£1,000
Between +£2,500 and +£3,499	+£3,000	0·25	+£ 750
	Mean/expected cash flow		+£2,000

At a discount rate of (say) 10%:

Project A Expected cash flow: −£1,000 + £2,000
          Expected NPV: −£1,000 + £2,000 $V'_{0\cdot10}$ = +£818

Project B Expected cash flow: −£1,000 + £2,000
          Expected NPV: −£1,000 + £2,000 $V'_{0\cdot10}$ = +£818

Sensitivity analysis The appraisal of almost any investment project in the real world will involve the making of a great number of estimates about, for example, the outlay required to undertake the project, its life, the annual cash inflows and outflows it will generate, the scrap value it will have, and even the correct rate of discount to reduce the cash flows to present values. Estimates will be made for all these factors and the project will then be appraised by calculating an expected net present value. If this ENPV is positive then the appraisal is in favour of acceptance but, in terms of down-side risk, the decision maker is also interested in how sensitive the advice is to the estimates made about the project. In other words, he is likely to be interested in the margin of error that there can be in the estimates made about the individual components of the project (i.e., outlay, life, etc.) before the advice that the appraisal gives (in this case to accept) becomes incorrect. The decision pivot therefore is the point at which the project's net cash flows produce a zero ENPV. Sensitivity analysis is the term used to describe the process where each estimated element of a project is taken in turn (with a *ceteris paribus* assumption holding all other estimates constant) to see the extent to which it can vary before the project's positive ENPV is reduced to a zero value. These sensitivity calculations are performed below for a simple example.

Suppose the following estimates have been made about an investment proposal:

Outlay	£1,000
Life	3 years
Annual cash inflows	£2,000[7]
Annual cash outflows	£1,500[7]
Appropriate discount rate[6]	10%

On the basis of these estimates, the expected NPV can be calculated as follows:

Year	0	1	2	3
Capital outlay	−£1,000			
Cash inflows		+£2,000	+£2,000	+£2,000
Cash outflows		−£1,500	−£1,500	−£1,500
Net expected Cash flows	−£1,000	+£ 500	+£ 500	+£ 500

$$\text{ENPV} = -1{,}000 + 500\ A_{3|0\cdot10} = \underline{+\pounds245}$$

Taking each of the five estimated factors in turn (and holding all the others constant at their initial estimated values), we shall examine the degree of variation necessary to reduce the +£245 ENPV to zero.

Outlay: Let the outlay value be x.

$$-x + 500\ A_{3|0\cdot10} = 0$$

$$\therefore \qquad x = 500\ A_{3|0\cdot10} = 1{,}245$$

The outlay can be as high as £1,245 before the appraisal advice to invest (i.e., +ENPV) becomes incorrect; in other words the original estimate can increase by £245 or by $245/1,000 \,.\, 100 = 24{\cdot}5\%$.

Life: Let the life be x years.

$$-1,000 + 500\, A_{x|0\cdot 10} = 0$$

$$A_{x|0\cdot 10} = \frac{1,000}{500} = 2{\cdot}0$$

Using linear interpolation, $A_{2|0\cdot 10} = 1{\cdot}74$ and $A_{3|0\cdot 10} = 2{\cdot}49$ and therefore the value of x can be approximated:

$$x = 2 + \left[\frac{2{\cdot}0 - 1{\cdot}74}{2{\cdot}49 - 1{\cdot}74} \cdot (3-2) \right] = \underline{\underline{2{\cdot}35 \text{ years}}}$$

The project life can be as short as 2·35 years before the advice of the original investment appraisal is incorrect; i.e. the original estimate can decrease by 0·65 year or by $0{\cdot}65/3 \,.\, 100 = 22\%$.

Cash inflows: Let the annual cash inflows be x.

$$-1,000 + x\, A_{3|0\cdot 10} - 1,500\, A_{3|0\cdot 10} = 0$$

$$x = \frac{1,000 + 1,500\, A_{3|0\cdot 10}}{A_{3|0\cdot 10}} = \underline{\underline{£1,902}}$$

Thus the annual cash inflows can be as low as £1,902, over the three years, before the original advice is incorrect; i.e., the original estimate can decrease by £98 per year or $98/2,000 \,.\, 100 = \underline{\underline{4{\cdot}9\%}}$.

Cash outflows: Let the annual cash outflows be x.

$$-1,000 + 2,000\, A_{3|0\cdot 10} - x\, A_{3|0\cdot 10} = 0$$

$$x = \frac{1,000 - 2,000\, A_{3|0\cdot 10}}{A_{3|0\cdot 10}} = \underline{\underline{-£1,598}}$$

The annual cash outflows can be as high as £1,598 in each of the three years before the original investment advice is incorrect; i.e., the original estimate can increase by £98 per year or $98/1,500 \,.\, 100 = \underline{\underline{6{\cdot}5\%}}$.

Discount rate: Let the discount rate be x.

$$-1,000 + 500\, A_{3|x} = 0$$

$$A_{3|x} = \frac{1,000}{500} = 2{\cdot}0$$

Using linear interpolation, $A_{3|0\cdot 20} = 2{\cdot}11$ and $A_{3|0\cdot 25} = 1{\cdot}95$

$$x = 0.20 + \left[\frac{2.11 - 2.0}{2.11 - 1.95} \cdot (0.25 - 0.20) \right] = \underline{\underline{0.234^8}}$$

Thus the estimate for the discount rate can be as high as 23.4% before the original investment advice is incorrect; i.e., the original estimate can be increased by 13.4% or $0.134/0.10 \cdot 100 = 134\%$.

Sensitivity table

Estimate Factor	Sensitivity %
Outlay	24·5%
Life	22 %
Cash inflows	4·9%
Cash outflows	6.5%
Discount rate	134 %

The sensitivity table shows that the decision to invest is most sensitive to the estimates of annual cash inflows (where an actual outcome of only 4.9% below estimate would cause the NPV decision advice to be incorrect) and the annual cash outflows (a decision sensitivity of 6.5%). The decision advice is fairly insensitive to all the other estimates. We could conclude from this that management should review both of these decision-sensitive estimates to ensure that they cannot be improved upon.

This example outlines the general approach of the sensitivity analysis technique, which is a good working tool in that it makes the decision maker more aware of the possible effects of uncertainty on his investment decisions. In addition, it can also help to direct attention to those particular estimates which require a special forecasting effort on account of their effect on the decision's sensitivity. However, the technique suffers in particular from an obvious and important drawback: the fact that each estimated component is varied in turn whilst all the others are held constant. Thus, in the example above, the discount rate can be as high as 23.4% (approximately) before the NPV calculation advises rejection of the project, but this degree of sensitivity *only* holds (except through a chance ordering of factors) if all the other estimates turn out to be accurate. In other words, the technique ignores the possible effects on the decision of two or more of the esimated components varying simultaneously.[9] But even if this problem with sensitivity analysis is set to one side, it can also be criticised on the basis that it makes no attempt to analyse risk in any formal way, nor does it give any indication as to what the decision maker's reaction should be to the data presented in a sensitivity table. In the example used above, the original NPV calculations indicated a decision to accept. Sensitivity analysis provides no rules to guide the decision maker as to whether the initial appraisal advice should or should not be amended in the light of the sensitivity data. With these limitations in mind let us now look at other approaches which may be used to deal with the problem of uncertainty in investment appraisal.

The risk-adjusted discount rate The risk-adjusted discount rate attempts to handle the problem of risk and uncertainty in a more direct and thoughtful way. In earlier chapters, when we discussed the rationale behind the use of a company's existing weighted average cost of capital as an investment appraisal discount rate, we specified that it was only applicable for appraising investment proposals which, if accepted, would leave the company's current business risk level unchanged. This stipulation was necessary because any market determined interest rate in an uncertain world represents a combination of two separate components: the marginal rate of time preference (MRTP) and a consideration (or premium) for the level of risk involved. Thus a company's WACC reflects not only a weighted average MRTP of the suppliers of its capital, but it also reflects the general level of risk involved with the company. It follows therefore, that a company's WACC can be split up into its MRTP component (often called the risk-free or default-free interest rate) and its risk premium component such that $K_o = K_i + K_r$, where K_i is the risk-free interest rate and K_r is the risk premium.

To use a risk-adjusted discount rate for investment, the company simply adds to the current risk-free rate at an additional premium the size of which is determined by the estimated riskiness of the project being appraised. On the assumption that investors are risk-averse, the greater the perceived risk of a project the greater will be the risk premium and therefore the greater will be the resulting discount rate used to appraise the project. Thus the risk-adjusted discount rate takes the commonsense approach to handling risk in investment appraisal of adjusting the 'height' of the 'acceptance hurdle' to correspond to the project's risk level. For example, a company's management may judge that the current rate of return on government long-term bonds is an adequate reflection of the risk-free interest/discount rate. Suppose this rate is 8%. Management may also decide to classify investment proposals into three broad categories, low, medium and high risk, and assign risk premiums of 3%, 5% and 9% respectively. Therefore the cash flows of low-risk projects would be discounted to present value using a discount rate of $8\% + 3\% = 11\%$, whilst projects of medium or high risk would be evaluated by discounting their cash flows to present value using 13% and 17% discount rates respectively.

In one very important way, the risk-adjusted discount rate approach to the problem of uncertainty is much more useful to the decision maker than sensitivity analysis in that it does actually produce decision advice, in the form of a risk-adjusted net present value. In addition, the method is easily understandable and appears to be intuitively correct: investors *do* require a higher expected return on riskier investments. However, the approach has drawbacks in two areas, one practical and one theoretical. The main practical problems concern the allocation of investments into risk categories (e.g., high, medium or low risk) and the determination of the risk premium appropriate for each category. The approach provides only rough and ready rule of thumb guidelines to these problems and this severely limits its reliability. The theoretical problem concerns the fact that the use of risk-adjusted discount rates implies assumptions about the nature of the relationship between project risk and time which may not apply in practice. For example, if the risk-free rate of discount is 8% and it is thought that medium-risk projects will be required to earn an additional 5% return, then consider a project which requires an initial outlay of £100 and produces a single cash inflow 12 months later. If the project were risk free, then to be just acceptable (i.e.. to produce a zero NPV), the year 1 cash inflow would have to be £108:

$$\text{Year} \quad 0 \quad 1 \quad \text{NPV}$$

$$-100 \quad \frac{+108}{(1+0.08)} = 0$$

Instead, if the project had a medium level of risk, the minimum acceptable year 1 inflow would be £113:[10]

$$\text{Year} \quad 0 \quad 1 \quad \text{NPV}$$

$$-100 \quad \frac{+113}{(1+0.13)} = 0$$

Thus a minimum additional cash inflow at year 1 of £5 (i.e. £113–£108) would be required by way of compensation for the project's riskiness.

Suppose that we take the same two examples (risk-free and medium-risk projects) but now examine the minimum cash inflow required for the projects to be acceptable if they arise in 24 months' time:

	Year	0	1	2		NPV
Risk-free project		-100	—	$\frac{+116.64}{(1+0.08)^2}$	$=$	0
Medium-risk project		-100	—	$\frac{+127.69}{(1+0.13)^2}$	$=$	0

In these circumstances, the risky project has to produce a minimum *additional* cash flow at year 2 of £11·05, in order to compensate for the risk. Thus the *average* annual risk premiums (K_r) required for the two risky projects can be calculated:

Medium-risk project

1-year life: $100(1 + K_r) = 105$
$$1 + K_r = 105/100$$
$$K_r = \underline{0{\cdot}05}$$

2-year life: $100(1 + K_r)^2 = 111{\cdot}05$
$$1 + K_r = \sqrt{111{\cdot}05/100}$$
$$K_r = \underline{0{\cdot}0538}$$

From this example can be seen the general principle that, because of the effects of compounding the risk premium, as a project's life gets longer so the size of the average annual risk premium increases: if this medium-risk project were to produce its single cash inflow at year 25, the annual average risk premium required would be equivalent to $11{\cdot}253\%$. The conclusion that can be reached from this example is that it would be incorrect to judge that all medium-risk projects should produce a risk premium of (say) 5%, without making reference to the project's life-span and from that, being satisfied that the resulting implied relationship between risk and time is appropriate.[11]

The use of the normal distribution Another attempt to take a more analytical approach to the problem of risk makes use of the properties of Normal probability distributions. The approach starts from the premise that if a project's risk can be defined as the degree of possible variability between its expected outcome and its actual outcome, then what is of prime importance to the risk-averse decision maker (or more correctly, the risk-averse owner on whose behalf the decision is being made) is just one side of this variability: the risk of project underperformance. Therefore, what would be of interest to the decision maker is the probability of the project actually producing a negative NPV, even though the *expected* result was a positive NPV. On the assumption that the range of possible outcomes for the project are normally distributed, then the properties of the Normal Curve can be used to provide the required probability.

A problem arises, however, in the choice of the discount rate to be used to calculate the possible NPVs of the project being appraised. One possibility is to use the risk-free discount rate. The investment decision advice is then based on whether or not the probability of a negative NPV exceeds some maximum acceptable probability, in such the same way as a risk-premium is utilized when using the risk-adjusted discount rate. If the probability of a negative NPV were sufficiently small, the project would be acceptable. An alternative approach is to discount the project cash flows using an appropriate *risk-adjusted* discount rate in order to calculate the expected NPV and then use the properties of the Normal Curve to estimate the probability of a negative NPV. This latter approach uses the probability of a negative NPV as an *additional* piece of decision information, almost as an extension of the sensitivity analysis concept. By contrast, the former approach attempts to use the properties of the Normal Curve to allow directly for risk in investment decision making. In doing so it avoids the element of 'double-counting' risk which occurs when using a risk-adjusted discount rate to calculate the range of possible NPVs.

A simple example, such as that set out in Table 11.4, can be used to explain the mechanics of both approaches. From the results of this example it can be seen that when using a risk free discount rate, the decision advice is based on whether a 13·8% probability of the project actually producing a return below the riskless return is acceptable for the perceived level of risk of the project concerned. Alternatively, the second approach informs the decision maker that the project can be expected to produce a positive NPV of £492 when discounted at a rate appropriate for its degree of risk, but that if a decision is made to accept the project, there is a 18·4% probability that this decision will turn out to be incorrect (i.e., the project actually produces a negative NPV).

In conclusion None of these rather simple approaches to the problem of risk can be said really to tackle the issue except by a rather intuitive, 'rule of thumb' method. In the next section we shall define risk much more carefully than we have done to date, and we shall use that as a basis for undertaking a more systematic and rigorous analysis of the problem and its possible solution.

Table 11.4

A project is under evaluation which is thought to involve a medium degree of risk. The risk-free discount rate is 4% and the appropriate risk premium is believed to be 6%. The project has the following estimated cash flows:

Cash outlay (year 0): £1,000

Cash inflows:

	Year:	1	2	3	Prob.
	Good	+1,000	+1,000	+1,000	0·1
	Med./good	+800	+800	+800	0·2
Market conditions:	Medium	+600	+600	+600	0·4
	Med./poor	+400	+400	+400	0·2
	Poor	+200	+200	+200	0·1
					1·0

(a) Using the risk-free discount rate of 4%:

Market conditions	NPV at 4% × Prob.			$(NPV - ENPV)^2$ × Prob.
Good	+1,775 × 0·1	=	+177·5	123210
Med./good	+1,220 × 0·2	=	+244·0	61605
Medium	+ 665 × 0·4	=	+266·0	0
Med./poor	+ 110 × 0·2	=	+ 22·0	61605
Poor	− 445 × 0·1	=	− 44·5	123210
	Expected NPV		+665·0	$\sqrt{369630}$ = 608 = Std. deviation

Probability of a negative NPV:

$$\frac{0 - 665}{608} = 1\cdot094 \text{ Std. units}$$

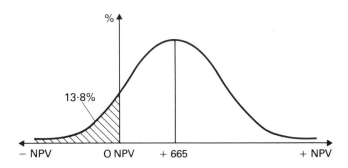

%

13·8%

− NPV   O NPV   + 665   + NPV

Using area under the Normal curve tables this gives a value for the shaded area (− NPV) of: 0·1379

Therefore there is a 13·8% probability that the project will produce less than the risk-free return of 4%.

(b) Using the risk-adjusted discount rate of 4% + 6% = 10%:

Market conditions	NPV at 10% × Prob.			$(NPV - ENPV)^2$ × Prob.
Good	+1487 × 0·1	=	+148·7	99002·4
Med./good	+ 989 × 0·2	=	+197·8	49401·8
Medium	+ 492 × 0·4	=	+196·8	0
Med./poor	− 5 × 0·2	=	− 1·0	49401·8
Poor	− 503 × 0·1	=	− 50·3	99002·4
	Expected NPV		+492·0	$\sqrt{296808\cdot4}$ = 545 = Std. deviation

Probability of a negative NPV:

$$\frac{0 - 492}{545} = 0\cdot903 \text{ Std. units}$$

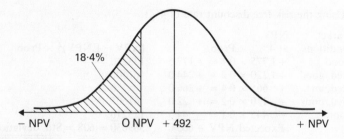

Using area under the Normal curve tables this gives a value for the shaded area (− NPV) of: 0·1841.

Therefore there is an 18·4% probability that the project will produce less than the required return of 10%.

11.2 The expected utility model

Introduction We are concerned with the construction of a theory of financial decision making by a company's management on behalf of its shareholders. Given the fact that management will have to take decisions about investment proposals whose outcomes are uncertain, it is important that we should be aware of how the individual shareholders would themselves come to a decision in such circumstances. Therefore we require a model which adequately reflects the risk attitudes of shareholders: how they perceive risk and how they react to its presence. Unlike our theory of financial decisions, which is a normative theory outlining how management *should* make financial decisions, the model of shareholders' risk attitudes needs to be a *positive* model – it should try to reflect their *actual* attitudes rather than what should be their attitudes. It is only in this way that we will be able to construct successfully a normative theory of managerial financial decision making based on shareholders' actual desires. To this end we have to make some carefully specified assumptions about shareholders and investors generally.

Investors' behaviour axioms Stated succinctly, we shall assume that when faced with making risky financial decisions, individual shareholders or investors act 'rationally' and 'consistently'. More specifically, we can formulate four basic axioms[12] regarding the behaviour of investors when making decisions:

1 Investors are able to choose between alternatives by ranking them, in some order of merit, i.e., they are capable of actually coming to a decision.

2 Any such ranking of alternatives is 'transitive', i.e., if alternative A is preferred to B and alternative B is preferred to C, then alternative A *must* be preferred to C.

3 Investors do not differentiate between alternatives which have the same degree of risk, i.e., their choice is dispassionate in that it is based solely upon consideration of the risk involved rather than on the nature of alternatives available.

4 Investors are able to specify for any investment whose returns are uncertain, an exactly equivalent alternative which would be just as preferable but which would involve a *certain* return, i.e., for any gamble investors are able to specify a 'certainty equivalent'.[13]

These four axioms of investor's decision-making behaviour can be used to construct an index or function of utility. This utility function[14] can then be used as the basis of a model of investors' risk attitudes which will enable us to explore the way in which individuals make decisions about risky alternatives, on the assumption that they do so in order to maximize their own utility index.

Given below is an example which goes through the process by which an individual's utility function may be derived. Although this process may appear rather unrealistic, it is perfectly practical as long as the individual's decisions are both consistent and rational, in line with the four axioms stated above.

Utility function construction Suppose that we inform an individual that a project will be made available to him and that we wish to know the maximum amount he would be willing to pay to be allowed to undertake it. There are just two possible outcomes from this project; the best possible is +£5,000 whilst the worst possible is −£2,000.

In order to construct the utility function we need a measure or index of utility. This measure is completely arbitrary, but for convenience we shall assign the utility index number of 1 to the +£5,000 outcome and 0 to the −£2,000 outcome:[15]

Outcome	Utility Function Index
+£5,000	1
−£2,000	0

Alternatively this could be written as:

$$U(+£5,000) = 1 \qquad U(-£2,000) = 0$$

and if the probability of an outcome of $+£5,000$ is ρ and of $-£2,000$ is $(1 - \rho)$, then the total utility of the product will be: $\rho U(+£5,000) + (1 - \rho)U(-£2,000)$. As $U(+£5,000) = 1$ and $U(-£2,000) = 0$, then the total utility of the project reduces to just ρ.[16]

From axiom 4 we assume that for any project with a risky outcome, an investor can specify an equivalent certain alternative: the certainty equivalent or $(C\text{-}E)$. This must represent the maximum sum he would be willing to pay to undertake the risky project. Using the example above, the utility of the certainty equivalent can be specified:

$$U(C\text{-}E) = \rho U(+£5,000) + (1 - \rho)U(-£2,000)$$

$$U(C\text{-}E) = \rho 1 + (1 - \rho)0 = \rho$$

We are now in a position to construct a utility function for a specific individual investor. However, before doing so, it is important to emphasize that the utility function we shall construct will be unique to this particular (hypothetical) investor. Different investors are likely to have different utility functions because they are based on each individual's *personal* attitude to risk.

The approach that we shall use is to ask the individual to state the maximum (certain) price he would be willing to pay to be allowed to undertake the project, for a whole range of different probabilities attached to the two outcomes. For example, if we said that the probability of the project producing $+£5,000$ is 0.80 and the probability of producing $-£2,000$ is $(1 - 0.80) = 0.20$, then he may state that he would be willing to pay a maximum of (say) £2,000. This is the project's certainty-equivalent, and its utility index can be calculated as:

$$U(C\text{-}E) = \rho U(+£5,000) + (1 - \rho)U(-£2,000)$$

$$U(+£2,000) = 0.80 . 1 + 0.20 . 0 = 0.80$$

Again we might specify that the probability of the project producing $+£5,000$ was 0.40, and the investor may allocate this project a certainty equivalent of (say) $-£500$. In other words, with probabilities of 0.40 and 0.60 attached to the project's two possible outcomes of $+£5,000$ and $-£2,000$ respectively, the investor would have to be *paid* £500 to induce him to undertake the project.

The utility index of this certainty equivalent would be:

$$U(-£500) = 0.40 . 1 + 0.60 . 0 = 0.40$$

This process could be carried on indefinitely, because there are an unlimited number of different pairs of probabilities (each adding up to unity) which can be attached to the project's two outcomes. Eventually we shall have gathered sufficient utility indices of certainty-equivalents to enable us to plot the individual's personal utility index. Figure 11.1 illustrates such a function.

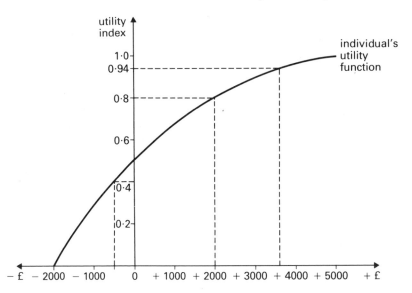

Figure 11.1

The general shape of this utility function is of some interest. Let us return to the first pair of probabilities attached to the project's outcome:

Project outcome	×	Probability	
+£5,000		0·80 =	+£4,000
−£2,000		0·20 =	−£ 400
		Expected outcome	+£3,600

The project's expected outcome had a value of +£3,600 whilst our individual assigned a certainty-equivalent of +£2,000. That is, the expected utility of the project to the individual is less than the utility of the project's expected value:

$$E(U(\text{PROJ.})) < U(E(\text{PROJ.}))$$

In this particular case, the expected utility of the project is the utility of the certainty equivalent value assigned by the individual of +£2,000, and the project's expected value is +£3,600. Using Figure 11.1 we obtain the following utility index values for these amounts:

$$\left.\begin{aligned} E(U(+£2,000)) &= 0·80 \\ U(E(+£3,600)) &= 0·94 \end{aligned}\right\} \quad \text{and } 0·80 < 0·94$$

With the second pair of probabilities that we used for illustration:

Project		
outcome	×	Probability
+£5,000		0·40 = +£2,000
−£2,000		0·60 = −£1,200
		Expected outcome +£ 800

Again, the project's expected outcome of +£800 is higher than the certainty equivalent assigned of −£500. We should find that this would hold for all the probability combinations offered to our investor: he would assign a certainty-equivalent value which was below the project's expected value. It is for this reason that the derived utility function is concave to the origin. If our individual always assigned a certainty-equivalent value which was *equal* to the project's expected value, the utility function would be a straight line, whilst if the individual assigned certainty-equivalent values consistently *greater* than the project's expected value, the utility function would be convex to the origin.

Because our individual consistently assigns certainty-equivalent values that are less than the project's corresponding expected value, he is termed 'risk-averse'. In other words he dislikes risk and shows this by being only willing to pay a sum of money to undertake the project (the *C-E*) which is less than the project's expected worth. The difference between the two figures is seen by the individual as the compensation he requires to bear the risk involved with the project. Thus when our individual indicated that £2,000 was the maximum he would pay to undertake a project with an expected value of +£3,600,

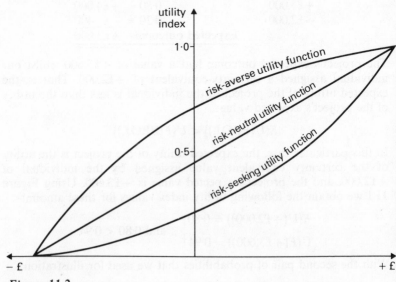

Figure 11.2

the difference of £1,600 is the expected compensation required because of the risk involved.

Similarly, if an individual assigns certainty-equivalents equal to the project's expected value, he is termed 'risk-neutral' in that he requires no compensation for undertaking a risky project. If the assigned certainty-equivalents are greater than the project's expected value, the investor is termed a 'risk-seeker' because he is willing to pay a premium in order to be allowed to bear a risk. Figure 11.2 illustrates the possible utility functions for these three categories of attitude to risk. It follows that the greater the aversion or attraction to risk, the more pronounced will be the concavity and convexity respectively of the utility functions, and vice versa.

Individual choice amongst risky investments Once an individual's utility function has been constructed in this way, it can be used to indicate how he would choose between alternative risky projects, on the assumption that he will attempt to achieve the greatest possible amount of utility, i.e., the individual selects whichever alternative is expected to produce the highest utility index value.

Suppose our individual, whose utility function is displayed in Figure 11.1, wishes to decide between two alternative investments: A and B. Once again we shall assume that the returns produced by both investments occur almost immediately after their required outlays so as to avoid the need for discounting. The possible net returns from these two investments and their relevant probabilities are set out in Table 11.5, together with the calculation of the utility that the individual would expect to derive from each. From this table it can be seen that although investment A has the largest expected return, the indi-

Table 11.5

Investment A Possible net return × Prob.				Investment B Possible net return × Prob.			
−£1,000	× 0·3 =	−£	300	+£ 500	× 0·2 =	+£	100
+£2,000	× 0·4 =	+£	800	+£1,500	× 0·6 =	+£	900
+£5,000	× 0·3 =	+£	1,500	+£2,500	× 0·2 =	+£	500
Expected return:		+£	2,000	Expected return:		+£	1,500

$$E[U(\text{Inv. A})] = 0 \cdot 3 \,.\, U(-£1,000) + 0 \cdot 4 \,.\, U(+£2,000) + 0 \cdot 3 \,.\, U(+£5,000)$$

$$E[U(\text{Inv. B})] = 0 \cdot 2 \,.\, U(+£500) + 0 \cdot 6 \,.\, U(+£1,500) + 0 \cdot 2 \,.\, U(+£2,500)$$

Using the utility function in Figure 11.1 to determine the utility index values:

$$E[U(\text{Inv. A})] = (0 \cdot 3 \times 0 \cdot 28) + (0 \cdot 4 \times 0 \cdot 8) + (0 \cdot 3 \times 1) = \underline{0 \cdot 704}$$

$$E[U(\text{Inv. B})] = (0 \cdot 2 \times 0 \cdot 59) + (0 \cdot 6 \times 0 \cdot 74) + (0 \cdot 2 \times 0 \cdot 85) = \underline{0 \cdot 732}$$

As $E[U(\text{Inv. B})] > E[U(\text{Inv. A})]$ the individual will select investment B in order to maximize his utility.

vidual would actually select investment B because it produces a higher level of expected utility: a utility index of 0·732 as opposed to 0·704. In other words, investment B is preferred because our risk-averse individual judges that it possesses a superior risk–expected return relationship than does investment A.

The problem with this expected-utility model of investment decision making is that its practical usefulness is virtually zero because of its elaborate procedure. To derive an accurate representation of an individual's utility function is both difficult and time-consuming. In addition, an individual's attitude to risk can be expected to change over time as his personal attitudes and circumstances change, thus necessitating a periodic re-estimation of the function. Furthermore, in terms of our normative theory of managerial financial decision making, the model presents another problem. Assuming that a company has several shareholders, the company's management would need to be aware of each individual's utility function. Even assuming that such a feat were possible, the utility functions of these individuals are likely to be different and there is no way in which they can sensibly be aggregated to assist managerial decision making. However, the expected utility model does provide a starting point for a more analytical approach to the problem of handling risk. In particular, of greatest interest is the fact that risk-averse investors generally are likely to have utility functions in the form of a quadratic equation: $U(x) = a + bx - cx^2$ as shown in Figure 11.1.

11.3 The approach to portfolio theory

Introduction Accepting the fact that the operational usefulness of the expected utility model is severely limited, we must look elsewhere for a means of measuring an investment's risk. One particularly successful approach that can be seen as having its foundations in the expected utility model is that of portfolio theory. This theory was originally developed within the context of a risk-averse individual investor concerned with combining shareholdings in different quoted companies, in order to build an investment portfolio which would maximize his level of expected return for a specified overall risk level. (Such a portfolio is termed an efficient portfolio). Initially, we shall outline its main characteristics in that context and then later turn to examine its validity in terms of managerial financial decision making.

We shall continue to avoid the problems that can arise through the discounting process by assuming that all shares/investments simply produce a single-period return. Therefore when referring to the return on an ordinary share, this term can be defined as:

$$\frac{\text{(Selling price} - \text{Purchase price)} + \text{Dividend received}}{\text{Purchase price}} = r$$

A note on notation Before going any further it is perhaps wise to specify and define some of the notation that it will be necessary to use in order to develop portfolio theory. This may be done in note form as follows:

1 As r, the single period return on an investment, is uncertain and therefore can take on a variety of values, it is termed a random variable and designated as $\tilde{r}$ (r tilde). A random variable will be assumed to take on the form of a Normal probability distribution.

2 An investment's expected or arithmetic mean return is designated as $E(\tilde{r})$ or $\bar{r}$.

3 The variance of possible returns around the expected return is designated as $\text{VAR}(\tilde{r})$ or σ_r^2 and can be defined as:

$$\text{VAR}(\tilde{r}) = E(\tilde{r}^2) - \bar{r}^2$$

4 The standard deviation of possible returns around the expected return is designated as σ_r and can be defined as:

$$\sigma_r = \sqrt{\text{VAR}(\tilde{r})}$$

Variance as a measure of risk Following on from the development of the expected utility model we can conclude that a risk-averse investor can be expected to have a utility function of the *general* form:

$$E(U(\tilde{r})) = a + b \cdot E(\tilde{r}) - c \cdot E(\tilde{r}^2)$$

That is, the utility that an individual investor expects to obtain from the return produced by a share is determined by the probability distribution of the share's possible returns and by the investor's personal attitude towards risk (which determines the values for the constants a, b and c).[17]

Given that $\text{VAR}(\tilde{r}) = E(\tilde{r}^2) - \bar{r}^2$, the general form of the investor's utility function can be rewritten as:

$$E(U(\tilde{r})) = a + b \cdot \bar{r} - c \cdot (\text{VAR}(\tilde{r}) + \bar{r}^2)$$

$$= a + b \cdot \bar{r} - c \cdot \sigma_r^2 - c \cdot \bar{r}^2$$

and from this we can see that the expected utility produced by an investment is determined by the three 'risk-attitude' constants plus two characteristics of the probability distribution of the investment's possible returns: the arithmetic mean ($\bar{r}$) and the variance (σ_r^2). Furthermore, if a share's return is known with certainty, then the variance has a value of zero; whilst if a share's actual return is uncertain the variance will have a positive value. However, because the constant multiple attached to the variance (c) will be negative for the risk-averse investor (it is this which causes the utility function to be concave to the origin), a positive variance results in a reduction in the value of the expected utility to be gained from a share. The more uncertain is the share's actual return, the greater will be the value of the variance and the less will be the share's expected utility to the risk-averse investor (however mild or extreme his degree of aversion).

This analysis allows us to draw the very important conclusion that the variance (or standard deviation) of a share's possible returns can act as a measure of its risk. However, one of two alternative conditions must also hold for this to be valid. The first is that the variance is acceptable as a measure of risk as long as the probability distribution of possible returns is symmetrical (e.g., Normal). If it is asymmetrical the distribution's mean and variance no longer provide a complete description, and a measure of distributional skew would have to be included in the analysis. Alternatively, the conclusion only holds if the utility functions of individuals do follow a quadratic form and therefore are solely determined by the expected return and variance of return variables. If utility functions are more complex, it follows that any measure of risk is also likely to be more complex.

We shall continue our analysis on the (not too unrealistic) assumption that variance of return is an adequate measure of risk. Even so, at this stage we are in a position to assist managerial decision making in two rather special cases only: on the assumption that shareholders are generally risk averse, if management have to choose between two investments with identical expected returns, they should select whichever has the smallest variance; whilst if choice is between alternatives with the same variance, the investment with the largest return should be undertaken. In both cases management will be able to select the project which will yield the greatest expected addition to their shareholders' utility levels. However, we still remain unable to determine whether the expected return on a single project will provide sufficient compensation for shareholders in terms of the risk it involves and their attitudes towards that risk. We are also not in a position to select between a pair of mutually exclusive projects, A and B, where:

$$\bar{r}_A > \bar{r}_B$$
$$\sigma_A^2 > \sigma_B^2$$

A possible solution to these two decision problems may lie in the conclusions we can derive from portfolio theory.

Some further notation At this stage it is necessary to introduce and explain some more of the notation used. An example will be found in an Appendix to this chapter, which illustrates all the computations referred to.

1 Given that $\tilde{r}$ represents a random variable of a share's period return and there are two different companies x and y, if their shares were combined the expected joint period return would be:

$$E(\tilde{r}_x + \tilde{r}_y) = E(\tilde{r}_x) + E(\tilde{r}_y)$$

2 Similarly, the variance of their joint period return would be:

$$VAR(\tilde{r}_x + \tilde{r}_y) = VAR(\tilde{r}_x) + VAR(\tilde{r}_y) + 2\ COV(\tilde{r}_x, \tilde{r}_y)$$

3 $COV(\tilde{r}_x, \tilde{r}_y)$ is the notation used for the 'covariance' which measures the degree to which the two random variables of the period return from company x and from company y move in unison. The covariance can be calculated as:

$$COV(\tilde{r}_x, \tilde{r}_y) = E(\tilde{r}_x, \tilde{r}_y) - \bar{r}_x \cdot \bar{r}_y$$

where $E(\tilde{r}_x, \tilde{r}_y)$ is found from the joint probability distribution of the two random variables. A more useful measure of the degree to which the two random variables of the period return from company x and from company y move in unison is the 'correlation coefficient', as this measure only takes on values between $+1$ and -1 and is unaffected by data magnitude. We will denote the correlation coefficient as $COR(\tilde{r}_x, \tilde{r}_y)$. It can be calculated as:

$$COR(\tilde{r}_x, \tilde{r}_y) = \frac{COV(\tilde{r}_x, \tilde{r}_y)}{\sigma_{r_x} \cdot \sigma_{r_y}}$$

Therefore the covariance can be redefined as:

$$COV(\tilde{r}_x, \tilde{r}_y) = \sigma_{r_x} \cdot \sigma_{r_y} \cdot COR(\tilde{r}_x, \tilde{r}_y)$$

Constructing a share portfolio Suppose an individual investor has a sum of money that he wishes to use to purchase ordinary shares in companies. In order to keep the calculations as simple as possible, we shall assume that he is going to buy the ordinary shares in two companies only, although we shall show later how the approach used can be expanded directly to involve shareholdings in many companies.

Let the two companies whose shares comprise the individual's investment portfolio be termed A and B. The individual uses a proportion, x, of his investment cash to buy shares in company A and $(1 - x)$ of his cash to buy shares in company B. We can then calculate the expected return $(\bar{r}_p)$ and the risk $(VAR[\tilde{r}_p])$ of the resulting investment portfolio:

$$\bar{r}_p = x \cdot \bar{r}_A + (1 - x) \cdot \bar{r}_B$$

$$VAR(\bar{r}_p) = x^2\ VAR(r_A) + (1 - x)^2\ VAR(r_B) + 2x(1 - x)\ COV(\tilde{r}_A, \tilde{r}_B)$$

This expression for the portfolio's risk can be rewritten as:

$$VAR(\tilde{r}_p)$$

$$= x^2 \cdot \sigma_{r_A}^2 + (1 - x)^2 \cdot \sigma_{r_B}^2 + 2 \cdot x \cdot (1 - x) \cdot \sigma_{r_A} \cdot \sigma_{r_B} \cdot COR(\tilde{r}_A, \tilde{r}_B)$$

In other words, the expected return from the portfolio $(\bar{r}_p)$ is simply an average of the expected returns from the two component investments $(\bar{r}_A$ and $\bar{r}_B)$, weighted by their respective importance in the overall portfolio. The risk or variance of the portfolio requires a somewhat different analysis. One way of viewing it is to say that its variance is a weighted average of the variance of the individual components (i.e. $x^2 \cdot \sigma_{r_A}^2 + (1 - x)^2 \cdot \sigma_{r_B}^2$), plus an additional factor: $2x(1 - x)\sigma_{r_A} \cdot \sigma_{r_B} \times COR(\tilde{r}_A \cdot \tilde{r}_B)$. However with portfolio risk, the weights – x and $(1 - x)$ – have been 'squared' and so, unlike the portfolio return calculation where $x + (1 - x) = 1$, with portfolio risk $x^2 + (1 - x)^2 < 1$. As a result, the portfolio variance given by the *first two* terms will be less than the weighted average variance.

It is the third term, however, which provides much of the interest in portfolio theory, and in particular the fact that the final factor in this term – the correlation coefficient – can take on any value between $+1$ and -1 (including zero).

If the correlation coefficient of the probability distribution of returns between the two companies is positive, then the whole of the final term will be positive and so add to portfolio risk. The greater the positive correlation, the greater will be the additional portfolio risk until, at the point of maximum positive correlation $(+1)$, the additional risk added by the third term results in the total portfolio risk being exactly equal to the weighted average risk. If the correlation coefficient is zero, then the whole of the third term becomes zero; whilst if the correlation coefficient is negative, the whole of the third term becomes negative and so *reduces* the portfolio risk. Obviously, the nearer the correlation coefficient comes to -1, the greater will be this reduction in portfolio risk.

Therefore we can conclude that the risk of a two-component portfolio will always be less than the weighted average risk of its two components, unless the returns of the two components are perfectly positively $(+1)$ correlated. In these latter circumstances, portfolio risk is then just a straight weighted average of the individual component risk.

An example Suppose that the ordinary shares of the two companies (A and B), with which the investor has chosen to construct his portfolio, exhibit the following characteristics:

Company A	Company B
$\bar{r}_A = 0\cdot25$	$\bar{r}_B = 0\cdot18$
$\sigma_{r_A} = 0\cdot08$	$\sigma_{r_B} = 0\cdot04$

From the foregoing analysis, we know that the expected return and risk of any portfolio made up of the shares in these two companies depends not only on the above information, but also on the proportions of the available funds invested in each company's shares (i.e., x and $(1-x)$) and the correlation coefficient of the probability distributions of the returns from each company's shares (i.e., $\text{COR}(\tilde{r}_A, \tilde{r}_B)$).

Figure 11.3 illustrates the range of possible portfolio risk and expected return that the investor could obtain by varying the proportions of his funds between the two companies, in three particular cases: when the correlation coefficient of returns has a value of $+1$, 0 and $(1-x)$) and the correlation coefficient of the probability distributions of the returns from each company's shares (i.e., $\text{COR}(\tilde{r}_A, \tilde{r}_B)$). duce an expected return of:

$$\tilde{r}_p = (0.5 \times 0.25) + (0.5 \times 0.18) = 0.215$$

The risk of this portfolio, however, varies, depending upon the value of the correlation coefficient:

x	$\text{COR}(\tilde{r}_A, \tilde{r}_B)$	$\tilde{r}_p$	σ_p
0·5	+1	0·215	0·06
0·5	0	0·215	0·04
0·5	−1	0·215	0·02

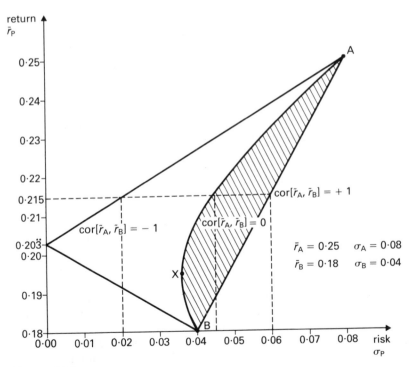

Figure 11.3

Thus portfolio risk is minimized where the two portfolio components are perfectly negative-correlated (i.e., $COR(\tilde{r}_A, \tilde{r}_B) = -1$) and maximized when the correlation coefficient is perfectly positive $(+1)$. For correlation coefficient variables between these two extremes, the portfolio risk (as measured by the standard deviation) is < 0.06 but > 0.02. However, this only applies in cases where the investor divides his money equally between the two companies. If, for instance, the returns of the two companies' shares were perfectly negative-correlated, then we can see from Figure 11.3 the range of different portfolios possible. At one extreme, there is the portfolio which consists solely in shares in company A, where $\tilde{r}_p = \tilde{r}_A = 0.25$ and $\sigma_p = \sigma_A = 0.08$, whilst at the other extreme is a portfolio which consists entirely of the ordinary shares in company B. One very interesting intermediate portfolio is the one in which one-third of the portfolio funds are invested in shares of company A, with the other two-thirds invested in the shares of company B. Such a portfolio would have an expected return[19] of $20\frac{1}{3}\%$ and zero risk.[20] The ability to reduce risk to zero in this way is a characteristic *only* of portfolios which consist of perfectly negative-correlated components. Where the correlation coefficient between portfolio components is greater than -1 (but less than $+1$), although the *reduction* of risk is possible, its total *elimination* is impossible.

In practice the ordinary shares of most companies exhibit correlation coefficients (with shares in other companies) with values greater than zero but less than $+1$, thereby limiting the degree of risk reduction possible through portfolio manipulation. The shaded area on Figure 11.3 therefore gives the likely risk–return combinations which might be possible in practice with a two-component portfolio consisting of ordinary shares in companies A and B.

It is also important to note, if we continue with the example where the two components are perfectly negatively correlated, that investors would not be interested in all of the possible portfolio combinations. In Figure 11.4, the line ACDEB can be termed the 'portfolio boundary' because it represents all possible portfolios constructed with the shares of the two companies. Point A represents the portfolio consisting solely of shares in company A, point B represents the portfolio consisting solely of shares in company B, and point D represents the portfolio where the investment is split one-third, two-thirds between companies A and B respectively and so eliminates risk. However, an investor imbued with the characteristics of rationality, consistency and risk-aversion would not be interested in any of the portfolio combinations lying along the portfolio boundary between points B and D. This is because there are always alternative portfolios available giving a higher expected return for the same level of risk. For example portfolios C and E have the same standard deviation of 3%, but whilst C gives an expected return of (approximately) 22.1%, E

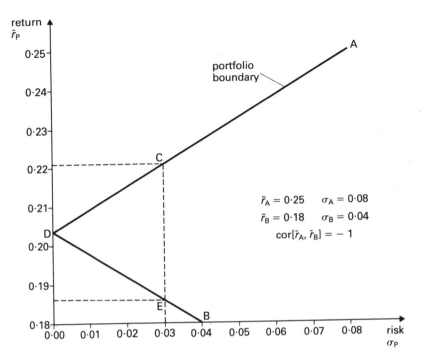

Figure 11.4

only gives an expected return of (approximately) 18·6%. Rational, risk-averse investors are always going to prefer portfolio C to E. The portfolios which lie along the boundary between points A and D are therefore termed 'efficient' in that each represents the maximum expected return for a given level of risk. Therefore, returning to Figure 11.3, along the portfolio boundary for when the correlation coefficient is zero, portfolios lying between points A and X are similarly efficient and those lying between points X and B, inefficient.

Multi-component portfolios So far, we have considered two-component portfolios only. However, the analysis can be quite easily extended to portfolios containing many components (e.g., the ordinary shares of many different companies), although the calculations become much more lengthy. The risk (measured by variance) and the expected return of a portfolio consisting of N different components can be calculated from the expressions given below, where x represents the proportion of funds invested in a particular component:

$$\bar{r}_p = \sum_{i=1}^{N} x_i \cdot \bar{r}_i$$

$$\mathrm{VAR}(\tilde{r}_p) = \sum_{i=1}^{N} \sum_{j=1}^{N} x_i \cdot x_j \cdot \sigma_{r_i} \cdot \sigma_{r_j} \cdot \mathrm{COR}(\tilde{r}_i, \tilde{r}_j)$$

It is the calculation of the portfolio variance that is particularly time-consuming because it is calculated as the sum of the weighted variance of all possible combinations of pairs of components. Table 11.6 illustrates the computations necessary for a simple three-component portfolio consisting of shares in companies A, B and C, in the respective proportions: 20%, 70%, 10%. The resulting portfolio, termed Z, has an expected return of 26·2% and a standard deviation of return of 8·04%.

Table 11.6

Investment	$\bar{r}$	σ_r	COR[$\tilde{r}, \tilde{r}$]		x
A	0·20	0·06	A, A	+1	0·20
			A, B	+0·7	
			A, C	+0·4	
B	0·30	0·10	B, A	+0·7	0·70
			B, B	+1	
			B, C	+0·8	
C	0·12	0·02	C, A	+0·4	0·10
			C, B	+0·8	
			C, C	+1	
					1·00

$$\bar{r}_{p_z} = \sum_{i=A}^{C} x_i \bar{r}_i$$

$$= (0·20 \times 0·20) + (0·70 \times 0·30) + (0·10 \times 0·12) = 0·262$$

$$\mathrm{VAR}[\tilde{r}_{p_z}] = \sum_{i=A}^{C} \sum_{j=A}^{C} x_i \cdot x_j \cdot \sigma_{r_i} \cdot \sigma_{r_j} \cdot \mathrm{COR}[\tilde{r}_i, \tilde{r}_j]$$

$$
\left.
\begin{aligned}
&= 0·20 \times 0·20 \times 0·06 \times 0·06 \times 1 && = 0·000144 \\
&\, 0·20 \times 0·70 \times 0·06 \times 0·10 \times 0·7 && = 0·000588 \\
&\, 0·20 \times 0·10 \times 0·06 \times 0·02 \times 0·4 && = 0·0000096 \\
&\, 0·70 \times 0·20 \times 0·10 \times 0·06 \times 0·7 && = 0·000588 \\
&\, 0·70 \times 0·70 \times 0·10 \times 0·10 \times 1 && = 0·0049 \\
&\, 0·70 \times 0·10 \times 0·10 \times 0·02 \times 0·8 && = 0·000112 \\
&\, 0·10 \times 0·20 \times 0·02 \times 0·06 \times 0·4 && = 0·0000096 \\
&\, 0·10 \times 0·70 \times 0·02 \times 0·10 \times 0·8 && = 0·000112 \\
&\, 0·10 \times 0·10 \times 0·02 \times 0·02 \times 1 && = 0·000004
\end{aligned}
\right\} +
$$

$$\mathrm{VAR}[\tilde{r}_{p_z}] = \underline{\underline{0·0064672}}$$

$$\sigma_{p_z} = \sqrt{\mathrm{VAR}[\tilde{r}_{p_z}]} = \sqrt{0·0064672} = 0·0804 \text{ (approx.)}$$

Therefore the portfolio (we shall term it portfolio Z), consisting of 20% of investment A, 70% of investment B and 10% of investment C has the following characteristics:

$$\text{Expected return: } \bar{r}_{p_z} = 26 \cdot 2\%$$
$$\text{Risk: } \sigma_{p_z} = 8 \cdot 04\%$$

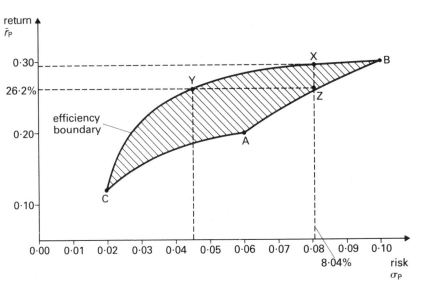

Figure 11.5

Whereas all possible portfolios that can be constructed from just two components (with a specified correlation coefficient) can be illustrated graphically as lying along a line (as in Figures 11.3 and 11.4), when dealing with multi-component portfolios, all possible combinations are represented by an area. Figure 11.5 illustrates the area of possible portfolios that may be obtained from combining the shares of companies A, B and C. Point Z represents the location of the portfolio actually constructed in Table 11.6. For the risk-averse investor however, the only portfolios of interest are those lying along the north-west boundary of the portfolio area, BXYC, the efficient boundary. These portfolios represent the greatest possible return for a given level of risk. Therefore a risk-averse investor would not be interested in holding portfolio Z: portfolio X would give a superior expected return for the same level of risk, whilst portfolio Y would give the same return for a much reduced level of risk. Indeed, all the portfolios lying along that part of the efficiency boundary between X and Y would be preferred to portfolio Z.

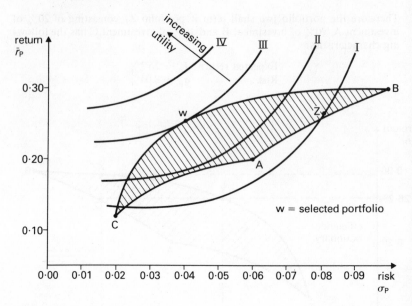

Figure 11.6

An investor faced with holding a portfolio consisting of shares in the three companies A, B and C would consider only the portfolios lying along the efficiency boundary and select the one which max- imized his utility, given his own particular attitude to risk and return. In terms of utility curves, the investor would select that portfolio which allowed him to obtain his highest possible utility curve. Figure 11.6 illustrates this situation.

Risk-free investments Up to this point, although the analysis has been useful in identifying that it is the risk–return characteristics of *combinations* of investments that are of importance, rather than the risk–return characteristics of single investments, the practical usefulness is limited. Individual investors themselves, never mind others who may be taking decisions on their behalf, are not likely to be aware of the nature of their set of utility curves. Thus in Figure 11.6, although in the circumstances given, portfolio W would be opti- mal for the investor with the set of utility curves (some of which are shown), in practice the investor can do little more than follow his own rather poorly-formed 'judgement' as to the combination of the three investments which will produce the 'best' risk–return combination. This example used only shares in three companies. In the real-world with the vast number of different investment opportunities available, he is unlikely to even be aware of the location of the efficiency boundary, let alone the optimal portfolio along that boundary.

However, a move towards greater practical usefulness can be made with the introduction of risk-free investments. The term risk-free is, to some extent, a misnomer. What is really meant is an investment whose *cash* return (not its real return) is known for certain.[21] Government bonds are usually credited with being such risk-free or default-free investments.

Let us start by examining the characteristics of a two-component

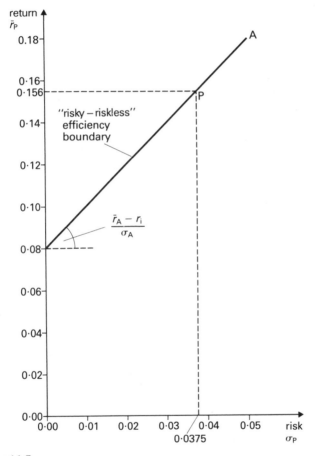

Figure 11.7

portfolio where one component is a risk-free investment (e.g., government bonds) and the other is a risky investment (e.g., the ordinary shares of a company). The risk-free return will be designated as r_i and because this return is certain, its risk – measured by either the standard deviation (σ_i) or the variance (σ_i^2) – is zero. The resulting portfolio has the following characteristics:

$$\bar{r}_p = x \cdot \bar{r}_A + (1 - x) \cdot r_i$$

$$\text{VAR}(r_p) = x^2\sigma_A^2 + (1 - x)^2\sigma_i^2 + 2x(1 - x)\text{COR}(\tilde{r}_A, \tilde{r}_i)$$

As the risk-free investment has a zero variance and standard deviation, the expression for portfolio risk reduces to:

$$\text{VAR}(r_p) = x^2 \cdot \sigma_A^2 \equiv \sigma_p = \sqrt{x^2 \cdot \sigma_A^2} = x \cdot \sigma_A$$

Figure 11.7 illustrates the range of portfolio risks and returns that are possible from combining a risky investment A with an expected return of 18% and a standard deviation of 5%, with a risk-free investment producing a certain 8% return. The efficiency boundary is linear because, as the expression above for portfolio risk shows, when combining a riskless and a risky investment, portfolio risk is a simple weighted average of the risk of the components. To identify this particular type of boundary, we will term it the 'risky–riskless' boundary. Portfolio P on this boundary consists of 75% of risky investment A and 25% of the risk-free investment, producing the following characteristics:

$$\bar{r}_p = (0.75 \cdot 0.18) + (0.25 \cdot 0.08) = \underline{\underline{0.155}}$$

$$\sigma_p = (0.75 \cdot 0.05) = \underline{\underline{0.0375}}$$

The slope of the efficiency boundary is particularly interesting, it is calculated as: $(\bar{r}_A - r_i)/\sigma_A$ and gives the additional amount of expected return produced by the portfolio for each unit increase in risk. Therefore in this example, every 1% increase in portfolio risk (σ_p) produces an extra $(0.18 - 0.08)/0.05 = 2.0$ or 2% of expected return. For example, if

$$\sigma_p = (x \cdot 0.05) = \underline{\underline{0.0475}}$$

$$x = \frac{0.0475}{0.05} = 0.95$$

and $$\bar{r}_p = (0.95 \cdot 0.18) + (0.05 \cdot 0.08) = \underline{\underline{0.175}}$$

The investment consists of taking on 4.75 'units' of risk $(\sigma_p = 0.0475)$ and so should provide a return of $4.75 \times 2\% = 9.5\%$ *over* the risk-free return of 8%: $8\% + 9.5\% = 17.5\%$.

Extending this approach further, suppose that an investor is faced with a choice amongst many alternative risky investments which result in the efficiency boundary AB shown in Figure 11.8. Portfolios lying along this line between the points A and B are said to be

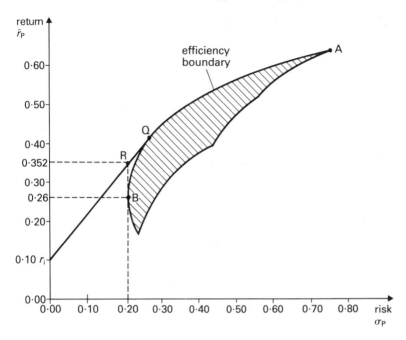

Figure 11.8

efficient because they produce the greatest expected return for each given level of risk. If the possiblity of undertaking a risk-free investment is now introduced, we can specify that the most advantageous portfolio of risky investments to combine with the risk-free investment would be that which gives the 'risky–riskless' boundary its steepest possible slope – in other words, the risky portfolio which results in the greatest increase in expected return per unit increase in risk. This portfolio is found at the point of tangency of a line from the risk-free rate of return to the risky portfolio efficiency boundary: Portfolio Q in Figure 11.8. From this figure we can see that with the introduction of a risk-free investment, portfolios lying along the lower part of the original efficiency boundary, between points Q and B, are no longer efficient, because a greater return for the same level of risk can be obtained by investors combining the portfolio of risky investment, Q, with the risk-free investment. For example, efficient portfolio B which produced an expected return of 20% with a standard deviation of 21% will be superseded by a combination of portfolio Q and the risk-free investment which produces an approximate expected return of 35·2% for an unchanged level of risk, designated portfolio R on Figure 11.8:

$$\bar{r}_B = \underline{\underline{0.26}} \qquad \bar{r}_Q = 0.415 \qquad r_i = 0.10$$

$$\sigma_B = \underline{\underline{0.21}} \qquad \sigma_Q = 0.265 \qquad \sigma_i = 0$$

80% of funds invested in Q,
20% of funds invested in risk-free bonds,
then:

$$\bar{r}_R = (0.80 \,.\, 0.415) + (0.20 \,.\, 0.10) = \underline{\underline{0.352}}$$

$$\sigma_R = 0.80 \,.\, 0.265 = \underline{\underline{0.21}}$$

The possibility of borrowing In the previous section we have seen how the shape of the efficiency boundary is modified and extended by the introduction of a risk-free investment. A complementary extension and modification can also be achieved by the introduction of the possibility that the investor can add to his investment funds by borrowing.

Given that the individual can borrow an unlimited amount (save that it must be within his ability to repay) at an interest rate of r_r and assuming that the loan and interest payments are certain, then Figure 11.9 illustrates the modification and extension possible to the original boundary of efficient investment portfolios: the line BD. The new efficiency boundary now becomes ABD where D extends without limit (unlimited borrowing capacity). Thus portfolios lying along the curve BC are no longer efficient: for example portfolio S is superseded by all portfolios lying to the north-west of S along BD, as each of these portfolios gives a higher expected return and/or a lower level of risk than does portfolio S.

Borrowing and lending possibilities Figure 11.10 combines the possibilities of borrowing money at an interest rate of r_r and lending money at the risk-free interest rate of r_i (i.e., buying Government bonds). The resulting efficiency boundary is given by the line ABCD. As this stands, we have not advanced the practicality of portfolio theory because we still have to rely on knowledge of the investor's utility curves in order to determine what portfolio of risky assets will be held. For example, Figure 11.10 shows the points of tangency between the utility curves and the efficiency boundary for three different investors: I, II and III.

Investor I will hold portfolio p_I, which produces an expected return and standard deviation of (reading from Figure 11.10) 12·8% and 0·93% respectively. This portfolio is achieved by investing two-thirds of his funds in portfolio B (which has the characteristics of

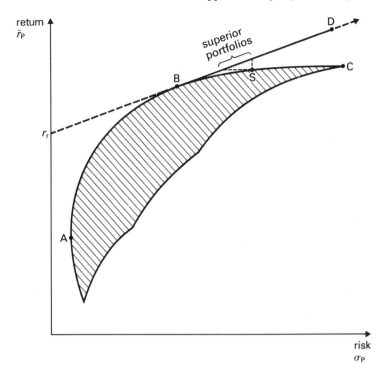

Figure 11.9

$\bar{r}_B = 0.172$, $\sigma_B = 0.014$) and one-third of his funds in risk-free bonds $(r_i = 0.04, \sigma_i = 0)$. This can be calculated as follows:

$$\begin{array}{l} \bar{r}_B = 0.172 \\ \sigma_B = 0.014 \\ r_i = 0.04 \\ \sigma_i = 0 \end{array} \left. \begin{array}{l} \\ \\ \end{array} \right\} \begin{array}{l} \text{From} \\ \text{Fig. 10} \end{array} \qquad \begin{array}{l} \bar{r}_{pI} = (0.6\dot{6} \times 0.172) + ((1 - 0.6\dot{6}) \times 0.04) \\ = \underline{\underline{0.128}} \\ \sigma_{pI} = \overline{0.6\dot{6} \times 0.014} = \underline{\underline{0.0093}} \\ \therefore \quad \bar{r}_{pI} = 12.8\% \quad \sigma_{pI} = 0.93\% \end{array}$$

Investor II will hold portfolio p_{II} which simply consists of risky investments and which has the characteristics of (reading from Figure 11.10) an expected return of 21.6% and a standard deviation of 2.2%. This investor will neither lend money at the risk-free rate of 4%, nor borrow money at the borrowing rate of 18%.

Investor III will hold portfolio p_{III} which has an expected return of 28.4% and a standard deviation of (approximately) 5.4%. This portfolio will be achieved by borrowing £0.73 at 18% interest, for every £1 of his own funds. The total amount (own funds plus borrowings) is

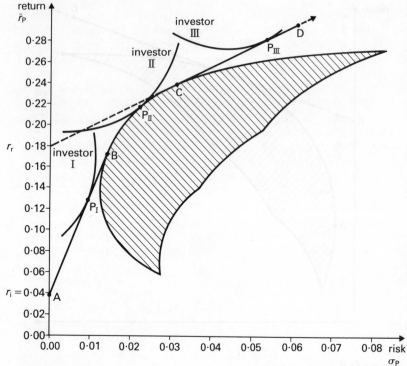

Figure 11.10

then invested in portfolio C. The characteristics of the resulting portfolio p_{III} can be calculated as:

$$
\begin{aligned}
\bar{r}_C &= 0.24 \\
\sigma_C &= 0.031 \\
r_r &= 0.18 \\
\sigma_r &= 0
\end{aligned}
\left.\begin{aligned}
\\
\text{From} \\
\text{Fig. 10}
\end{aligned}\right\}
\begin{aligned}
\bar{r}_{pIII} &= (1.73 \times 0.24) + ((1 - 1.73) \times 0.18) \\
&= 0.416 - 0.132 = 0.284 \\
\sigma_{pIII} &= 1.73 \times 0.031 = 0.0537 \\
\bar{r}_{pIII} &= 28.4\% \quad \sigma_{pIII} = 5.4\% \text{ (approx.)}
\end{aligned}
$$

The separation theorem From the above example and as can be seen
from Figure 11.10, the only efficient portfolios of risky investments lie
along that part of the total efficiency boundary represented by BC.
Investor I held a portfolio which partially consisted of efficient portfolio B; Investor III held a portfolio which consisted of portfolio C
plus borrowings; whilst Investor II held an intermediate portfolio of
risky investments: portfolio p_{II}. Therefore given a risk-free lending
rate of 4%, a borrowing rate of 18% and a range of risky investments
which can be combined to produce any risk–return combination
given by the shaded area of Figure 11.10, risk-averse individuals are

going to be interested only in those combinations of risky investments which lie along the curve BC. Furthermore, the smaller the gap between the borrowing (r_r) and lending (r_i) rates, the smaller will be the segment of efficient risky investment portfolios of interest to the risk-averse investor.

The extreme case is where an individual can lend *and* borrow at the risk-free interest rate. Figure 11.11 illustrates the revised efficiency boundary, now called the Capital Market Line (CML): AMC. This figure shows that if an investor wishes to hold any portfolio between points A and M (e.g. portfolio X) this can be achieved by placing part of the total available funds in the risk-free investment and part in the portfolio of risky investments, portfolio M. Similarly, if an investor wishes to construct a portfolio lying between points M and C on the efficiency boundary (e.g. portfolio Y), this is achieved by borrowing additional funds (in a proportion to the investor's own funds which is determined by the location of his desired portfolio along MC) and investing both his own funds plus the borrowed funds in the portfolio of risky investments: portfolio M. Finally, there is the third case where investing the whole of his own funds only in portfolio M produces the desired risk and return.

This extreme case, where investors can both lend and borrow at the risk-free interest rate, is important because of the fact that, in such circumstances, *all* risk-averse investors will be interested in only *one* portfolio of risky investments: portfolio M. They will either put all their funds into this portfolio, or only part of their funds and lend the rest at the risk-free rate, or borrow additional funds and put both their own funds and the borrowed funds into portfolio M. Therefore, for the first time we should be able to identify the portfolio of risky investment that an investor would wish to hold, *without any knowledge of his personal attitude to risk* (except that he is generally risk-averse). This is the so-called Separation Theorem, which has a significance similar to the Separation Theorem of the two-period investment–consumption ·decision model we developed in earlier chapters: investment decisions can be made on behalf of the investor without the need for any knowledge about the specific characteristics of his utility curves.

The market portfolio If all investors display the characteristics we ascribed earlier to a single investor – general risk-aversion, rationality and consistency – then under the assumptions listed below, *all* investors will wish to invest some or all of their funds in portfolio M of Figure 11.11. Furthermore, this will be the *only* combination or portfolio of risky investments, termed the Market Portfolio, that will be of interest to investors. It follows, therefore, that all the different risky investments available to investors must have a market price (and, therefore, an expected return and associated risk) which makes them

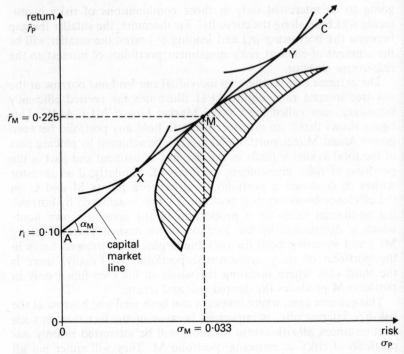

Figure 11.11

acceptable for inclusion within the market portfolio; i.e., all risky investment must be included in the market portfolio because the market portfolio is the only risky investment investors are willing to hold. This conclusion concerning the market prices of risky investments, which arises out of portfolio theory, is termed Capital Market Theory.

Most of the assumptions necessary for these conclusions will be familiar to the reader because they were used earlier in our development of a theory of financial management decision making:

1 All investors can lend and borrow unlimited amounts of cash at the risk-free interest rate.

2 No taxation.

3 No transaction costs.

4 All investors have the same knowledge and expectations about the future and have access to the complete range of investment opportunities.

5 All investors have the same decision-making time horizon, i.e., the expected return on investments arises from expectation over the same period.

The price of risk The slope (α_m) of the Capital Market Line is of interest. It can be calculated as: $(\bar{r}_m - r_i)/\sigma_m = \alpha_m$, where $\bar{r}_m$ and σ_m represent the expected return and the standard deviation of the market portfolio[22] and r_i represents the risk-free rate of return. The slope of the CML indicates the risk–return relationship of the whole investment market: in other words it indicates the reward provided to investors for accepting risk. Using the data of Figure 11.11 as an example, where:

$$\bar{r}_m = 0\cdot225 \qquad \alpha_m = \frac{0\cdot225 - 0\cdot10}{0\cdot033} = \underline{\underline{3\cdot78}}$$
$$r_i = 0\cdot10$$
$$\sigma_m = 0\cdot033$$

Therefore, for every 1% of risk (i.e., standard deviation) held, the market yields an expected return 3·78% above the risk-free return. If an investor were willing to hold risk equivalent to a standard deviation of 2% he would be able to construct a portfolio yielding an expected return of:

$$0\cdot10 + (2 \times 0\cdot0378) = \underline{\underline{0\cdot1758}}$$

In general terms the expected return from an efficient portfolio J which consists of a holding of the market portfolio plus either the lending or borrowing of funds at the risk-free rate can be defined as:

$$\bar{r}_J = r_i + \alpha_m \cdot \sigma_J, \qquad \text{where } \alpha_m = \frac{\bar{r}_m - r_i}{\sigma_m}$$

which is the expression for the Capital Market Line. An alternative way of explaining the meaning of this expression is that the expected return on an efficient portfolio (efficient in the sense of lying on the CML) is equal to the risk-free return (r_i) plus a premium for risk: $\alpha_m \sigma_J$. This premium reflects the portfolio's own risk (σ_J), together with the market's risk attitude or risk–return trade-off (α_m).

Summary This very brief analysis of portfolio theory can be summarized as follows. Investors can reduce the risk of their investment portfolios by a judicious combining of risky investments, having regard not only to their risks and expected returns but also to the covariances or correlation coefficients of their expected returns to those of other risky investments. Risk can be minimized for a given level of expected return from a portfolio of risky investments by the selection of a portfolio lying along the so-called efficiency boundary.

With the introduction of the ability both to lend and to borrow at the risk-free rate of interest, the range of efficient portfolios of risky investments of interest to the investor is reduced to just one: the market portfolio. As all the risky investments in a market must be held by someone, it follows from the fact that investors will only be interested in holding the market portfolio, that the market portfolio must contain *all* risky investments. Therefore, in a perfect market for risky investments, the individual market prices must adjust so that the expected return and risk characteristics of individual investments are acceptable for inclusion within the market portfolio.

Each investor will place a proportion of his funds in the market portfolio,[23] the size of the proportion being determined by his set of utility curves and their point of tangency with the Capital Market Line. Investors with a high degree of risk-aversion are likely to place only a small proportion of their funds in the market portfolio, with the balance invested in risk-free Government bonds. Conversely, an investor with a low degree of risk-aversion is likely to place all of his own funds in the market portfolio and borrow additional funds (at the risk-free rate of interest) and place these in the market portfolio as well.

11.4 The capital asset pricing model

Introduction Throughout this book, we have taken as the objective for financial decision making, the maximization of shareholder wealth, which has translated into the maximization of the market price of the ordinary share capital. In this chapter we will develop a model of share price behaviour which may be superior to the dividend valuation model, because it explicitly allows for the risk attached to an ordinary share as well as the future flow of benefits it is expected to generate.

The model is called the Capital Asset Pricing Model, and it arises directly out of the ideas and conclusions of portfolio theory. However, it also involves the many unrealistic assumptions of portfolio theory. Nevertheless, the model is useful in that it provides a number of significant insights into the major factors of share price determination, and so is of direct interest to decision makers within companies.

Derivation of the security market line The Capital Market Line function provides an expression for the return that can be expected (assuming market equilibrium) from an 'efficient' investment, i.e., an investment in the market portfolio, plus either lending or borrowing at the risk-free rate of return. It can also be used to derive an expression for the expected return from an *inefficient* investment, such as a risky portfolio other than the market portfolio or an investment in the ordinary shares of a single company.

One of the simplest ways of deriving an expression for the expected return on an inefficient investment is to examine the characteristics of a two-component (inefficient) portfolio consisting partly of shares in company Y and partly of the market portfolio. The risk and expected return characteristics of the resulting portfolio, p*, are as follows:

$$\bar{r}_{p*} = x \cdot \bar{r}_y + (1 - x)\bar{r}_m$$

$$\sigma_{p*}^2 = x^2 \cdot \sigma_y^2 + (1 - x)^2 \cdot \sigma_m^2 + 2x(1 - x) \cdot \text{COV}[\tilde{r}_y, \tilde{r}_m]$$

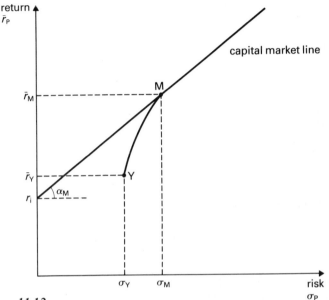

Figure 11.12

Figure 11.12 illustrates the range of possible risk–return combinations, YM, for portfolio p* (assuming a modest positive correlation coefficient between the return from investing in shares of company Y and the return from the market portfolio).

By the use of calculus, the slope of the line YM at point M can be found, and from this can be derived a general expression for the expected return from an inefficient investment in an equilibrium market:

$$\bar{r}_{p*} = x \cdot \bar{r}_y + (1 - x)\bar{r}_m$$

$$\frac{\partial \bar{r}_{p*}}{\partial x} = \bar{r}_y - \bar{r}_m \tag{1}$$

$$\sigma_{p*}^2 = x^2 \cdot \sigma_y^2 + (1 - x)^2 \cdot \sigma_m^2 + 2x(1 - x) \cdot \text{COV}[\tilde{r}_y, \tilde{r}_m]$$

$$\sigma_{p*} = \sqrt{x^2 \cdot \sigma_y^2 + (1 - x)^2 \cdot \sigma_m^2 + 2x(1 - x) \cdot \text{COV}[\tilde{r}_y, \tilde{r}_m]}$$

$$\frac{\partial \sigma_{p*}}{\partial x} = \frac{x \cdot \sigma_y^2 + x \cdot \sigma_m^2 - 2x \, \text{COV}[\tilde{r}_y, \tilde{r}_m] + \text{COV}[\tilde{r}_y, \tilde{r}_m] - \sigma_m^2}{\sigma_{p*}} \tag{2}$$

Expressions (1) and (2) are of the marginal expected return and marginal risk, respectively. At point M on the line YM, x (the proportion of investment funds placed in the shares of company Y) equals zero and therefore $\sigma_{p*} = \sigma_m$. As a result expression (2) reduces to:

$$\frac{\partial \sigma_{p*}}{\partial x} = \frac{\text{COV}[\tilde{r}_y, \tilde{r}_m] - \sigma_m^2}{\sigma_m} \tag{3}$$

Dividing expression (1) by expression (3):

$$\frac{\partial \bar{r}_{p*}}{\partial x} \cdot \frac{\partial x}{\partial \sigma_{p*}} = \frac{\sigma_m(\bar{r}_y - \bar{r}_m)}{\text{COV}[\tilde{r}_y, \tilde{r}_m] - \sigma_m^2} \tag{4}$$

This expression (4) provides the slope $(\partial \bar{r}_{p*}/\partial \sigma_{p*})$ of the line YM at point M. However, at this point the slope of YM must also equal the slope of the CML, i.e.,

$$\frac{\sigma_m(\bar{r}_y - \bar{r}_m)}{\text{COV}[\tilde{r}_y, \tilde{r}_m] - \sigma_{m2}} = \frac{\bar{r}_m - r_i}{\sigma_m} \tag{5}$$

Rearranging, an expression can be found for $\bar{r}_y$:

$$\bar{r}_y = r_i + \left\{ \frac{\bar{r}_m - r_i}{\sigma_{m2}} \right\} \cdot \text{COV}[\tilde{r}_y, \tilde{r}_m] \tag{6}$$

This expression gives the return that can be expected from an inefficient investment (shares in company Y) in an equilibrium market. It is a straight-line function of three variables: the risk-free rate of return, the market's risk–return trade-off, and the covariance between the inefficient investment's return and the market's return. In other words, the expected return from a single risky investment, Y, is equal to the risk-free return (r_i) plus a premium for risk:

$$\left\{ \frac{\bar{r}_m - r_i}{\sigma_{m2}} \right\} \cdot \text{COV}[\tilde{r}_y, \tilde{r}_m].$$

Function 6 is termed the Security Market Line (SML).

Systematic and unsystematic risk The Security Market Line function can be rearranged to give the Capital Asset Pricing Model (CAPM). We have defined earlier the slope of the CML (α_m) as $(\bar{r}_m - r_i)/\sigma_m$ and interpreted it as expressing the risk–return relationship of the market or as 'the market price of risk'. Using this expression, the required return on single risky investment can be given as:

$$\bar{r}_y = r_i + \frac{\alpha_m}{\sigma_m} \cdot \text{COV}[\tilde{r}_y, \tilde{r}_m] = r_i + \frac{\alpha_m}{\sigma_m} \cdot \sigma_y \cdot \sigma_m \cdot \text{COR}[\tilde{r}_y, \tilde{r}_m]$$

$$= r_i + (\alpha_m \cdot \sigma_y \cdot \text{COR}[\tilde{r}_y, \tilde{r}_m])$$

This expression is of considerable interest and provides us with the main conclusion of the CAPM. The expected return on a single risky investment $(\bar{r}_y)$ depends upon the risk-free return, plus a premium for the risk involved. This premium is composed of three elements: the market price of risk, the individual investment's own risk (i.e., the standard deviation of its expected return), and the correlation of returns between the individual investment and the investment market as a whole.

If we accept that the risk-free return (r_i) and the market price of risk (α_m) are given, then the size of the risk premium attached to a risky investment can be seen to depend not only upon the investment's own risk (σ_y) but also on how this risk is related to the general investment market, i.e. $\sigma_y \cdot COR[\tilde{r}_y, \tilde{r}_m]$. An example, such as shown in Table 11.7, will help to illustrate the importance of this point.

From Table 11.7 it can be seen that where the correlation coefficient is positive, the risk premium is also positive, and so the expected return on the risky investment is above the risk-free return. This is what we would expect but, where the correlation coefficient is zero, so too is the risk premium, and thus the risky investment's expected return is just equal to the risk-free return; and apparently more puzzling still is the case where the correlation coefficient is negative, which results in the expected return on the risky investment

Table 11.7

$$\text{Given:} \begin{cases} r_i = 0.06 \\ \bar{r}_m = 0.14 \\ \sigma_m = 0.04 \\ \sigma_y = 0.025 \end{cases} \qquad \alpha_m = \frac{0.14 - 0.06}{0.04} = 2$$

We can examine what would be the required or expected return on investment Y, for a whole range of different correlation coefficients between the returns from investment Y and the returns from the market:

$$
\begin{array}{llll}
r_i & + (\alpha_m \cdot \sigma_y & \cdot COR[\tilde{r}_y, \tilde{r}_m]) = \bar{r}_y \\
0.06 + (2 & .\ 0.025\ . & -1) & = 0.01 \\
0.06 + (2 & .\ 0.025\ . & -0.5) & = 0.035 \\
0.06 + (2 & .\ 0.025\ . & 0) & = 0.06 \\
0.06 + (2 & .\ 0.025\ . & +0.5) & = 0.085 \\
0.06 + (2 & .\ 0.025\ . & +1) & = 0.11 \\
\end{array}
$$

being *below* the return on a risk-free investment. This last result appears to go against all that we have discussed previously about the relationship between risk and return: because investors are assumed to be generally risk-averse, the greater the risk of an investment, the greater will be its expected return. However, this result is in fact perfectly consistent with our assumed relationship between risk and return, when it is placed within the context of portfolio theory.

If risky investment Y had a correlation coefficient with the return on the market of (say) -0.5, then we know that if it were to be included in the market portfolio, its effect would be to reduce the overall risk of that portfolio. Consequently, such a risky investment would be in great demand and only a low return would be expected from it (3.5% in the example used) because of its ability to help reduce overall risk.[24] Hence, we have the important conclusion that what is of interest to an investor is not only an investment's risk, but also the nature and degree of its association with the return on the market.

An alternative way of expressing this conclusion is to say that the total risk of an individual investment (measured by the standard deviation of its return) can be split into two separate components. One of these components is of little interest however, because it can be eliminated through diversification (i.e., it can be eliminated by holding the investment as part of an efficient portfolio). The other component is of interest, because it cannot be eliminated and therefore affects the overall risk of the portfolio of which it is a part. For example, suppose a particular investment had a standard deviation of return of 8% and its correlation coefficient with the market was $+0.6$. The investment's risk can then be split up as follows (using the CAPM):

Risk type
Systematic: $0.08 \times (+0.6)$ $= 0.048$
Unsystematic: $0.08 \times (1 - 0.6) = 0.032+$
                                  Total risk $= \overline{0.08}$

That is, of the total risk of 8%, 3.2% can be eliminated through efficient diversification, but 4.8% cannot be so eliminated and therefore remains to affect the overall risk of the portfolio in which the investment is included. The risk component which can be eliminated is called 'Unsystematic Risk', whilst the component that remains is termed 'Systematic Risk'. Given that the required return on a risky investment is given by the risk-free return plus a premium for risk, this premium is determined not on the overall risk of the investment but only on its systematic risk.

The β measure Expressing the CAPM as:

$$\bar{r}_y = r_i + \frac{\bar{r}_m - r_i}{\sigma_m^2} \cdot \text{COV}[\tilde{r}_y, \tilde{r}_m]$$

and letting $$\beta_y = \frac{\text{COV}[\tilde{r}_y, \tilde{r}_m]}{\sigma_m^2}$$

then the CAPM can be rewritten in simplified (and most commonly expressed) form as: $\bar{r}_y = r_i + (\bar{r}_m - r_i)\beta_y$, with the risky investment's β value indicating its degree of responsiveness to changes in the return on the market portfolio. For example, if the expected return on the market portfolio rises or falls by (say) 10%, then:

$\bar{r}_y$ will rise or fall by $> 10\%$ if $\beta_y > 1$
$\bar{r}_y$ will rise or fall by $< 10\%$ if $\beta_y < 1$
$\bar{r}_y$ will rise or fall by $\quad 10\%$ if $\beta_y = 1$

The significance of a share's β value is clear as far as stock market investment tactics are concerned: if the stock market in general (i.e., $\bar{r}_m$) is expected to rise, it is worth buying shares with high β values because they can be expected to rise faster than the market. Conversely, if the market is expected to fall, then shares with low β values are more attractive because they can be expected to fall less than the market generally.

The measurement of β Ideally, the β value should reflect expectations about the *future* responsiveness of a share's return to changes in the return on the market. An acceptable surrogate may perhaps be found from a regression line plotted through historical data, in circumstances where it is reasonable to assume that the past relationship

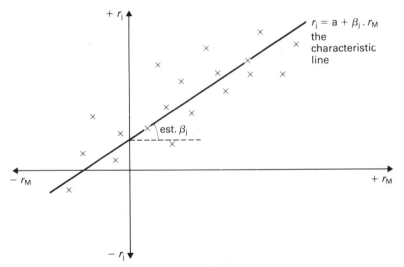

Figure 11.13

between a share's return and the market's return will hold good in the future. In such circumstances, the slope of the regression line will serve as the estimate of the share's β value. Figure 11.13 illustrates such an approach. This regression line is often termed the Characteristic Line.

The significance of portfolio theory for the investment decision As far as our theory of financial decision making is concerned and in particular the investment decision, portfolio theory has a number of significant conclusions. On the basis that the various supportive assumptions behind portfolio theory hold (these were detailed earlier, but prime amongst them is the existence of a perfect capital market), we can conclude that there is no particular merit in a company concerning itself with its overall risk level and whether it is changing to become more or less risky. Shareholders are able to adjust their individual portfolios to take account of changed risk much more easily than can the company management, who can only manipulate the company's risk level through project selection with this aim in mind. As a result, we can conclude that each project should be evaluated in terms of its expected return and its *own* systematic risk – whether or not the company's existing selection of projects combines with the new project in such a way as to eliminate all of that project's unsystematic risk. The problem as far as the practical application of this conclusion is concerned is that the project's β value has to be based on estimates of the future which are likely to be highly subjective.

However, this theoretical conclusion does help to illuminate a failing of the weighted average cost of capital approach to the discount rate for investment appraisal. The WACC is a single-figure discount rate applicable to appraising *all* projects, on the proviso that they are marginal and do not affect the overall risk of the company. Using instead the discount rate supplied by the CAPM (and therefore using the project's β value), this rate varies from project to project, depending on the systematic risk of each investment proposal. Thus situations are likely to occur where a project is unacceptable as far as the WACC approach is concerned (i.e. it has a negative NPV when discounted by K_o), but when computing its required return in relation to its systematic risk, the project in fact achieves an acceptable level of return. Alternatively, it would be just as possible for a project to be acceptable as far as the WACC criterion was concerned, but to fail to produce a sufficiently high return when its systematic risk was taken explicitly into account.

Under the assumptions of portfolio theory, individual investor portfolio diversification and corporate diversification are perfect substitutes. When we move away from the perfect world of the theory, however, we may well find that the company should pay greater attention to its overall risk than portfolio theory concludes. In such circumstances, although they are not directly applicable in pure form, the company management may well find significance in the general concepts of portfolio theory in that they may wish to view the collection of possible investment projects undertaken by the firm as a portfolio. Thus they should aim to combine these investment possibilities in such a way as to locate the firm on its own 'efficiency boundary'. In other words, they should ensure that, for the overall risk level of the company, they would be generating the best possible return. Shareholders would then simply have to decide whether the risk–return combination produced by the company matched their own personal requirements. In such circumstances the company could appraise projects on the basis of an acceptable rate of return – derived from the CAPM – which is acceptable relative to the risk of the project which cannot be diversified away by the company's existing cash flows, i.e., the project's systematic risk is not measured in the absolute terms of a perfect world, but in terms of the risk remaining once the project is contained within the company's portfolio of projects.

One substantial problem with using portfolio theory and the ideas of the CAPM in even this very rough-and-ready way is that the analysis is essentially a single-period analysis, whilst investment appraisal normally will require a multi-period analysis. However, one possible way around the problem would be to utilize the idea of the weighted average cost of capital, but to use the CAPM (rather than the dividend valuation model and the interest valuation model) to estimate the cost (or expected return) on debt and equity capital, and then to combine these into a weighted average cost of capital. This would require β values for both the debt and the equity capital of the company, which could be obtained by performing regression analysis on the appropriate historical data.

In conclusion We can say in conclusion that when risk is explicitly involved within our theory of financial decision making, perhaps more questions are posed than answered. However, it is likely that the analysis is taking the theory in the right direction for a more complete solution to be found in the future.

Appendix .

Given the following information:

$\tilde{r}_x$	Prob.	$\tilde{r}_y$	Prob.	
0·10	0·20	0·05	0·10	
0·20	0·60	0·10	0·20	Individual
0·30	0·20	0·15	0·40	probability
		0·20	0·20	distributions
		0·25	0·10	

Joint Probability Distribution

$\tilde{r}_x$

	0·05	0·10	0·15	0·20	0·25
0·10	0·05	0·05	0·03	0·02	0·05
0·20	0·02	0·10	0·30	0·15	0·03
0·30	0·03	0·05	0·07	0·03	0·02

$\tilde{r}_y$

$\tilde{r}_x$ × Prob.	$\tilde{r}_x^2$ × Prob.
$0.10 \times 0.20 = 0.02$	$0.01 \times 0.20 = 0.002$
$0.20 \times 0.60 = 0.12$	$0.04 \times 0.60 = 0.024$
$0.30 \times 0.20 = \underline{0.06}$	$0.09 \times 0.20 = \underline{0.018}$
$E[\tilde{r}_x] = \underline{\underline{0.20}}$	$E[\tilde{r}_x^2] = \underline{\underline{0.044}}$

$$E[\tilde{r}_x] = \bar{r}_x = \mathbf{0.20} \qquad VAR[\tilde{r}_x] = E[\tilde{r}_x^2] - \bar{r}_x^2 = 0.044 - 0.2^2 = \mathbf{0.004}$$

$\tilde{r}_y$ × Prob.	$\tilde{r}_y^2$ × Prob.
$0.05 \times 0.10 = 0.005$	$0.0025 \times 0.10 = 0.00025$
$0.10 \times 0.20 = 0.020$	$0.0100 \times 0.20 = 0.00200$
$0.15 \times 0.40 = 0.060$	$0.0225 \times 0.40 = 0.00900$
$0.20 \times 0.20 = 0.040$	$0.0400 \times 0.20 = 0.00800$
$0.25 \times 0.10 = 0.025$	$0.0625 \times 0.10 = 0.00625$
$E[\tilde{r}_y] = \underline{\underline{0.150}}$	$E[\tilde{r}_y^2] = \underline{\underline{0.0255}}$

$$E[\tilde{r}_y] = \bar{r}_y = \mathbf{0.15} \qquad VAR[\tilde{r}_y] = E[\tilde{r}_y^2] - \bar{r}_y^2 = 0.0255 - 0.15^2 = \mathbf{0.003}$$

$$E[\tilde{r}_x + \tilde{r}_y] = E[\tilde{r}_x] + E[\tilde{r}_y] = 0.20 + 0.15 = \mathbf{0.35}$$

$$VAR[\tilde{r}_x + \tilde{r}_y] = VAR[\tilde{r}_x] + VAR[\tilde{r}_y] + 2\,COV[\tilde{r}_x, \tilde{r}_y]$$

$$= 0.004 + 0.003 + 2\,COV[\tilde{r}_x, \tilde{r}_y]$$

$$COV[\tilde{r}_x, \tilde{r}_y] = E[\tilde{r}_x, \tilde{r}_y] - \bar{r}_x \cdot \bar{r}_y$$

$$\bar{r}_x \cdot \bar{r}_y = 0.20 \times 0.15 = \mathbf{0.03}$$

$E[\tilde{r}_x, \tilde{r}_y] = \tilde{r}_x$ × $\tilde{r}_y$ × Prob. $\tilde{r}_x\tilde{r}_y$	
$0.10 \times 0.05 \times 0.05$	$= 0.00025$
$0.10 \times 0.10 \times 0.05$	$= 0.00050$
$0.10 \times 0.15 \times 0.03$	$= 0.00045$
$0.10 \times 0.20 \times 0.02$	$= 0.00040$
$0.10 \times 0.25 \times 0.05$	$= 0.00125$
$0.20 \times 0.05 \times 0.02$	$= 0.00020$
$0.20 \times 0.10 \times 0.10$	$= 0.00200$
$0.20 \times 0.15 \times 0.30$	$= 0.00900$
$0.20 \times 0.20 \times 0.15$	$= 0.00600$
$0.20 \times 0.25 \times 0.03$	$= 0.00150$
$0.30 \times 0.05 \times 0.03$	$= 0.00045$
$0.30 \times 0.10 \times 0.05$	$= 0.00150$
$0.30 \times 0.15 \times 0.07$	$= 0.00315$
$0.30 \times 0.20 \times 0.03$	$= 0.00180$
$0.30 \times 0.25 \times 0.02$	$= 0.00150$
	$E[\tilde{r}_x, \tilde{r}_y] = \underline{\underline{0.02995}}$

$$COV[\tilde{r}_x, \tilde{r}_y] = 0.02995 - 0.03 = \mathbf{-0.00005}$$

$$VAR[\tilde{r}_x + \tilde{r}_y] = 0.004 + 0.003 + (2 \times -0.00005) = \mathbf{0.0069}$$

$$COR[\tilde{r}_x, \tilde{r}_y] = \frac{COV[\tilde{r}_x, \tilde{r}_y]}{\sigma_{r_x} \cdot \sigma_{r_y}} = \frac{-0.00005}{\sqrt{0.004} \cdot \sqrt{0.003}} = \frac{-0.00005}{0.00346} = \mathbf{-0.0144}$$

In summary:

Company x	Company y	Company x + y
$\bar{r}_x = 0.20$	$\bar{r}_y = 0.15$	$\bar{r}_{x+y} = 0.35$
$\sigma_x^2 = 0.004$	$\sigma_y^2 = 0.003$	$\sigma_{x+y}^2 = 0.0069$
$\sigma_x = 0.063$	$\sigma_y = 0.055$	$\sigma_{x+y} = 0.083$
		$COR[\tilde{r}_x, \tilde{r}_y] = -0.0144$

NOTE: The calculations implicitly assume that the combination of companies x and y is in equal proportions.

Selected references

C. Alderfer and H. Bierman, 'Choices with Risk: Beyond the Mean and Variance', *Journal of Business*, July 1970.

F. Black, M. C. Jensen and M. Scholes, 'The Capital Asset Pricing Model: Some Empirical Tests', in *Studies in the Theory of Capital Markets*, ed. M. Jensen, New York, Prager, 1972.

M. E. Blume, 'Portfolio Theory: a Step Towards its Practical Application', *Journal of Business*, April 1970.

M. E. Blume, 'On the Assessment of Risk', *Journal of Finance*, March 1971.

J. R. Brick and H. E. Thompson, 'The Economic Life of an Investment and the Appropriate Discount Rate', *Journal of Financial and Quantitative Analysis*, December 1978.

E. F. Fama, 'The Behaviour of Stock Market Prices', *Journal of Business*, January 1965.

E. F. Fama, 'Risk, Return and Equilibrium: Some Clarifying Comments', *Journal of Finance*, March 1968.

E. F. Fama, 'Risk Adjusted Discount Rates and Capital Budgeting under Uncertainty', *Journal of Financial Economics*, August 1977.

I. Friend, Y. Landskroner and E. Losq, 'The Demand for Risky Assets under Uncertain Inflation', *Journal of Finance*, December 1976.

I. Friend, R. Westerfield and M. Granito, 'New Evidence on the Capital Asset Pricing Model', *Journal of Finance*, June 1978.

C. J. Grayson, 'The Use of Statistical Techniques in Capital Budgeting', in *Financial Research and Management Decisions*, ed. A. Robichek, New York, John Wiley, 1967.

D. B. Hertz, 'Risk Analysis in Capital Investment', *Harvard Business Review*, January–February 1964.

D. B. Hertz, 'Investment Policies that Pay Off', *Harvard Business Review*, January–February 1968.

J. Klammer, 'Empirical Evidence of the Adoption of Sophisticated Capital Budgeting Techniques', *Journal of Business*, July 1972.

D. Leuhari and H. Levy, 'The Capital Asset Pricing Model and the Investment Horizon', *Review of Economics and Statistics*, February 1977.

H. Levy and M. Sarnat, 'Diversification, Portfolio Analysis and the Uneasy Case for Conglomerate Mergers', *Journal of Finance*, September 1970.

W. G. Lewellen, 'A Pure Financial Rationale for the Conglomerate Merger', *Journal of Finance*, May 1971.

J. Lintner, 'The Valuation of Risk Assets and the Selection of Risky Investments in Stock Portfolios and Capital Budgets', *Review of Economics and Statistics*, February 1965.

J. Lintner, 'Security Prices, Risk, and the Maximal Gains from Diversification', *Journal of Finance*, December 1965.

J. H. Lorie and M. T. Hamilton, *The Stock Market: Theories and Evidence*, New York, Irwin, 1973.

J. F. Magee, 'Decision Trees for Decision Making', *Harvard Business Review*, July–August 1964.

J. F. Magee, 'How to Use Decision Trees in Capital Investment', *Harvard Business Review*, September–October 1964.

J. C. Mao and C. E. Sarndal, 'A Decision Theory Approach to Portfolio Selection', *Management Science*, April 1966.

H. Markowitz, 'Portfolio Selection', *Journal of Finance*, March 1952.

H. Markowitz, *Portfolio Selection: Efficient Diversification of Investments*, New York, Wiley, 1959.

R. C. Merton, 'An Inter-temporal Capital Asset Pricing Model', *Econometrica*, September 1973.

F. Modigliani and G. A. Pogue, 'An Introduction to Risk and Return: Concepts and Evidence', *Financial Analyst's Journal*, March–April, May–June 1974.

J. Mossin, 'Equilibrium in a Capital Asset Market', *Econometrica*, October 1966.

S. C. Myers and S. Turnbull, 'Capital Budgeting and the Capital Asset Pricing Model: Good News and Bad News', *Journal of Finance*, May 1977.

J. W. Pratt, 'Risk Aversion in the Small and in the Large', *Econometrica*, January–April 1964.

A. Rappaport, 'Sensitivity Analysis in Decision Making', *Accounting Review*, July 1967.

A. Robichek and S. C. Myers, 'Conceptual Problems in the Use of the Risk Adjusted Discount Rate', *Journal of Finance*, December 1966.

R. Roll, 'A Critique of the Asset Pricing Theory's Tests', *Journal of Financial Economics*, March 1977.

S. A. Ross, 'The Current Status of the Capital Asset Pricing Model', *Journal of Finance*, June 1978.

B. Schwab, 'Conceptual Problems in the Use of Risk Adjusted Discount Rates with Disaggregated Cash Flows', *Journal of Business Finance and Accounting*, Winter 1978.

W. F. Sharpe, 'Capital Asset Prices: a Theory of Market Equilibrium Under Conditions of Risk', *Journal of Finance*, September 1964.

W. F. Sharpe, 'A Simplified Model for Portfolio Analysis', *Management Science*, January 1965.

W. F. Sharpe, *Investments*, Englewood Cliffs, N.J., Prentice-Hall, 1977.

R. C. Stapleton, 'Portfolio Analysis, Stock Valuation and Capital Budgeting Decision Rules for Risky Projects', *Journal of Finance*, November 1971.

R. O. Swalm, 'Utility Theory – Insights into Risk Taking', *Harvard Business Review*, November–December 1966.

J. Tobin, 'Liquidity Preference and Behaviour Towards Risk', *Review of Economic Studies*, February 1958.

J. Tobin, 'The Theory of Portfolio Selection', in *The Theory of Interest Rates*, ed. F. H. Hahm and F. P. R. Brechling, London, Macmillan, 1965.

Postscript

This book has attempted to present a reasoned development of a theory of financial decision making, covering in particular the three principal long-term decisions, about the investment choice, the financing method and the dividend policy. Right from the opening paragraphs of the first chapter, it was emphasized that the book set out to develop a normative theory, in other words, how these long-term financial decisions *should* be made, rather than how they are *actually* made. The idea behind the approach can be found in the quotation by Paarlberg made in the preface: the distinction between theory and practice is a barren boundary which serves little practical purpose. The real distinction is to be made between good and bad in both theory and practice. This book makes no claims that the theory of financial decision making which it contains is necessarily good theory, but just that it presents, in outline, the theory that has been slowly constructed over the last thirty years, and which is still developing and changing.

As far as financial decision making is concerned, the theory is currently being actively advanced and consolidated along several fronts, but the practice lags no little way behind, hampered by – amongst other things – the different conceptual bases of financial and management accounting. It will not be until these two areas of practical accounting are in step with one another, that we shall be able really to test that what we have is both good theory and good practice.

Finally, it is hoped that the reader who manages to 'stay the course' of this book will be spurred on to further, more advanced reading and to wider reading. If nothing else, the modern theory of financial decision making lays itself open to the criticism that it takes too narrow a view of what is an immensely complex process. But more than this, it is hoped that this book will spur the reader on to a greater thoughtfulness about how managements should undertake their task of financial decision making.

Selected Questions

(Model answers to these questions are available to lecturers and instructors free of charge on application to the Publishers.)

1 Barye Ltd, Bassa Ltd and Bawden Ltd are three companies which are all believed to fall within the same business risk class. Barye Ltd and Bassa Ltd both have mixed capital structures, whilst Bawden Ltd is an all-equity company. You are given the following information:

Barye Ltd		
		1–∞
	annual dividends	£ 30,000
	annual interest	£ 10,000
	annual earnings	£ 40,000
Bassa Ltd		
	annual dividends	£ 74,769
	annual interest	£ 22,031
	annual earnings	£ 98,000
Barye Ltd		
	total market value equity	£250,000
	total market value debt	£250,000
Bassa Ltd		
	total market value equity	£249,230
	total market value debt	£550,770

The shareholders in Bawden Ltd earn a 10% return on their capital.

Capital markets are perfect, there are no transaction costs and no taxation. The ordinary shares in Bawden Ltd and the debenture capital market are both believed to be in equilibrium.

Required:

(a) Analyse the above situation. What would your advice be to shareholders in Bayre Ltd and Bassa Ltd?

(b) Mr Bellini has £100 worth of shares in Bayre Ltd. Advise him how he may gain from arbitrage whilst keeping his current level of financial risk constant. Assume that he may borrow money at an annual interest rate of 4%

(c) If in equilibrium, a company's cost of equity capital can be estimated by the expression:

$$K_E = K_O + (K_O - K_D)\frac{D}{E}$$

estimate both the cost of equity capital and the weighted average cost of capital of Bayre Ltd if many shareholders undertake market transactions similar to Mr Bellini's.

2 Cipriani Ltd are considering an investment opportunity which, if accepted, would leave the company's operating risk unchanged. It would require an immediate cash outlay of £3,250,000 and would produce annual net cash earnings of £1,150,000 in perpetuity.

The company is currently entirely financed by 10 million 25p ordinary shares, each of which has a market value of 360p. The company has consistently followed a policy of paying out the whole of each year's net cash earnings as a dividend, and shareholders expect the policy to continue. Without acceptance of the new project, the company's annual earnings are expected to be £6 million in perpetuity. The current dividend is due to be paid in two weeks' time.

Two possible financing methods for the project are under consideration. It could be financed either by retaining a sufficient proportion of the forthcoming dividend or alternatively by making an issue of irredeemable debentures with a coupon rate equal to the current debt interest rate of 8%. If this latter financing method is undertaken, it is expected that shareholders will require an extra 2% return to compensate them for the resulting financial risk.

Required:
(a) Evaluate the project and the two alternative methods of financing outlined above. What course of action is likely to lead to the greatest increase in shareholder wealth?

(b) If a rights issue were substituted for the alternative of retaining part of the current dividend, how would your solution to part (a) be affected? If the rights issue were to be made at £2.60 per share, what would be the theoretical nil-paid rights price?

3 Blake Ltd is considering the construction of an underground car park. Preliminary studies have yielded the following information:

1 The car park could commence operation in two years' time if its construction was commenced immediately.

2 The site could be purchased for £2 million, £1 million payable immediately and the balance in 24 months' time.

3 Construction costs have been estimated (in present day/current terms) at £1 million in the first year and £2 million the year after. Assume that these costs are paid at the end of the year to which they relate.

4 The car park will be for all-day parking with a maximum capacity of 5,000 cars. It will be open 250 days a year and it is expected to operate at a utilization rate of 80%.

5 The operational life of the car park is expected to be five years.

6 At the end of its life the building will be demolished at an estimated cost (allowing for inflation) of £200,000. The site would then be sold.

7 The real value of the site is likely to increase by 5% per annum.

8 The company intends to set the car parking charge per car at the start of each year, raising charges each time in line with the retail price index. Assume that all this revenue is received by the company at the end of each year in which it arises.

9 The company expects a 6% return on its capital, in real terms. The retail price index is likely to show an annual increase of 8% in the foreseeable future. Construction costs are expected to rise by 12% per year.

Required:
Calculate the price that Blake Ltd should charge per car, per day in the first year of operation in order that the project should produce the required return.

4   Cortona Ltd has discovered the following investment opportunities (none of which can be undertaken more than once):

				£000's		
Project Year	0	1	2	3	4
name					
A	− 50	− 20	+ 50	+ 200	0
B	− 100	+ 110	+ 40	+ 80	+ 100
C	0	0	− 1000	+ 500	+ 800
D	− 300	− 100	− 100	+ 400	+ 400
E	− 100	+ 50	+ 50	0	0

The company's cost of capital, which reflects the shareholders' opportunity cost of money, is 10%. When discounted at this rate the projects display the following NPVs:

Project	NPV 10%
A	£+ 71,800
B	£+ 161,460
C	£+ 99,890
D	£+ 200,060
E	£− 13,225

None of these projects can either be delayed or have its starting date brought forward.

Required:
(a) If there is only £300,000 of investment cash available at time O, but it is freely available thereafter, of which projects would you recommend acceptance, on the assumption that none of the investment opportunities are divisible?

(b) If the projects *were* infinitely dividible, how would your investment advice in (a) above differ?

(c) If investment capital available from external sources is limited to £300,000 in time 0, zero in time 1 and £500,000 in time 2, but is unlimited thereafter, formulate the problem into a linear programme. Assume that all projects are infinitely divisible and that money can be placed on deposit from time 0 to time 1 at an 8% interest rate and from time 1 to time 2 and time 2 to time 3 at an annual interest rate of 6%.

(d) Explain the circumstances under which the solution to the linear programme may suggest using the money deposit facility referred to in (c) above.

5   Endoios Ltd has an all-equity capital structure. Foppa Ltd is very highly geared. Both companies come within the same business risk class. You are given the following information:

	Foppa Ltd Yrs 1–∞	Endoios Ltd Yrs 1–∞
Annual dividends	100,000	180,000
Annual interest	80,000	—
Total annual cash earnings	180,000	180,000
Total market value of equity	400,000	1,800,000
Total market value of debt	1,000,000	—

There is a perfect capital market, no taxation, no transaction costs and no difference between corporate and private gearing.

Required:
(a) State what you would conclude from the above information.

(b) Draw a diagram, or diagrams (not to scale) to illustrate the current situation and to show what would happen if arbitragers entered the market.

(c) Illustrate the gain to be made from arbitrage by an individual currently holding £1,000 worth of shares in one of the above companies (i.e., there are arbitrage gains to be made only from trading one way, and you therefore have initially to specify the direction of arbitrage).

Assume: The ordinary shares of Endoios Ltd and the debentures of Foppa Ltd are in equilibrium.

6   The Guas Co Ltd have a very old air-conditioning plant operating in their steel smelting plant. If it were replaced now, it could be sold for scrap to yield £10,000 net of dismantling costs. Alternatively, it could be repaired to make it operational for a further year at a cost of £30,000. Its subsequent net scrap value is estimated at £12,000.

To replace the present equipment, the company have approached a specialist air-conditioning firm. Because work at present is slack, Guas Ltd have been offered a replacement system for immediate installation, at a cost of £200,000. However, if the company waited for a further year before replacement, the new equipment would have to be purchased at its normal price of £220,000.

The specialist manufacturers estimate that the equipment will need a £50,000 overhaul at the end of 4 years, which should be sufficient to ensure a total operational life of 7 years. Because of its specialist nature, the new equipment's scrap value is independent of its age or condition and it is estimated that it would be £40,000.

Guas Ltd intend buying identical replacement equipment for the foreseeable future.

The company use a risk-adjusted discount rate for investment appraisal purposes with the following risk premia:

Low risk   4%
Medium risk   9%
High risk   15%

The Government's minimum lending rate is currently 6%.

Required:
Advise management on the replacement decision.

7   Lomazzo Ltd has an issued capital of 2 million ordinary shares of 50p each and no fixed interest securities. It has paid a dividend of 70p per share for several years, and the stock market generally expects that level to continue. The market price is £4·20 per share, *cum div.*

The firm is now considering the acceptance of a major new investment which would require an outlay of £500,000 and generate net cash receipts of £120,000 per annum for an indefinite period. The additional receipts would be used to increase dividends.

Lomazzo is appraising three alternative sources of finance for the new project:

(i) Retained earnings. The usual annual dividend could be reduced. Lomazzo currently holds £1·4 million for payment of the dividend which is due in the near future.

(ii) A rights issue of ordinary shares. One new share would be offered for every ten shares held at present at a price of £2.50 per share; the new shares would rank for dividend one year after issue, when cash receipts from the new project would first be available.

(iii) An issue of ordinary shares to the general public. The new shares would rank for dividend one year after issue.

Assume that, if the project were accepted, the firm's expectations of future results would be discovered and believed by the stock market, and that the market would perceive the risk of the firm to be unaltered.

Required:
(*a*) Estimate the price *ex div* of the ordinary shares, following acceptance of the new project, if finance is obtained from (i) retained earnings or (ii) a rights issue.

(*b*) Calculate the price at which the new shares should be issued under option iii assuming the objective of maximizing the gain of existing shareholders.

(*c*) Calculate the gain made by present shareholders under each of the three finance options.

(*d*) Discuss the advantages and disadvantages of each of the three sources of finance.

Ignore taxation and issue costs of new shares for (*a*), (*b*) and (*c*) but *not* (*d*).

8 The Ostendorfer Co. Ltd faces an imperfect capital market and in addition it has trouble in obtaining supplies of some of its basic manufacturing inputs for its major area of production: industrial and commercial mouse-traps.

The Management Accounting Department within the Business Opportunities Division has identified three major investment possibilities, the cash flows of which are given below:

Project	0	1	2	3	4
A	− 1000	− 4000	+ 5000	+ 5000	0
B	− 2000	− 2000	+ 8000	+ 5000	0
C	− 3000	+ 100	+ 2000	+ 3000	+ 4000

The company's cost of capital has been calculated as 10% and at this discount rate all projects have positive NPVs. However, the company does not have sufficient capital: only 4000 is available now and a further 3000 will be available at Period 1.

We also have the following information:

1 Money can be transferred from Period 0 to Period 1 via a Bank deposit which earns 5% interest.

2 Money can be transferred from Period 1 to Period 2 via a Bank deposit which earns 4% interest.

3 A fixed overhead of £1500 per year, payable at the end of each year, has to be allowed for.

4 This year's dividend is now due. We must pay at least £800. The company's dividend policy is such that the dividend in any one year must not be less than the dividend paid in the previous year.

5 During Period 1, a raw material that is required for Projects A and B will be in short supply. Only 55,000 tons will be available. Project A requires 38,000 tons and Project B requires 44,000 tons.

6 The directors believe that it will be possible to raise an additional £2500 of capital via a rights issue at Period 1. Shareholders would require their normal return on this capital.

7 None of the projects can be delayed – for fear of competitive activity. All the projects are infinitely divisible, but each can only be undertaken once.

Required:

(a) Formulate the problem into a linear programme so as to maximize the present value of the shareholders' dividend flow through time.

(b) State your assumptions and explain in what circumstances the company might take advantage of the opportunity to place money on deposit at the Bank.

9   Osona Ltd manufacture a wide range of stationery goods. At the present time the directors are considering the extension of the product range to include felt-tipped pens. The company's market research agency believes that they will be able to capture and retain 5% of the UK market (which currently stands at 40 million pens per year and is expected to remain static), by simply trading on the Osona name and reputation. The sales pattern for felt-tipped pens remains steady over the 250-day trading year. Pens would be wholesaled to shops at £95 per 1,000, with a recommended retail price of 13p each.

A specialized felt-tipped pen machine has recently been introduced on to the market which the company is considering purchasing. It costs £23,000 and is capable of an annual output of 10 million pens. Its technological life is expected to be 5 years at the end of which its scrap value will be virtually nil. The machine's manufacturer estimates that set-up costs are likely to be £450 per production run, irrespective of the size of the run. Osona's management accounting department have determined that the variable input costs using this machine (including marketing and storage costs, but excluding batch set-up costs) will be 9p per pen. It is planned that the company would manufacture the annual sales requirement in two equal sized batches each year, with the pens being left in stock and issued as required.

The machine's capital cost, together with the additional working capital required, would be funded by the company's retained earnings (and in doing so, would not displace any other investment). The appropriate cost of capital is 10%.

As an alternative, the company already owns a ball-point pen machine which is disused and has a current scrap value of £8,000. This machine could be converted at a cost of £2,000 to produce felt-tipped pens at an output rate of 4 million per year. It is believed that the converted and overhauled machine would have a productive life of 5 years. It would be less efficient than the specialized machine, with variable input costs (excluding set-up costs) estimated at 9·2p per pen, but the company's previous operating experience with it in ball-point pen production, suggests that batch set-up costs will only be £287·50, irrespective of batch size.

Required:
(a) Assess the desirability of operating the specialized machine for five years using the production plan proposed.

(b) Prepare calculations to show how this proposed production plan can be improved. What impact does this improvement have on the specialized machine's desirability?

(c) Suggest which machine (i.e., the specialized or converted machine) the company should use to manufacture felt-tipped pens, if at all.

Assume all cash flows occur on the last day of the year in which they arise, with the exception of the machine purchase/conversion cost and the working capital requirement, which are both payable immediately the decision is made to invest. Ignore taxation and inflation.

10　Praxitiles Ltd is investigating the introduction of a new alcoholic drink to be called Theed. Extensive market research by an outside agency, at a cost of £10,000, has suggested that a price of £5 per bottle to the retail trade would be acceptable.

Production of Theed will require specialized distilling and flavouring equipment which, it is estimated, would cost £200,000. As with most distilling equipment, this installation is likely to have a long productive life but, because of its rather specialized nature, when production of Theed ceases it will only be able to be sold for scrap at around £2,000 (net of dismantling costs). Variable costs of production are estimated at £3 per bottle, and overheads are estimated at £25,000 per year, avoidable only if production ceases.

At the proposed selling price, the drink trade is expected to demand 50,000 bottles per year, well within the capacity of the production equipment, but after four years interest is expected to decline and so production will cease. However, the company believes that it may well be able to extend product life for a further two years either by running a small trade advertising campaign at the start of years 5 and 6 at a cost of £10,000 per year, or alternatively by reducing the price per bottle by 40p in these two years. The market research company believes that the two alternatives would achieve similar sales results, but just what those sales would be is uncertain. If the campaign is successful in year 5 then sales of 35,000 bottles could be expected in that year, with sales of 28,000 or only 9,000 bottles being equally likely in year 6; or alternatively the year 5 promotion may be relatively unsuccessful with sales of only 7,000 bottles in that year and an equal likelihood of either 12,000 or 5,000 bottles in the following year. The market research agency believes that the campaign has only a 60% chance of being successful in year 5.

All expenses and revenues will be paid or received in cash at the end of the year in which they arise, with the exception of the production equipment, for which payment is due at the start of the first year of manufacture, and the advertising expenditure, which must be paid for at the start of each year in which a campaign is mounted. The directors estimate that 10% is the appropriate rate of discount at which projects should be evaluated.

Required:

(a) Evaluate the financial feasibility of the proposed new drink, in respect of its normal expected life of 4 years, including in your presentation details about the sensitivity of the decision advice to changes in the estimates made.

(b) Evaluate which of the two alternative methods (if any) should be used to extend the product life.

11　The Troostwijck Town Council are planning to build a bridge over the local river, in order to enlarge their town's trade catchment area. Plans have already been drawn up by the Surveyor's Department, and if the decision to go ahead is taken, building will start in two year's time. The following estimates have been presented to the chief executive of the Planning Department.

The bridge would require initial capital expenditure of £14m, of which £6m would be payable at the start of building and the balance payable 24 months later. Construction work is expected to take five years in total. Labour costs are forecast at £2m per year over this period and general material costs at £3.5m per year. Once completed, the bridge is expected to have a very long economic life (at least 80 years), but it would require repainting each year at an annual cost of £1m, and in addition a major overhaul would be required at the end of the first ten years of use. This overhaul would cost £5m, expenditure being evenly divided between labor and materials.

All these costs are expressed in present-day prices and, for evaluation purposes, costs which in practice are likely to be spread evenly over a year can all be assumed to arise on the last day of the year, except where stated otherwise. Labour wage rates over the next 25 years are expected to rise steadily at an average annual rate of 4%. Material costs are expected to inflate at the same rate over the next 10 years and then become stable.

The Town Council propose to raise the required finance from a variety of sources. The Treasurer's Department estimate that the market discount rate over the next 7 years will be around 14.4%. Thereafter, they estimate the annual opportunity cost of capital to be 8% in present-day terms.

It is proposed to charge a toll for use of the bridge (which would be a monopoly), which would be increased each year in line with the general level of inflation within the economy. This rate is expected to be a constant 4% per year.

The Traffic Department have supplied estimated vehicle usage rates for the proposed bridge as follows:

No. of Crossings per day	Probability
8,000	0·1
10,000	0·2
12,000	0·4
14,000	0·2
16,000	0·1

Based on a 350-day year

Required:

(a) Estimate the break-even toll charge per crossing which should be charged during the bridge's first year of operation, based on the above estimates. Assume that total annual toll payments arise on the last day of each year.

(b) Discuss briefly the main areas in which your analysis would be improved.

12 In the context of the capital-asset pricing model, what is the expected return of Sambin Ltd if it has the following characteristics and if the following information holds for the market portfolio?

Standard Deviation, Sambin Ltd	0·20
Standard Deviation, Market Portfolio	0·15
Expected Return, Market Portfolio	0·10
Correlation between possible returns for Sambin Ltd and the market portfolio	0·80
Risk-free rate	0·04

(a) What would happen to the required return if the standard deviation of Sambin Ltd were higher?

(b) What would happen if the correlation coefficient were less?

(c) What is the functional relationship between the required return for a security and market risk?

13 The following portfolios are available in the market:

Portfolio	Expected Return	Standard Deviation
A	0·13	0·11
B	0·05	0·02
C	0·11	0·08
D	0·15	0·15
E	0·09	0·05

(a) Assume that you can invest in only one of these portfolios: that is, it is not possible to mix portfolios. Plot the risk–return trade-off. Which portfolio do you prefer?

(b) Assume now that you are able to borrow and lend at a risk-free rate of 4%. Which portfolio is preferred? Would you borrow or lend at the risk-free rate to achieve a desired position? What is the effect of borrowing and lending on the expected value of return and upon the standard deviation?

14 Two companies, Ricca Ltd and Ribera Ltd, are undertaking business operations with identical levels of risk. Ricca Ltd is an all-equity company with annual net cash earnings of £800,000, at which level they are expected to remain for the foreseeable future. The company has issued 6·25 million 5p ordinary shares and has a current market capitalization of £5 million. Ribera Ltd has a mixed capital structure and has annual net cash earnings, before

interest, of £500,000. This level is expected to remain unchanged in the fore-seeable future. The company has issued 5 million 25p ordinary shares and £1 million 5% irredeemable debentures. The equity has a current market capitalization of £2·5 million, and the debentures currently stand in the market at 80%. Both companies follow a policy of distributing the whole of each year's net cash earnings as dividends and interest.

Henry Redman has a shareholding in Ribera Ltd which is currently valued by the market at £3,000. His broker has informed him that Ribera's equity is thought to be overvalued and that he stands to make a financial gain by switching his shareholding into Ricca Ltd.

Required:

(a) Outline a means by which Henry Redman might use to switch his share-holding whilst retaining his current level of financial risk. Calculate the gain he could expect to make from such a switch.

(b) On the assumption that the current market price of both Ricca's ordinary shares and Ribera's debentures are in equilibrium, calculate the eventual market capitalization of Ribera's equity after several other shareholders have undertaken similar switching arrangements as in (a) above. What would happen if the market value of Ribera's equity fell below this level?

(c) Briefly discuss the implications of your calculations for the determination of the optimal financial structure of a company. Be careful to specify the assumptions used.

Ignore taxation.

15   Teniers Ltd is considering investing in a new product line, currently referred to as 'Project X'. The expected value and standard deviation of the probability distribution of possible net present values for the product line are £12,000 and £9,000 respectively.

The company has two existing lines which may be referred to simply as A and B. The expected values of net present value and standard deviation for these product lines are:

	NPV £	σ £
Product A	16,000	10,000
Product B	10,000	4,000

The correlation coefficients of the returns between each product line are estimated as:

	A	B	X
A	1·00	—	—
B	0·90	1·00	—
X	0·40	0·80	1·00

Capacity constraints dictate that it is possible for the company to operate only two production lines at any one time, and having made the decision it would not be possible to change because of tooling and marketing problems. Available portfolios, including the proportions invested in each production line are:

	Proportion invested in:		
Portfolio	A	B	X
A	1·00	—	—
B	—	1·00	—
X	—	—	1·00
A & B	0·50	0·50	—
A & X	0·50	—	0·50
B & X	—	0·50	0·50

Required:
(a) Advise the Company on the most suitable combination of product-lines, and state the assumptions made in relation to the Company's objectives and attitudes to risk.

You may assume that the proportion invested in each project and the NPV are linearly related.

(b) State what additional information you would need in order to select an 'optimal' portfolio.

16 Santi and Sambin are considering setting up an independent company called Regnault Ltd, with an initial injection of £100,000 of equity capital. The purpose of the company is to undertake the production of some specialized agricultural equipment for which there is some short-term unsatisfied demand. The company will require machinery at a cost of £80,000, and the remaining £20,000 of start-up equity will be used to finance working capital. The market for the equipment is expected to last for four years, at the end of which time the machinery will be sold for scrap to net an estimated £5,000. The company will be wound up at the end of the following year.

The machinery will be depreciated straight-line in the accounts, spread over a four-year life. The two owners intend to pay a total dividend (i.e., gross) of £20,000 in each year 1–4 with the remainder of the cash flow accumulating in a bank current account. A final liquidation dividend is to be paid at the end of year 5.

Corporation tax is charged at 40%, payable 12 months in arrears, and an imputation system is used in respect of dividends (except for liquidation dividends). The equipment attracts 100% capital allowances. The basic income tax rate is 30% but both pay 50% tax on marginal income. Capital Gains Tax is levied at 30%.

The following estimates have been made about the project:

Year	Sales Income	Wage Costs	Material Costs	Depreciation	Sundry Expenses
1	85,000	10,000	8,000	18,750	5,000
2	95,000	12,000	10,000	18,750	3,000
3	85,000	14,000	10,000	18,750	2,000
4	95,000	17,000	12,000	18,750	2,000

The company does not intend to undertake any other activities. Santi and Sambin believe that an alternative investment involving similar uncertainties would yield a return of 4% per annum after tax, in real terms. Over the next twelve months, the general rate of inflation is expected to run at 3·8%. Thereafter, the annual rate is expected to increase to 5·8%.

Required:
Advise Santi and Sambin on the worthwhileness of the venture.

Ignore any legal constraints on dividend distribution. Assume that working capital cannot be liquidized until the end of year 5 and that it does not bear any taxation.

17   Soest Ltd is presently financed entirely by equity capital. Its issued capital comprises one million ordinary shares of £1 each, and the shares have a current market value of £2·40 each. On average, the entire after-tax net cash flow from operations has been distributed and has yielded a dividend of 51p per share (net) for many years; you may assume that it is generally expected to continue at this level. The last dividend was paid recently.

The directors are now considering a major new investment. It would require an outlay of £1 million and would yield expected net cash receipts of £370,000 per annum (before tax) indefinitely, before deducting any interest on long-term debt capital. Finance for the project would be obtained by issuing £1 million of debentures at par, at a coupon rate of 18%.

The new project would involve a level of uncertainty similar to that of existing activities. However, the issue of debentures, in conjunction with the acceptance of the project, would cause the rate of return required by ordinary shareholders to increase to 25%.

Corporation tax is charged at 50%, payable immediately upon assessment at the end of each year to which it relates.

Required:
(a) Give calculations to show whether acceptance of the new project would be worthwhile on the alternative assumptions that:

(i) The change in gearing involved in accepting the project could be achieved only in conjunction with the acceptance of the new project.

(ii) The gearing ratio implied by the proposals could be obtained independently of acceptance of the new project, as a result of proposed additional investments.

(b) Explain shortly the reasons why the distinction between (a), (i) and (ii) may be important.

18   Pontormo Ltd is a large company operating mainly within the process chemical sector of the economy. Currently its corporate planning team are formulating the investment, dividend and financing plans over the next five years. The following information has been assembled:

1 *Investments*
The following investment opportunities have been identified:

Project Code	0	1	2	3	4	5
A	− 2000	− 1500	+ 1000	+ 1000	+ 1000	+ 1000
B	− 3000	+ 2000	+ 2500	+ 1000		
C		− 6000	− 4000	+ 5000	+ 5000	+ 5000
D	− 1000	+ 400	+ 600	+ 800		
E			− 1500	+ 500	+ 800	+ 400
F		− 1000	0	− 1000	+ 3000	− 800

Annual Year-end Cash-Flow, £000s

The start-up dates of all these projects cannot be delayed for fear of competitive activity. Neither can any project planned to start later than time 0 be commenced earlier because of research and development considerations. All the project cash flows given above represent the maximum possible investment, but they can be proportionally reduced if required.

Projects B and D would both require a special uranium isotope which, world wide, is in limited supply. Project B would require a maximum of 33 lbs and D, 18 lbs. It has been pointed out that project A produces this isotope as a by-product, but only a maximum of 5 lbs is thought to be recoverable. The company believes that it will be able to obtain up to 25 lbs on the open market.

2 *Finance*
It has been estimated that the company will be able to make available only £3·5m in time 0 and £2m in both times 1 and 2 to support the corporate plan. These amounts can be increased by the cash flow generated by investment in the above projects. In addition, it is believed that the company could make a rights issue in two years' time to yield a maximum of £3m.

3 *Dividends*
The company, which has an all-equity capital structure, has grown steadily over the last 10 years at an average compound rate of 8% and is generally expected to continue doing so. The current dividend of 12p per share has recently been paid, in line with expectations.

The directors believe that the previous investments made by the company are sufficient to maintain the level of this year's dividend, and they are looking to the investment plan currently under consideration to generate the dividend growth expected by shareholders. Next year the corporate plan *must* provide an 8% dividend increase. Additionally, it must also provide for an annual average dividend growth rate of at least 8% compound over the planning period. In the event of a rights issue being made, the additional dividends required will be supplied by cash flow generated from the company's existing investments. It is company policy never to reduce an annual dividend. The company has 250 million ordinary shares in issue, quoted at 130p ex div.

(*a*) Convert the information given above into a *formulation* suitable for being solved by linear programming, keeping in mind the company's objective of maximizing the current market value of the equity capital. Do not solve the linear programme.

(*b*) Discuss any reservations you might have about the plan which would subsequently be produced.

(*c*) The linear programme has produced the following dual values (amongst others):

Cash	Uranium isotopes	Rights issue
$t_0 = 13\cdot241$	98·270	10·901
$t_1 = 11\cdot420$		
$t_2 = 10\cdot901$		
$t_3 = 1\cdot247$		
$t_4 = 0\cdot516$		
$t_5 = 0\cdot819$		

Explain and comment upon the following four dual values:

(i)   Cash at $+1$.
(ii) Cash at $+4$.
(iii) Uranium Isotopes.
(iv) Rights Issue.

19   Pisano Ltd and Zille Ltd are two companies operating in the same industrial sector and are considered to face similar levels of risk. Both companies also have a similar asset structure and reported operating earnings (before interest and tax) of approximately £1m per annum. The only difference between the two firms is their capital structures.

Pisano Ltd has an all-equity financial structure comprising five million shares at £1 nominal value each. Zille Ltd has three million shares of £1 and £2m of irredeemable 10% debentures.

The market for securities in both companies is active, and current share prices stand at

Pisano Ltd   £1·33 per share
Zille Ltd   £1·78 per share

Required:
(*a*) Compute the average weighted cost of capital for both companies and briefly comment on the results.

(*b*) Mr Zille is a shareholder in Zille Ltd with a 5% shareholding. Advise him whether at current market prices he should transfer his investment to Pisano Ltd if he intends to maintain his financial risk at a constant level.

(*c*) On the assumption that the market considers the current return from an equity holding in Zille to be acceptable in relation to its business risk, prepare calculations to show the price at which Pisano's shares are likely to settle if investors find it profitable to buy into Pisano's equity.

(*d*) Comment on any reservations you may have regarding the above results with particular reference to the likely influence of corporate taxation.

20 Zoffany Ltd operate internationally, specializing in the survey of ocean floor sub-structures for possible mineral deposits. They are currently evaluating the investment potential of a deep-sea algon gas field that has been recently discovered in the Irish Sea. Current estimates are that there is a 70% probability that the field will have a five-year production life and a 30% probability that it will have an eight-year life. The estimated annual extraction tonnages are given below:

5-year life Million ton/year	Probability	8-year life Million ton/year	Probability
40	0·45	35	0·85
60	0·55	60	0·15

The UK Government stipulates that it shall have sole purchasing rights of the algon gas and it is expected that a price of £40 per ton will be paid. However, there is a 20% probability that a world shortage of the gas will cause the Government to offer a price of £65 per ton. Whatever final price is fixed, it is expected to remain constant throughout the life of the field.

Extraction costs vary, but it is estimated that a field with a five-year life, in this type of location, will have extraction costs of £30 per ton. If the field is found to have an eight-year life, the lower rate of extraction will mean lower extraction costs at around £28 per ton.

The fixed costs of operating the extraction platform and pipeline are estimated at £140 million per year.

The Irish Government, under an international agreement, is legally entitled to a royalty payment which, it is estimated, will be levied at £4 per extracted ton.

Zoffany Ltd has already spent £10·5 million on survey work and preliminary well drillings, but an additional capital outlay of £1,4000 million for the necessary field support structures will be required before production can commence. £1,000 million of this capital cost will be payable immediately the decision is taken to proceed with developing the field, and the remaining £400 million will become due for payment two years later. Twelve months after this second payment, the first production operating costs and revenues will arise and can then be assumed to arise at each following year end.

The appropriate discount rate for project appraisal purposes is 10% per annum.

Required:
(a) Calculate the expected net present value of the investment proposal and, on the basis of this figure, advise the management of Zoffany Ltd about the desirability of the investment.

(b) The Irish Government have yet to fix firmly the royalty levels. How sensitive is the decision given in your answer to (a) above to changes in the present estimates of £4 per ton?

Ignore inflation and taxation (with the exception of the royalty payments).

21   Neeffs Ltd is considering the investment of capital to be raised from a new issue of ordinary shares and fixed interest capital which will hold its current gearing ratio approximately constant. It wishes to calculate a discount rate to be used to appraise projects which would be small relative to the company's present scale of operations and whose acceptance would leave the company's risk level unchanged.

It has been proposed that an average of the costs of the individual sources of the company's capital, weighted by their proportion in the overall capital structure, would provide an appropriate figure.

The company has an issued share capital of two million 75p ordinary shares which have a current middle market price of 236p cum div. In addition £500,000 of 5% preference shares were issued five years ago which are currently capitalized in the market at £400,000 ex div. At the same time the company made a £2 million issue of 8%, 25 year debentures, redeemable at par. The current ex-interest market price of these is £100 per cent.

A summary of the most recent balance sheet of Neeffs Limited runs as follows:

Ordinary Share Capital	750,000
Preference Share Capital	500,000
Reserves	2,825,000
Debentures	2,000,000
Corporation Tax	1,000,000
	7,075,000
Fixed Assets less depreciation	4,575,000
Current Assets 4,000,000	
− Current Liabs. 1,500,000	2,500,000
	7,075,000

Dividends and earnings have been as follows:

	Net Div per share	E.P.S. after tax
19 × 5	20p	28·6p
19 × 6	21p	30p
19 × 7	22½p	32·2p
19 × 8	23½p	38·6p
19 × 9 (current)	25p	35·75p

Assume that there have been no changes in the systems or rates of taxation during the last five years. Corporation tax, levied on the imputation system, is 50%, and the standard rate of income tax is 33%.

Required:

(a) Carry out the calculations necessary to provide the required investment appraisal discount rate.

(b) Discuss any difficulties and uncertainties in your answer to (a) above.

22   Pollock Ltd is a well-diversified manufacturing company with a good record of profitability. Its capital structure is composed of 6 million 25p ordinary shares and £4 million 12% debentures, redeemable 2005 – 2009. The company's after-tax weighted average cost of capital is 16%. Currently the directors are considering expanding one of the company's areas of operation by the purchase of some high technology production equipment.

The equipment can be installed almost immediately the decision is made to undertake the investment, and it qualifies for a 100% Capital Allowance. It will cost a total of £0·5 million, 40% of which is payable immediately, with the balance being paid twelve months later (i.e., at the end of the year). The equipment is expected to have an economic life of five years ·and will depreciate down to a zero value over this period, using the straight-line method. Any scrap proceeds are expected to be very small and are likely to be fully absorbed by the dismantling costs.

The company intends to finance the investment, which is small relative to the size of the company, through a long-term £300,000 bank loan at a variable rate of interest computed at 3% above Base Rate and through £200,000 of retained earnings. The proposed financing method is unlikely to cause any serious disturbance to the company's overall gearing, and the investment, if accepted, will have no impact on the company's business risk level. Corporation Tax is levied at an annual rate of 45%, payable twelve months in arrears. Taxable profits can be simply defined as income less direct costs, depreciation and interest payments. The company is expected to generate a high level of taxable profits over the next 10 to 15 years.

The following forecasts have been made with respect to the project's performance:

Year	£ 000's				
	1	2	3	4	5
Sales income	200	200	250	300	350
Direct materials	40	45	48	54	60
Direct labour	20	20	25	25	30
Depreciation	100	100	100	100	100

Required:

(a) Calculate the project's NPV, stating any reservations that you may have about the decision advice it produces.

(b) Below what percentage would the Capital Allowance have to fall before the decision advice given in (a) above were overturned?

Ignore inflation.

23   Antenor Ltd are considering starting an airship service between London and Aberdeen to specialize in the transportation of heavy oil rig drilling equipment. The following estimates have been made:

1 Two airships will be required at a cost of £1·5 million each. They must be ordered now and will be delivered and paid for in 12 months' time.

2 Every flying day, each airship will undertake one journey.

3 The maximum load per journey is 100 tons. Revenue will be generated at a flat rate of £100 per ton.

4 Fixed costs of airship crew, ground staff, and service facilities will be £500,000 per year.

5 The construction of an airship terminal at Aberdeen and enlarging the London terminal is expected to cost a total of £8·5 million. £4 million of this would be payable immediately the decision to undertake the project was made and the balance in 12 months' time. The construction work is expected to take one year.

6 The airship service would commence immediately the terminals were finished.

7 The London Weather Bureau has supplied the following historical data:

Year	No. suitable flying days/year
19 × 3	320
19 × 4	280
19 × 5	330
19 × 6	290
19 × 7	305
19 × 8	275

8 The company's market research department has supplied the following estimates of capacity utilization per journey (i.e., a capacity utilization of 90% would mean a load of 90 tons was transported):

Av. capacity utilization	Prob.
90%	0·10
80%	0·15
70%	0·25
60%	0·25
50%	0·15
40%	0·10

9 The airships have a working life of 5 years. Antenor Ltd do not intend to continue the service beyond this time.

10 The appropriate discount rate for this project is believed to be 10%.

Required:
(a) Appraise the project's viability in terms of the net present value it is expected to generate.

(b) Examine the sensitivity of the project to the estimates of:
   (i) Terminal construction time.
   (ii) Number of suitable flying days per day.

Assume that all cash flows arise at the end of the year to which they relate, except for the construction costs and the airship purchase.

Ignore inflation and taxation.

Notes

Chapter 1

1 Be these either large stock exchange quoted companies such as ICI or Unilever, or small unquoted companies such as a local printing company or car rental company.

2 The terms decision 'making' and decision 'taking' can be used synonymously. However, the term decision 'making' will be used in this book because of its more positive emphasis on deliberate creative action.

3 We will carefully define just what financial decisions are, but for now this covers such things as a decision to invest in a new machine, to borrow money from the bank or a decision to 'pass' (i.e. not pay) an annual dividend that shareholders were expecting.

4 There are many variants of capitalism (which in itself is just one type of economic system; for example, alternatives could include socialist, feudal and primitive communal economies) but its two general features are the private ownership of property and the allocation of the economy's resources (land, labour and machinery) through a supply and demand price mechanism.

5 Indeed, we shall also occasionally allude to the psychological processes behind firms' financial decisions.

6 In a way, in specifying this second necessary condition, we are ignoring the situation where a decision *has* to be made even though this second condition does not exist. For instance, if you are out for a walk with no particular destination in mind and you come to a crossroads, a decision *has* to be taken on what direction to go, even though the second necessary condition is really unfulfilled. Such situations are of little interest as far as the decision *process* is concerned; we could call them indifference decisions.

7 For the present, we shall ignore the possibility of multiple objectives, although we shall touch upon it later. However we may observe that where multiple objectives exist in real life, one objective is often regarded (either implicitly or explicitly) as being of overriding importance, with the other objectives acting as constraining factors or considerations.

8 In abstract terms we can define a company as a collection of assets. The owners of the company have therefore pooled their funds to assemble such a collection and are logically only likely to do so in order to bring benefit (either directly or indirectly) to themselves.

9 The term 'privately owned companies' can be a source of confusion. It refers to all companies which are owned by individuals, either singly or collectively, whether or not they are 'publicly quoted' on a stock exchange or otherwise. Thus both public and private companies (in financial nomenclature) are privately owned companies.

10 See, for instance, Ivy Papps, *Government and Enterprise*, Hobart Paper No. 61, Institute of Economic Affairs, 1975.

11 We shall be ignoring the effects of inflation until later.

12 This is obviously a simplification, as in practice each share has two equilibrium prices a buying price and a selling price. The former will be the higher of the two, and the difference constitutes the jobber's 'turn'.

Chapter 2

1 Although this point will be expanded upon later, it is worth specifying now that an investment's 'cost' can be defined as all cash outflows and/or reduced cash inflows through time that result (either directly or indirectly) from the investment decision. Similarly, an investment's 'benefit' can be described as all cash inflows and/or reduced outflows through time that result (directly or indirectly) from the investment decision. Thus all costs and benefits of an investment are defined in terms of being incremental to the firm, through time and expressed in cash terms.

2 Various empirical surveys both in the UK and the USA and elsewhere have shown that these two methods are by far the most popular investment appraisal methods used in business. Their familiarity and directness will make the task of replacing them by superior appraisal techniques a difficult one.

3 Not least amongst these diverse considerations is the decision maker's own psychology.

4 There are a variety of names given to this method. Others include: payback period, pay-off period, capital recovery period, cash recovery factor.

5 The term 'mutually exclusive' when applied to investment projects is best explained by means of an example. Suppose a company requires a new warehouse and there are two possible sites under consideration, then the decision could be analysed in terms of two mutually exclusive investments: building the warehouse at Site A and building the warehouse at Site B. The projects are said to be mutually exclusive because only *one* new warehouse is required, so if it is built at Site A, the acceptance of this project excludes the other project from being chosen, and vice versa. More generally a pair of projects are mutually exclusive if the acceptance of one means that the other would not or could not be accepted. This definition can be extended to any number of alternative investment projects of which only one can be chosen.

6 It is important to note that throughout this book we shall use the following convention when dealing with all types of financial flows (e.g. profit, dividend, cash or tax flows): all flows will occur instantaneously on the last day of the time period. Thus a dividend flow in year 2 will be assumed to arise on the last day of year 2. This rather unrealistic assumption is made purely for arithmetical convenience and does not affect the realism of our results in any substantial way (see the section on Compounding and Discounting). Period 0 is defined as the *start* of the first period.
Diagrammatically, using periods of one year:

Thus time point 0 refers to the start of the year 1 or 'now', point 1 refers to the *end* of year 1 and the start of year 2, and so on.

7   Project independence can be defined as a situation where the expected financial flows that arise from a project will occur irrespective of any other project being or not being undertaken.

8   There do exist special cases where the payback decision rule effectively allows for the time value of money, but such situations are simply fortuitous and of little more than arithmetical interest.

9   This may be especially true of very small companies which may be lacking the resources and knowledge to undertake a more complex appraisal.

10   Even this is really open to doubt. Original writers on the topic such as Joel Dean and Ezra Solomon believed that payback could be used as a coarse screening device to pick out projects whose desirability (in terms of profitability) is so obvious as to remove the need for more refined appraisal. For similar reasons it is held that the method could also be used to reject 'obviously' highly unprofitable projects. There is little evidence to support this belief, neither has there been an operational definition of 'obvious' in this context.

11   Diagrammatically, it is easy to see why the project's scrap value is added to the capital outlay to calculate the average capital employed:

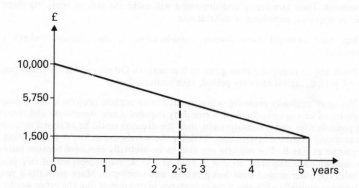

12   Even allowing for the payback variant referred to in note 9 (above), payback still carries the major criticism of not considering a project's financial flows outside the payback period.

Chapter 3

1   This approach was first used by the American economist Irving Fisher (and hence has become known as Fisherian Analysis) in *The Theory of Interest* (New York, Macmillan, 1930). Its use was revived specifically in terms of financial decision theory by Jack Hirshleifer, 'On the Theory of Optimal Investment', *Journal of Political Economy*, Vol. 66, No. 4 (August 1958) pp. 329–52. This article is reprinted in B. Carsberg and H. Edey (Eds.), *Modern Financial Management* (Harmondsworth, Penguin Books).

2   Alternatively we could say that all investment opportunities have a life-span of just one period of time, from period 0 to period 1.

3   In this assumption of no risk, we are also implicitly assuming that our investor will be alive in period 1 to enjoy the fruits of his decisions made in period 0.

4 We are also assuming here that the relative price levels of these factors of production are unchanging and so no 'holding gains' (in inflation accounting parlance) are possible.

5 Here we are using the term 'spare cash' in the sense of the residual cash resources of a company after allowing for the claims of all creditors.

6 In this simple case we are obviously ignoring the possible constraining influence of government legislation in respect of company dividends.

7 We can define a consistent criterion for investment decisions as one which would produce the following decision: if Project A is preferred to Project B and Project B is preferred to Project C, then the decision criterion should result in Project A being preferred to Project C. If not, the criterion is not producing consistent decisions.

8 This rate of time preference could be either positive or negative. For instance, an individual could be willing to take 5p less 'next year' for every £1 invested 'now', so his exchange rate would be $95/100 - 1 = -0.05$ or -5%. However, there is considerable evidence to suggest that RTPs are usually positive with the ultimate, although somewhat morbid, argument being the inevitability of death. So in a two-period case, in order to be persuaded to forgo £1 of consumption 'now', the owner will have to be offered £1 + 'next year', just to cover the risk that he may not be around next year to collect the return from the investment – he may be dead!

As an individual's rate of time preference is likely not to remain constant but to change with events, it is more correct to call any RTP a *marginal* rate of time preference.

9 The literature gives this curve a variety of names, e.g., investment opportunity line, productive opportunity line or time-exchange function.

10 The term 'maximum consumption combinations' is meant in the sense that with any given amount of current consumption, no higher consumption next year is possible with the company's existing resources and similarly, with any given amount of consumption next year, no higher level of current consumption is possible.

11 As a result of this arrangement and of our assumption that all physical investment opportunities are infinitely divisible and display decreasing returns to scale, the physical investment line is likely to be generally smooth and concave to the origin.

12 The return on the marginal investment – the marginal return – can properly be found from the first derivative of the physical investment line. In terms of Figure 1, it can be *very* roughly approximated by:

$$\frac{OD - CA}{CA} = \frac{OD}{CA} - \frac{CA}{CA} = \frac{OD}{CA} - 1$$

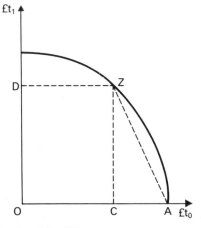

Therefore if the company has a total value now of £1,000 (OA) of which the owner consumes £600 (OC) and invests the remainder (CA) in order to produce £450 (OD) next year, we can obtain a rough approximation of the return on the marginal project (point Z) as:

$$\frac{450}{400} - 1 = 0.125 = 12\tfrac{1}{2}\%$$

Graphically, we are finding the slope of the dotted line ZA.

13   It is worth noting that under our present assumptions it makes no difference to our analysis whether or not the company represents the owner's *sole* source of consumption. However, we shall see later that when some of the assumptions are varied, this factor becomes one of importance.

14   The concept of a perfect capital market will prove extremely important to us, in later developments of the theory. For the time being we shall define it as a market where everyone can borrow or lend as much money as they wish (within their ability to repay) at a single rate of interest which is applicable to all, whether borrowing or lending. Additionally there are no transaction costs involved in using the market.

15   Up to this point, no mention has been made of taxation. It is easiest to assume that taxation does not exist, but it makes little difference to the analysis if tax is levied on gain as long as all investors face the same level of taxation and there is no differentiation between gain from physical and capital market investment. In such circumstances the return on investment referred to in the analysis is, of course, the after-tax return.

16   The reader must be careful not to be misled here. The test of being 'better off' or increasing welfare is whether or not a higher utility curve is reached. So we could just as easily get a situation where the shareholder achieves a higher utility curve through using the capital markets but this results (say) in a decrease in consumption 'now' and an increase 'next year'. As a higher utility curve has been reached the reduction in consumption 'now' *must* be more than offset (in the shareholder's mind) by the gain in consumption 'next year'.

17   It would be possible, although somewhat unlikely, for all of a company's shareholders to have an identical set of utility curves/marginal rate of time preference. In such cases the Separation Theorem would lose its importance.

18   In fact there do exist chance circumstances when ROCE will provide correct investment appraisal advice, but such situations are likely to be highly artificial and of little practical significance.

19   Having said this, it is still undoubtedly true that although the payback and return on capital employed appraisal rules have been losing popularity in practice ever since these shortcomings started to receive fairly wide publicity in the late 1950s and early 1960s, they are still very widely used by managements through the whole spectrum of company size and operations. For instance, a survey in the USA by Fremgen (*Management Accounting*, N.Y., Vol. 54, May 1973, pp. 19–25) showed that of 177 responding companies, although 71% used the IRR, 20% used NPV and 6% used the Present Value Index, 67% of companies continued to use Payback and 49% used ROCE. Increasing company size only appeared to affect whether appraisal techniques were used per se; thus companies in Fremgen's largest category (capital budget over $100 million annually) not only were the largest percentage users of IRR and NPV techniques, they also were the highest percentage users of Payback, ROCE and a variety of other methods (such as return on sales, discounted payback and earnings per share effects).

20   It may be wise to correct here a mistaken impression that the reader could possibly gain from this presentation and development of the theory. Payback and ROCE were derived (largely) in ignorance of the two-period investment–consumption model. It is therefore not surprising that neither method meets the model's requirement for an investment appraisal technique. However, the two major discounted cash flow methods were *not* developed in isolation from the model but arise out of the logic

which lies behind the model's construction. The reader should not hold the belief that it is just fortuitous that these later two methods of investment appraisal accord (as we shall see) with the model.

Chapter 4

1   There is a widely used DCF method of investment appraisal variously called the 'excess present value index', the 'profitability index', the 'discounted profitability index', or even the 'benefit–cost ratio'. This method arises directly out of the NPV method (and so gives equivalent decision advice) and can be defined as:

$$\frac{\text{Present Value of Project Cash Inflows}}{\text{Present Value of Project Cash Outflows}}$$

If the index is less than 1, the project should be rejected (equivalent to a negative NPV). If the index is greater than or equal to zero, the project should be accepted. Thus in terms of Project B4:

$$\text{Index} = \frac{827 \cdot 09}{1000 \cdot 00} = 0 \cdot 8271$$

as the index < 1, Project B4 should be rejected.

2   We earlier referred to the 'discounted payback method'. The criterion is that a project may be accepted only if it pays back its initial investment outlay within a specified maximum time, where both the initial outlay and the paying-back inflows are expressed in terms of present value cash flows.

3   To a limited extent a similar analysis can be performed on the vertical axis in terms of net *terminal* values (i.e. at t_1) rather than net present values. For instance, in the situation illustrated in Figure 4.1, OF represents the terminal value of the sum of dividend OD in t_0 and OC in t_1; OC represents the terminal value of the cash inflows generated from the company's investments; and CF represents the terminal value of the company's period 0 dividend of OD.

4   Notice that if the company were to overinvest up to point W, the total net present value of its investment decision would be negative. In other words, the shareholders would have been better off if management had undertaken no investment at all, rather than overinvesting to such an extent. This analysis does serve to support management's general inclination to invest conservatively (i.e., a tendency to underinvest or invest less than the optimal amount). Under-optimal investment must always lead to an increase in shareholders' wealth, relative to their wealth if management undertook zero investment, as long as negative NPV projects are not undertaken. However, with over-investment a situation like point W *is* possible where shareholders are actually *worse* off as a result of the company's investment decisions. In the real world, a management with poor forecasting ability may well do right to err on the side of conservatism rather than taking a very sanguine or cavalier attitude to investment decisions.

5   This method of investment appraisal has unfortunately suffered a confusing array of alternative names in the past, such as the 'marginal efficiency of capital', 'true yield' and even (to really add to the confusion) 'discounted cash flow'. Some of these alternatives still persist in the literature, but it is now most widely known as the 'internal rate of return'.

6 For instance, discounting Project B7 by 15% produces an NPV of +£5·10 and discounting by 18% produces an NPV of +£1·12. Diagrammatically:

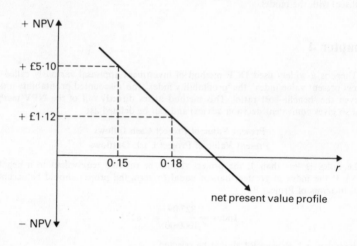

net present value profile

Assuming a straight line net present value profile, the gradient of the line is given by:

$$\frac{5·10 - 1·12}{0·15 - 0·18} = \frac{3·98}{-0·03} = -132·67$$

The general equation for a straight line is $y = a + bx$ where a is the y intercept and b the gradient. In terms of our graph therefore: NPV $= a - 132·67r$, and substituting one of our points into this equation to find a, say $(0·15, 5·10)$: $5·10 = a - (132·67 . 0·15)$ which gives a value for a of 25·00. Therefore, the equation of our line is: NPV $= 25 - 132·67r$. As we wish to find the value of r when the net present value is zero, solving:

$$0 = 25 - 132·67r$$

$$r = 25/132·67 = 0·1884 \text{ or } 18·84\%$$

and this is our approximation of the IRR.

7 In these terms, 'cost' is really Opportunity Cost. If the firm borrows the money from the capital market in order to make the investment, it has to pay the market rate of interest on that borrowed amount and so that is its cost. If the firm uses internally generated cash (i.e., retained earnings) to make the project investment, it forgoes the opportunity to lend this money on the capital market at the market rate of interest and so once again the interest rate is the cost of the funds invested in the project. For a full discussion on this important concept, see J. R. Gould: 'Opportunity Cost – The London Tradition' in *Debits, Credits, Finance and Profits*, ed. H. Edey and B. S. Yamey (Sweet and Maxwell).

8 These are not the original six assumptions made at the start of Chapter 3. We dropped the original assumption 3 when we introduced the possibility of financial as well as physical investment opportunities. In doing so however, we introduced the assumption of a perfect capital market.

9 This term has been defined earlier. It applies to situations where there are a series of alternatives, the acceptance of any one of which excludes or prevents the remaining alternatives from being chosen. Common industrial examples could include

a decision to build a new factory when a variety of alternative locations are under consideration, or a choice between several different makes of machine which all essentially carry out the same task.

10   From this point on, the discount factors given in the tables at the end of the book will be used instead of setting out the discount expression in full. For example, 0·6302 will be given instead of

$$\frac{1}{(1 + 0·08)^6}$$

11   There are two additional assumptions here. First, that the correct alternative investment is chosen initially, and second, that the actual performance of this chosen alternative is at least as good as was expected (and embodied in the NPV calculation based on the project's expected cash flow).

12   For example, a situation which involved three alternatives with operational lives of 3, 4 and 5 years respectively. Here the alternatives would have to be compared over a 60-year time-span!

13   For details of method, see the appendix on compounding and discounting.

14   In the case where the *costs* (and not the benefits) of each alternative were being compared, then whichever alternative had the *smallest* annual equivalent cost would be chosen.

15   Having examined this third type of interdependence of project cash flow, the reader should be aware that the second type, the replacement cycle problem, is really only a special case of the third type, which is in turn a special case of the basic mutually exclusive investments situation.

16   The processes of discounting and compounding can be viewed simply as a method of assigning weights to cash flows.

17   The IRR calculation simply involves finding the roots of a polynomial equation of n terms (where n = the number of periods of the project's life). In general, the IRR equation of a project which lasts for n years will have n roots or solutions or IRRs. However, with a conventional type of cash flow, only one of these solutions is a *real* number and the rest will be imaginary (i.e. $\sqrt{-2}$), with mathematical, but no economic importance. However, a non-conventional project cash flow can produce a polynomial equation of a type which may have *several* real number roots, each one of which is an equally valid IRR.

18   The use of these terms should not lead the reader into the all too easy substitution of 'usual' and 'unusual'. Non-conventional cash flows are extremely common in practice, as we shall discover when we examine the impact of taxation on investment appraisal.

19   The IRR is said not to exist only as a 'real' number, in such cases. It will exist, and so there will be roots to the polynomial, in terms of imaginary numbers. This mathematical result, however, has little relevance for our purposes.

20   Even this may be a disadvantage in that management may falsely believe that the IRR is essentially the same as the Accounting Rate of Return (ROCE), when in fact the two measures are totally distinct.

Chapter 5

1   It is important to remember that the effects or relaxing many of the rather more unrealistic assumptions of the investment–consumption model remain to be examined.

2   We have referred earlier to the distinction between certainty and risk/uncertainty. We shall deal more formally with the problem in a later chapter.

3   For the purposes of attempting to explain the concept of risk, we shall be assuming that physical investments are undertaken using borrowed money and therefore they must produce at least sufficient return to repay this borrowed capital plus interest. However, the analysis equally applies (given a perfect capital market) to the case where the investor's *own* funds are used, because now the investment must produce at least sufficient return to replace the capital outlay *and* the interest that the capital market would have paid but was forgone by applying the capital to a physical investment (i.e., the opportunity cost).

4   Except under very exceptional circumstances, such as liquidation.

5   This is assuming that the rate of discount remains a constant at $12\frac{1}{2}\%$ in perpetuity. Alternatively, we could view the $12\frac{1}{2}\%$ as the (weighted) *average* rate of discount over this time period.

6   It is interesting to note that this assumption of a constant dividend in perpetuity also implicitly assumes that the company never retains any of its annual net cash flow, but pays it all out as dividend. Thus, specifying the assumption more rigorously, the company's net annual surplus cash flow is a constant in perpetuity and all of this is paid out each year as dividend, a surplus being defined as the amount remaining after retaining sufficient cash to maintain the required rate of return in the future.

7   The middleman who makes the market for shares on the floor of the London Stock Exchange is called a jobber or dealer. The difference between the bid and offer price represents his profit or 'turn'.

8   Alternatively, we could assume that as the jobber's turn is a relatively small percentage of a share's value, then taking the mid-point between the bid and offer price is likely to be a satisfactory approximation.

9   For a detailed explanation of immediate annuities, see the appendix on compounding and discounting.

10   We have only examined the situation where a single annual dividend is paid. Where, say, dividends are paid twice a year (an interim and a final dividend) there are, in effect, two ex/cum dividend situations. For example, suppose a 5p per share dividend is paid half-yearly on a share with an ex div market value of 100p. We cannot say that $K_e = 10/100 = 0·10$ as this only represents the share's nominal annual return. The effective annual return would be given by:

$$100 = \frac{5}{K_e} + \frac{5(1 + K_e)}{K_e}$$

so that $K_e = 10/95 = 0·105$ or $10\frac{1}{2}\%$.

11   This assumption could be relaxed so that dividends through time, *on average*, are assumed to be a constant, but to do so can lead to problems where the discount rate changes over time.

12   This assumption is crucial to the operation of the dividend growth model. If $K_e = g$ the share price would be infinitely large, and if $K_e < g$ the share price would be negative. The latter, especially, is a nonsensical result.

13 I.e., $I/(1 - I)(d_1 - d_0) \equiv (\text{ACT}_{d_0} \cdot g)$ where ACT_{d_0} is the ACT payable on the time 0 net dividend. For example, if

$$I = 0.33, d_0 = 8\text{p} \quad \text{and} \quad g = 0.02,$$

then
$$d_1 = 8(1 + 0.02) = 8.16\text{p}$$

$$\frac{0.33}{0.67}(8.16 - 8) = \left(8 \cdot \frac{33}{67}\right) \cdot 0.02 = 0.0788 \text{ (approx.)}$$

14 Irredeemable or undated debentures do exist, where the loan is never repaid (except in liquidation), but are very rare.

15 A recent development has been the issuing of debentures with variable coupon rates to try to protect the subscribers against extreme movements in market interest rates.

16 Just like ordinary shares, debentures are not homogeneous in terms of risk. The riskiness of any particular debenture depends upon a number of factors including the riskiness of the company issuing debentures, the security (if any) attached to the debenture and how it ranks for payment with other fixed-interest capital issued by the company.

17 Such a belief really arises from an incorrect interpretation of the word 'cost'. Cost of capital does not refer to how much the capital costs the company to buy, but the best available return that is forgone if the firm applies the capital to a project: its *opportunity* cost.

18 There will be no problems with multiple IRRs because debentures will always have 'standard' cash flows.

Chapter 6

1 Either by making the company more risky or less risky.

2 For the moment, we shall assume a tax-free world.

3 We are deliberately ignoring the fact here that the issue of debenture capital affects the company's capital structure and so affects the weights and hence the value of K_0. The effect of this change, and whether or not the company's existing K_0 or new K_0 should be used as the discount rate, will be dealt with later.

4 The word 'leverage' is used in the United States.

5 This is not quite true; as we have seen, the taxation régime also can play a part in determining this opportunity cost.

6 Which therefore does implicitly assume that there are no retained earnings!

Chapter 7

1 The prices of individual goods and services may rise faster or slower than this average or general rate of increase (or they may even decline). The point of this definition of inflation is that the general tendency of prices in such an economy is to rise.

Chapter 8

1   We are assuming that the company has located projects which would produce the return that would normally be required by the capital markets in a situation where capital rationing did not exist.

2   This return would be the project's IRR. For simplicity, we are abstracting from the problems which may arise in calculating or using an IRR.

3   If not, any book on Management Accounting will outline the basic principles.

4   This second alternative may *not* be part of a simple rationing problem – for example, where there is multi-period capital rationing and where outside fund sources are strictly limited but the level of internally generated funds that can be applied to new investment projects fluctuates with the level of internally generated funds provided by past investments. In other words, this second alternative will only hold necessarily in a soft rationing situation.

5   The company's discount rate is the external weighted average cost of capital and, in so defining it, we are making all the assumptions which lie behind its use (i.e., not including any internal opportunity costs caused by the fact that capital is in limited supply).

6   Note that Project B violates our alternative assumption for a simple rationing situation, because its capital requirements are spread over two periods. In particular, take care to notice how this project's benefit–cost ratio is calculated.

7   If the £460 were raised from internal funds, the equity market value would increase by the amount of the total positive NPV. If the £460 were raised through a new equity issue, then the market value of the equity would rise by £460 + £283·09 = £743·09, i.e., it would increase by the amount of + NPV, *plus* the amount of newly injected capital.

8   This analysis could be undertaken in terms of benefit–cost ratios rather than in terms of rates of return.

9   In addition, there may be a very much longer term capital budget which might stretch as far as 20–25 years ahead, depending upon the company and the industry in which it operates and upon the gestation period of its major capital investment projects.

10   It could be argued that even this internally imposed capital rationing is, in reality, produced by external – but not exclusively financial – market inefficiencies, in that there is a time-lag between demand signals and the subsequent supply.

11   In advocating the use of K_0 in such circumstances, all the usual assumptions that accompany its use must still hold.

12   The primal solution reads: a = 0, b = 0, c = 1, d = 1, e = 0·3, f = 0·6.

13   By including 'chance' constraints into the LP formulation, whereby some level of cash flow must be provided by the solution, with a given level of probability.

14   It is possible, although rather unlikely, for a constraint to be fully utilized but non-binding in the sense that, if the constraint were relaxed, it would not be any further utilized than it was beforehand.

15   Project E produces a total NPV of +£83,662. 0·001% of this amount is £0·837, the dual value for year 1. This information on how the dual value arises is supplied by the computer solution to the problem. In a more complex example the source of the dual value is likely to involve more than merely an adjustment to the level of investment in a single project.

16   We are assuming here that liquidation can be achieved without incurring costs.

Chapter 9

1   An investment which has a rather unusual cash flow:

$$+ \; - \; - \; - \; - \; - \; - \; ...$$

2   It is necessary to leave a minute amount so as not to liquidate the company totally.

3   A not entirely surprising result, in view of the large numbers of rather unrealistic assumptions made in order to reach the conclusions of the analysis.

4   There are numerous definitions of gearing in use, perhaps the most common of which is the ratio of the market value of debt capital to *total* market value (i.e. debt plus equity).

5   In fact, remembering the objective function we have assigned to management decision making, we really want to know whether the gearing ratio can affect the market value of a company's *equity* capital. We shall later reconcile changes in total market value and equity market value.

6   In other words, it is assumed that if the company becomes bankrupt it will be possible to liquidate its assets and distribute them amongst the various claimants without cost.

7   The analysis could be carried through (in a slightly different way) to the same conclusions if the stock market had placed a *lower* value on the geared company. We shall refer to this case later.

8   There is no reason to assume anything other than that the company's debt capital will remain correctly valued on the market at £4,000, since we assume the interest rate to be constant.

9   An equilibrium point (i.e. where their WACCs equate) for the two share prices could occur anywhere between the two existing share prices, and could be calculated by just specifying *one* of the resulting share prices.

10   In some equivalent fashion.

11   From this point on, K_D will refer to the before tax cost of debt capital. References to the after-tax cost of debt will be designated $K_{D_{AT}}$, as before.

12   This is an approximation. The tax relief on debt interest is slightly more risky because the rate of corporation tax levied (and hence the level of tax relief) is uncertain.

13   This is not to say that K_E is falling, but that it is not rising as rapidly as it would have done otherwise.

14   Although the point has yet to be dealt with formally, it is important to note that in terms of risk – and it is this which largely governs the 10% capitalization rate – $\bar{X}$ and $\bar{X}(1-T)$ are identical (on the assumption of a constant rate of tax). It is only their *magnitudes* and not their *riskiness* which differs. The fact that an all equity company has only $\bar{X}(1-T)$ available for distribution, whilst the (virtually) all-debt company has $\bar{X}$ available – it will pay no tax because all its pre-tax cash flow is paid out as debt interest – does not affect the riskiness of the cash flow.

15   The problem of capital structure is complicated because it is many-faceted. One facet that we have not referred to is the differential taxation rates for individuals between unearned income (say from dividends) and capital gains. As a result, share-

holders who have high marginal tax rates may well prefer the company to retain earnings – and this retention be reflected in the share price showing a capital gain – rather than pay them out as dividends. This conclusion obviously clashes with the 99% gearing argument and would tend to favour a substantial amount of company financing through earning retention, at the expense of debt capital.

Chapter 10

1   Including preference share capital.

2   The reader may find it worth while to reflect how the M.M. dividend irrelevancy hypothesis is also just a natural continuation of their capital structure hypothesis.

3   The model's numerator is slightly more fully defined than when it was first introduced.

4   So-called because it is one which is widely held amongst both stock market investors and analysts.

5   A third possible alternative is a combination of the two courses of action.

6   For simplicity, we are assuming here that shares are divisible. The fact that this is not true in practice can be viewed as a slight market imperfection.

7   Notice that our analysis started with the assumption of certainty. With the introduction of debt capital, this assumption is implicitly being relaxed. The analysis is largely unaffected as long as it can be assumed instead that investors all have the same perception of uncertainty.

8   It is important to notice that constant dividends are not being advocated, but a constant *policy*. This policy may be to treat dividends as a residual of the investment decision and hence may result in a highly erratic dividend *flow*, but a constant policy.

9   A cost which will ultimately be felt by the shareholders.

Chapter 11

1   So as not to become embroiled in side-issues we will define this term at a later stage.

2   There are two assumptions about the nature of financial decision makers and decision making, which we have held throughout the analysis. Rational has been defined as always preferring more money (or a higher return) to less money (or a lower return), whilst risk aversion has been defined as disliking risk and requiring a reward or compensation for bearing it.

3   A basic knowledge of descriptive and inferential statistics will be useful in this and the following sections of the chapter.

4   Or, more correctly, arithmetic mean NPV.

5   Most introductory books on Operational Research give details about the use of decision trees.

6   We shall have more to say about the 'appropriate' discount rate in a later section.

7   We shall assume that these values are the arithmetic means of subjective probability distributions.

8   This, of course, is the project's internal rate of return.

9 In theory this problem can be overcome by use of the O.R. technique of simulation, but in practice this does little to enhance and clarify the decision maker's view of the effects of uncertainty on a project's desirability.

10 The discount rate of 13% arises from the sum of the risk-free rate of 8% and the medium-risk premium of 5%.

11 Of course the implied risk premiums calculated from the examples used are only averages. There are an infinite number of actual year-by-year risk premiums possible for a project with a life extending over more than one period. For example, taking the medium-risk project with a single cash flow at year 2, although the implied average annual premium is approximately 5·38%, the *actual* premiums could be (say) 5% in year 1 and (approximately) 5·76% in year 2:

$$100(1 + 0.05)(1 + 0.0576) \approx 111.05$$

The use of risk-adjusted discount rates does not necessarily imply (as is often stated) that risk is an increasing function of time; there are in fact an infinite number of relationships which could be implied by the specification of any particular single-figure risk premium.

12 An axiom can be defined as a statement which is generally accepted without any need for proof or verification.

13 For example, suppose an investor is offered an investment which has a 60% chance of producing £5,000 and a 40% chance of producing only £1,000. We are assuming that the investor will be able to specify a *certain* sum of money which would be equally acceptable as this uncertain investment. This sum might be £3,000. Thus £3,000 is said to be the certainty-equivalent of the above uncertain investment: the investor would be indifferent between receiving £3,000 for certain or receiving £5,000 with a 60% probability and £1,000 with a 40% probability.

14 We have already come across the idea of utility or indifference curves in the development and use of the two-period investment–consumption model.

15 Quite literally any utility index numbers could be used; for instance we could give +£5,000 an index of 75 and −£2,000 an index of 36 if we wished. The advantage of assigning index numbers of 1 and 0 to these two outcome extremes is simply that it eases the arithmetic.

16 $\rho \cdot 1 + (1 - \rho) \cdot 0 = \rho$.

17 The c constant is negative to ensure that the utility function is that of a risk-averse individual and hence concave to the origin.

18 With the variance of the portfolio, the weights (x and $(1 - x)$) are squared to match the fact that the individual variances are themselves the squares of the standard deviations.

19 In the case of zero risk, the expected return will also equal the actual return.

20 This particular portfolio could be found from inspection of Figure 11.3, but more accurately from solving the quadratic equation:

$$\text{VAR}(\tilde{r}_p) = 0.08^2 x^2 + 0.04^2(1 - x)^2 + 2x(1 - x)0.08 \cdot 0.04 \cdot -1 = 0$$

$$= 0.0144x^2 - 0.0096x + 0.0016 = 0$$

The solution gives x the unique value of 0·333.
Thus if $x = 1/3$, $(1 - x) = 2/3$, then:

$$\tilde{r}_p = (0.33 \cdot 0.25) + (0.66 \times 0.18) = 0.2033 \text{ or } 20\tfrac{1}{3}\%.$$

21   The real return from such an investment is of course uncertain because it depends upon the general movement of prices within the economy (e.g., inflation, deflation).

22   In practical terms $\tilde{r}_m$ and σ_m could be estimated from the historical period return and standard deviation of the all-share index of an efficient stock market.

23   In the extreme case of *total* risk-aversion this proportion will be zero.

24   It hardly needs to be said that individual investments which are negatively correlated to the market are very rare (if they exist at all) and hence almost all risky investments have an expected return greater than the risk-free return.

Compounding and Discounting Tables

Table A Compound interest factors $(1 + i)^N$

i	0·04	0·06	0·08	0·10	0·12	0·14	0·16	0·18	0·20
N1	1·0400	1·0600	1·0800	1·1000	1·1200	1·1400	1·1600	1·1800	1·2000
2	1·0816	1·1236	1·1664	1·2100	1·2544	1·2996	1·3456	1·3924	1·4400
3	1·1249	1·1910	1·2597	1·3310	1·4049	1·4815	1·5609	1·6430	1·7280
4	1·1699	1·2625	1·3605	1·4641	1·5735	1·6890	1·8106	1·9338	2·0736
5	1·2167	1·3382	1·4693	1·6105	1·7623	1·9254	2·1003	2·2878	2·4883
6	1·2653	1·4185	1·5869	1·7716	1·9738	2·1950	2·4364	2·6996	2·9860
7	1·3159	1·5036	1·7138	1·9487	2·2107	2·5023	2·8262	3·1855	3·5832
8	1·2686	1·5939	1·8509	2·1436	2·4760	2·8526	3·2784	3·7589	4·2998
9	1·4233	1·6895	1·9990	2·3580	2·7731	3·2519	3·8030	4·4335	5·1598
10	1·4802	1·7909	2·1589	2·5937	3·1058	3·7072	4·4114	5·2338	6·1917
11	1·5395	1·8983	2·3316	2·8531	3·4785	4·2262	5·1173	6·1759	7·4301
12	1·6010	2·0122	2·5182	3·1384	3·8960	4·8179	5·9360	7·2876	8·9161
13	1·6651	2·1329	2·7196	3·4523	4·3635	5·4924	6·8858	8·5994	10·6993
14	1·7317	2·2609	2·9372	3·7975	4·8871	6·2613	7·9875	10·1472	12·8392
15	1·8009	2·3966	3·1722	4·1773	5·4736	7·1379	9·2655	11·9737	15·4070

Table B Present Value Factor $(1 + i)^{-N}$

i	0·04	0·06	0·08	0·10	0·12	0·14	0·16	0·18	0·20
N1	0·9615	0·9434	0·9259	0·9091	0·8929	0·8772	0·8621	0·8475	0·8333
2	0·9246	0·8900	0·8573	0·8264	0·7972	0·7695	0·7432	0·7182	0·6944
3	0·8890	0·8396	0·7938	0·7513	0·7118	0·6750	0·6407	0·6086	0·5787
4	0·8548	0·7921	0·7350	0·6830	0·6355	0·5921	0·5523	0·5158	0·4823
5	0·8219	0·7473	0·6806	0·6209	0·5674	0·5194	0·4761	0·4371	0·4019
6	0·7903	0·7050	0·6302	0·5645	0·5066	0·4556	0·4014	0·3704	0·3349
7	0·7599	0·6651	0·5835	0·5132	0·4523	0·3996	0·3538	0·3139	0·2791
8	0·7307	0·6274	0·5403	0·4665	0·4039	0·3506	0·3050	0·2660	0·2326
9	0·7026	0·5919	0·5002	0·4241	0·3606	0·3075	0·2630	0·2255	0·1938
10	0·6756	0·5584	0·4632	0·3855	0·3220	0·2697	0·2267	0·1911	0·1615
11	0·6496	0·5268	0·4289	0·3505	0·2875	0·2366	0·1954	0·1619	0·1346
12	0·6246	0·4970	0·3971	0·3186	0·2567	0·2076	0·1685	0·1372	0·1122
13	0·6006	0·4686	0·3677	0·2897	0·2292	0·1821	0·1452	0·1163	0·0935
14	0·5775	0·4423	0·3405	0·2633	0·2046	0·1597	0·1252	0·0985	0·0779
15	0·5553	0·4173	0·3152	0·2394	0·1827	0·1401	0·1079	0·0835	0·0649

Table C Terminal value of an annuity $S_{n]i}$

i	0·04	0·06	0·08	0·10	0·12	0·14	0·16	0·18	0·
N1	1·0000	1·0000	1·0000	1·0000	1·0000	1·0000	1·0000	1·0000	1
2	2·0400	2·0600	2·0800	2·1000	2·1200	2·1400	2·1600	2·1800	2·
3	3·1216	3·1836	3·2464	3·3100	3·3744	3·4396	3·5056	3·5724	3
4	4·2465	4·3746	4·5061	4·6410	4·7793	4·9211	5·0665	5·2154	5·
5	5·4163	5·6371	5·8666	6·1051	6·3528	6·6101	6·8771	7·1542	7·
6	6·6330	6·9753	7·3359	7·7156	8·1152	8·5355	8·9775	9·4420	9
7	7·8983	8·3938	8·9228	9·4872	10·0890	10·7305	11·4139	12·1415	12·
8	9·2142	9·8975	10·6366	11·4359	12·2997	13·2328	14·2401	15·3270	16·
9	10·5828	11·4913	12·4876	13·5795	14·7757	16·0853	17·5185	19·0859	20·
10	12·0061	13·1808	14·4866	15·9374	17·5487	19·3373	21·3215	23·5213	25·
11	13·4864	14·9716	16·6455	18·5312	20·6546	23·0445	25·7329	28·7551	32·
12	15·0258	16·8699	18·9771	21·3843	24·1331	27·2707	30·8502	34·9311	39·
13	16·6268	18·8821	21·4953	24·5227	28·0291	32·0887	36·7862	42·2187	48·
14	18·2919	21·0151	24·2149	27·9750	32·3926	37·5811	43·6720	50·8180	59·
15	20·0236	23·2760	27·1521	31·7725	37·2797	43·8424	51·6595	60·9653	72

Table D Present value of an annuity $A_{n]i}$

i	0·04	0·06	0·08	0·10	0·12	0·14	0·16	0·18	0·20
N1	0·9615	0·9434	0·9259	0·9091	0·8929	0·8772	0·8621	0·8475	0·8333
2	1·8861	1·8334	1·7833	1·7355	1·6901	1·6467	1·6052	1·5656	1·5278
3	2·7751	2·6730	2·5771	2·4869	2·4018	2·3216	2·2459	2·1743	2·1065
4	3·6299	3·4651	3·3121	3·1699	3·0373	2·9137	2·7982	2·6901	2·5887
5	4·4518	4·2124	3·9927	3·7908	3·6048	3·4331	3·2743	3·1272	2·9906
6	5·2421	4·9173	4·6229	4·3553	4·1114	3·8887	3·6847	3·4976	3·3255
7	6·0021	5·5824	5·2064	4·8684	4·5638	4·2883	4·0386	3·8115	3·6046
8	6·7327	6·2098	5·7466	5·3349	4·9676	4·6389	4·3436	4·0776	3·8372
9	7·4353	6·8017	6·2469	5·7590	5·3282	4·9464	4·6065	4·3030	4·0310
10	8·1109	7·3601	6·7101	6·1446	5·6502	5·2161	4·8332	4·4941	4·1925
11	8·7605	7·8869	7·1390	6·4951	5·9377	5·4527	5·0286	4·6560	4·3271
12	9·3851	8·3838	7·5361	6·8137	6·1944	5·6603	5·1971	4·7932	4·4392
13	9·9856	8·8527	7·9038	7·1034	6·4235	5·8424	5·3423	4·9095	4·5327
14	10·5631	9·2950	8·2442	7·3667	6·6282	6·0021	5·4675	5·0081	4·6106
15	11·1184	9·7122	8·5595	7·6061	6·8109	6·1422	5·5755	5·0916	4·6755

Table E Sinking Fund Factor $S_{\overline{n}|i}^{-1}$

i	0·04	0·06	0·08	0·10	0·12	0·14	0·16	0·18	0·20
N1	1·0000	1·0000	1·0000	1·0000	1·0000	1·0000	1·0000	1·0000	1·0000
2	0·4902	0·4854	0·4808	0·4762	0·4717	0·4673	0·4630	0·4587	0·4545
3	0·3203	0·3141	0·3080	0·3021	0·2963	0·2907	0·2853	0·2799	0·2747
4	0·2355	0·2286	0·2219	0·2155	0·2092	0·2032	0·1974	0·1917	0·1863
5	0·1846	0·1774	0·1705	0·1638	0·1574	0·1513	0·1454	0·1398	0·1344
6	0·1508	0·1343	0·1363	0·1296	0·1232	0·1172	0·1114	0·1059	0·1007
7	0·1266	0·1191	0·1121	0·1054	0·0991	0·0932	0·0876	0·0824	0·0774
8	0·1085	0·1010	0·0940	0·0874	0·0813	0·0756	0·0702	0·0652	0·0606
9	0·0945	0·0870	0·0801	0·0736	0·0677	0·0622	0·0571	0·0524	0·0481
10	0·0833	0·0759	0·0690	0·0627	0·0570	0·0517	0·0469	0·0425	0·0385
11	0·0741	0·0668	0·0601	0·0540	0·0484	0·0434	0·0389	0·0348	0·0311
12	0·0666	0·0593	0·0527	0·0468	0·0414	0·0367	0·0324	0·0286	0·0253
13	0·0601	0·0530	0·0465	0·0408	0·0357	0·0312	0·0272	0·0237	0·0206
14	0·0547	0·0476	0·0413	0·0357	0·0309	0·0266	0·0229	0·0197	0·0169
15	0·0499	0·0430	0·0368	0·0315	0·0268	0·0228	0·0194	0·0164	0·0139

Table F Annual Equivalent Factor $A_{\overline{n}|i}^{-1}$

i	0·04	0·06	0·08	0·10	0·12	0·14	0·16	0·18	0·20
N1	1·0400	1·0600	1·0800	1·1000	1·1200	1·1400	1·1600	1·1800	1·2000
2	0·5302	0·5454	0·5608	0·5762	0·5917	0·6073	0·6230	0·6387	0·6545
3	0·3603	0·3741	0·3880	0·4021	0·4163	0·4307	0·4453	0·4599	0·4747
4	0·2755	0·2886	0·3019	0·3155	0·3292	0·3432	0·3574	0·3717	0·3863
5	0·2246	0·2374	0·2505	0·2638	0·2774	0·2913	0·3054	0·3198	0·3344
6	0·1908	0·2034	0·2163	0·2296	0·2432	0·2572	0·2714	0·2859	0·3007
7	0·1666	0·1791	0·1921	0·2054	0·2191	0·2332	0·2476	0·2624	0·2774
8	0·1485	0·1610	0·1740	0·1874	0·2013	0·2156	0·2302	0·2452	0·2606
9	0·1345	0·1470	0·1601	0·1736	0·1877	0·2022	0·2171	0·2324	0·2481
10	0·1233	0·1359	0·1490	0·1627	0·1770	0·1917	0·2069	0·2225	0·2385
11	0·1141	0·1268	0·1401	0·1540	0·1684	0·1834	0·1989	0·2148	0·2311
12	0·1066	0·1193	0·1327	0·1468	0·1614	0·1767	0·1924	0·2086	0·2253
13	0·1001	0·1130	0·1265	0·1408	0·1557	0·1712	0·1872	0·2037	0·2206
14	0·0947	0·1076	0·1213	0·1357	0·1509	0·1666	0·1829	0·1997	0·2169
15	0·0899	0·1030	0·1168	0·1315	0·1468	0·1628	0·1794	0·1964	0·2139

Index